EMBODIED CONFLICT

Our abilities to learn and remember are at the core of consciousness, cognition, and identity, and are based on the fundamental brain capacity to encode and store perceptual experience in abiding neural structures. These neural structures are the mechanisms by which we know, think about, create beliefs about, and understand the world in which we live. This includes the social world in which we experience conflict with others; our conflicts are largely about differences in what we know, think, believe, and understand. A number of characteristics of the neural encoding function are at the root of and help to explain conflict in our social relations and why some conflicts are difficult to prevent and resolve.

Embodied Conflict presents the neural encoding function in layman's terms, outlining seven key characteristics and exploring their implications for communication, relationship, and conflict resolution. In doing so, *Embodied Conflict* situates the field of conflict resolution within the long arc of human history and asks whether and how conflict resolution practice can take another step forward by considering the neural experience of parties in conflict. The book includes many case examples and offers some suggestions for how conflict resolution practitioner training might be expanded to include this theoretical framework and its implications for practice.

Tim Hicks has been a conflict resolution practitioner and teacher for 25 years. From 2006 to 2014, he was the first director of the conflict resolution Master's degree program at the University of Oregon.

EMBODIED CONFLICT

The Neural Basis of Conflict
and Communication

Tim Hicks

Routledge
Taylor & Francis Group

NEW YORK AND LONDON

First published 2018
by Routledge
711 Third Avenue, New York, NY 10017

and by Routledge
2 Park Square, Milton Park, Abingdon, Oxon, OX14 4RN

Routledge is an imprint of the Taylor & Francis Group, an informa business

© 2018 Tim Hicks

Library of Congress Cataloging-in-Publication Data
A catalog record for this title has been requested

ISBN: 978-1-138-08711-8 (hbk)
ISBN: 978-1-138-08712-5 (pbk)
ISBN: 978-1-315-11066-0 (ebk)

Typeset in Bembo
by Swales & Willis Ltd, Exeter, Devon, UK

CONTENTS

PREFACE

We've been on this planet as humans (homo sapiens) for some 300,000 years or so,[1] have evolved from our proto-human ancestors, have come down from the trees, have made our way from the caves through the agricultural revolution and the industrial revolution to this present moment in our story. It's been a long journey of challenge and struggle. Survival has not been easy. For these millennia, we have witnessed conflict in our personal and public lives, have seen power dynamics play out against the backdrop of the competition/cooperation balance, have lived the narratives of us and them, friend and foe, have often wondered why so much self-inflicted suffering exists, what are its causes, and whether and how we can prevent or reduce power abuses and violence. Our journey continues.

We are social beings and it is in the nature of social engagement to struggle with issues of power and dominance, agency and control, and diversity and hierarchy as we navigate the terrain of our social relations. Conflict will arise because we are each different from the other, because we each see the world from our own vantage point, because we are motivated by personal survival needs and fears and will often allow perceived self-interest to determine behavior that denies the other's self-interest, and because we affiliate within groups that define themselves in opposition to other groups. And yet, as we negotiate our paths through the complex webs of social interaction, we must coordinate our behaviors for personal and group survival.

We engage in destructive conflict in our families and with those whom we love most. We see wasteful conflict in our workplaces. We see destructive and dangerous conflicts at the international level. We see poorly managed conflict everywhere two or more people live or work together. If we define conflict as the coming up against differences (of goals, objectives, interests, perceptions, perspectives, understanding, expectations, intentions, preferences, styles, beliefs, values, motives, abilities, backgrounds, experience, etc.), then conflict is not a bad thing in itself. It is to be expected. It is in the nature of being human together with other humans. We will not be rid of conflict in the social realm any more than we will be rid of the physics of friction in the world of objects. It is not so much the presence of conflict that is the problem. Rather, it is in our response to differences that we create harm and waste.

The incidence of conflict and our responses to conflict are core and prominent themes in our individual lives and in the life of our species, along with the counterbalancing experiences of love, compassion, inclusion, and altruism. Looking at the arc of human history, one interpretation of our species biography is that it has been a quest to learn how to live together more harmoniously in the face of our differences, how to negotiate collaborative action in the presence of disagreement, how not to abuse other individuals as we live our own biography, how not to allow our self-interests to deny the self-interests of others, how to be in relationships with more responsibility, less violence, less power-abuse. The puzzle is not an easy one to solve, particularly because some of our biologically inherent and often unconscious characteristics, evolutionarily determined, tend towards fear-based and dominance-seeking responses. But it is a noble endeavor based on concepts that define what we sometimes call our higher natures, concepts of doing good, of not harming the other, of recognizing the legitimacy of the other equal to our own, concepts that arise in part from our ability to empathize.

For all their continuing shortcomings in practice, social concepts of participatory and inclusive democracy with equal representation for all, equality before the law and equal access to a fair justice system, gender equality and norms of domestic relations that don't tolerate or expect domination one over the other, civil and human rights universally declared and applied, non-discriminatory social standards, equitable economic policies, and universally accessible education, are indications of a trend line. The field of conflict resolution is another expression of this trend in our human development, a reflection of our yearning to create a present and a future less characterized by abuses of power and destructive responses to differences.

Arguably, the pressure is increasing to improve our ability to prevent destructive conflict and better manage the conflicts that inevitably arise. Perhaps it's that the stressors of population growth, environmental impact, climate change, and the clash of cultures brought together in heterogeneous societies by what we call globalization face us with increasingly dire prospects if we are unable to find better solutions. Perhaps it's just that this is the time in human development that it is, this moment in our search, our introspection, and our scientific advances, this moment at which we look in the mirror and again ask who we are, who we can be, who we wish to be, and how we can do better at living here, together. Perhaps it's that the more we know and understand of ourselves, the closer the elusive grail appears and the more intense and earnest our motivation to find and seize it. In any case, whether or not the stakes are increasing, we continue to try to better meet the challenges of social relating.

It's interesting to think about the violence we see in the world, whether at the level of interpersonal relationships or at the societal and global levels, as a public health issue. It is clear that the health of a community is harmed by violence, in whatever form, as is the health of an interpersonal relationship harmed by dominance, subjugation, or violence. Apparent short-term gains by perpetrators are more than offset by long-term and aggregate loss. Just as we contend with diseases that harm our physical health, so also do we face destructive relational conflict that harms our psychosocial health. Precise figures on death and injuries by violence are difficult to gather and decipher, and associated well-being costs are even more difficult to measure,[2] but we can be certain that public and private health are undermined by the incidence of violence, whether physical or psychological, and are improved as violent responses to differences are reduced. What follows from this framing are questions about the epidemiology of the public health threat as a prerequisite for considering possible strategies to remedy. Some of the causes will be contextual and others will be inherent to the organism.

Our myths speak of the battle of good and evil, god and the devil, the noble and the base, in reflection of the twin aspects of our nature. In large part, these twin aspects get played out in the arena of our social relations and in how we deal with the differences and disagreements among us. In the face of these differences and disagreements, the field of conflict resolution seeks to promote our better angels by fostering methods of decision-making that are inclusive and collaborative, processes based on mutual respect and a recognition that those affected by a decision should be part of the decision-making. It is an adolescent field, eager, active, limber, adventurous, and ambitious, seeking maturity but still relatively inexperienced and incompletely formed. In an interview conducted by Robert Benjamin for Mediate.com,[3] mediator Bernie Mayer expressed his belief that we've not developed sufficient intellectual bedrock for the conflict resolution field. It has also been commonly noted that the field is inherently interdisciplinary since, in conflict resolution work, we're dealing with humans in all their diversity and complexity, and the various disciplines we refer to when speaking about the field's interdisciplinary nature (psychology and social psychology, decision sciences, rhetoric, history, political science, international studies and diplomacy, law, negotiation studies, anthropology, neuroscience and the science of perception, and a few more) have to do with how humans function and behave. But bandwidth constraints in education, training, and practice, and the reality of academic siloing impede informative cross-disciplinary fertilization of the field's theory and practice development.

We are a supremely inquisitive species and we inquire into the nature of ourselves as we inquire into every other nook and cranny of the universe within the limits of our perceptual capacities. We are self-reflective. We seek to satisfy our curiosity, a curiosity sculpted by evolutionary fitness pressures and enabled by our complex nervous system, itself sculpted by those same pressures. We are a species that seeks self-improvement. We have what we call moral values and a moral compass. We don't accept without question our behavior. This characteristic of our species, the ability to reflect upon our behavior, to measure it against arbitrary standards, and to manage and change our behavior to some degree, means that natural selection is not the only formative factor in our evolution. With our capacity to be self-reflective comes the responsibility, it may be said, to work to change the behaviors we find inimical to healthy social life, however we define that.

As we have reflected on our behavior, we have aspired to more peaceful and harmonious, more cooperative and collaborative relations even as we have so often engaged and witnessed ourselves engaging in battles to win, control, and dominate. We've struggled to make sense of our violence as we perceive ourselves distinguished by our moral attributes. We don't like the battles, even as we find ourselves repeatedly engaging in them, because they threaten our lives, hurt our loved ones, are costly, and rob us of tranquility. We have sought remedies and solutions, preventative, mitigating, or corrective – laws and decision-making rules and processes, religious and behavioral practices, cultural norms and standards, codes of conduct, enforcement strategies. Faced with our survival concerns, we have struggled with the balance between trust and suspicion, cooperation and competition.

Our self-study has been apparent in the writings and reports of the earliest philosophers, both east and west, who wondered about human nature and the nature of our social relations, and has continued over the centuries. It took a leap in the west with the work of Freud, William James, and others in the early days of modern psychology, and continues with the evolution of our investigations in social psychology, cognitive psychology, and our current scientific investigations into the workings of the brain and its extended nervous system, the seat of consciousness, cognition, identity, and behavior.

If the conflict resolution field is to continue to improve in its ability to help people better manage conflicts and avoid the destructive consequences of poorly managed conflicts, it will do so by keeping pace with and incorporating the knowledge advances in the other relevant disciplines, thereby building the more solid foundation for theory and practice that Mayer noted remains incomplete. Of the various frontiers of human inquiry, developments in neuroscience are likely to provide some of the most insightful pathways to understanding ourselves. We are coming to terms with the fact that we're physical organisms that function in ways determined by the body's physiology.[4] In the medical field, we have been inquiring for centuries into how the body functions as we've sought to better prevent, treat, and manage physical disease and injury. The enterprise continues now in psychology with the development of neuropsychology and neuropsychoanalysis.[5] It seems reasonable to presume that better understanding of how the nervous system works, the system that allows for and produces perception, consciousness, cognition, and identity, will help us better prevent and manage conflict in our social relations. That said, the application of neuroscientific insights to improve self-regulation and social management will not always be simple or obvious.

Let's remember how deep and real, how destructive and cruel poorly managed conflict can be. Our efforts to improve conflict resolution practice are not merely a theoretical or a purely intellectual exercise; conflict is part of the flesh and blood of our lives, the reality of our living together, a visceral reality for all of us. In an interview for the *New York Times* discussing the question of violence in human relations, Simon Critchley, a professor of philosophy at The New School, observes, "The danger of easy pacifism is that it is inert and self-regarding. It is always too pleased with itself. But the alternative is not a justification of war. It is rather the attempt to understand the deep history and tragic complexity of political situations."[6] In seeking to reduce the incidence of poorly managed conflict, we also face the danger of Pollyannaish thinking. The causes of conflict are deeply rooted, as are our less-than-ideal responses to conflict; indeed, they are of the very soil of our selves. We will not rid the soil of those elements. But similarly to Critchley's comment, our alternative is not resignation to and acceptance of destructive responses to conflict. Differences will always be difficult, to one degree or another, from simple problems to deep disagreements and seemingly intractable opposition. But we can see in our own lives, and we see in conflict resolution practice, that change is possible, change based on learning and what we call personal growth. I remember one of my daughters, 12 years old at the time, saying to me, when I'd been practicing in the field for about a year, after two years of intensive study prior to practicing, "Pops, I'm sure glad you got into this conflict resolution stuff because you're a much better dad now." She was right. I was a better dad because I was better at understanding and managing my own responses to differences, disagreements, and conflicts. With deeper understanding of ourselves, and particularly how and why we behave in response to differences, the promise is that we can better prevent or manage the conflicts that are an inherent part of social experience.

My goal with this book is to help link conflict resolution theory and practice to the basic physiological function by which perceptual experience is encoded in neural structures of meaning. By neural encoding I mean the creation of networks of connections among individual neurons in response to perceptual stimuli. This is the faculty that allows for learning, memory, cognition, and identity. Making this link, we can add another perspective to our understanding of human behavior in conflict circumstances and possibly deepen conflict resolution practice. The painter needs to understand how colors mix but does not need to understand the chemistry that underlies the recipes. The wood worker needs to know the characteristics of different woods but not necessarily the biology that produces those characteristics. But what about the conflict worker? How much of the inner workings of the human organism will it be helpful for us to understand as we work with parties in conflict? Dan Sperber, co-author of the recent *The Enigma of Reason* (Mercier and Sperber, 2017), in a talk about his work, put it this way:

> If we want to have a more ambitious understanding of how social life functions, of the mechanisms involved, the challenge is to achieve continuity with neighboring natural sciences. The obvious neighbors to begin with are cognitive neuroscience, ecology, biology, and others.[7]

The premise upon which my discussion in this book is based is that our experiences of knowing and meaning, of perception and communication are rooted in and emerge from our physical bodies, particularly what we call our nervous system and its central organ, the brain. As much as we tend to perceive ourselves in other ways, we are living organisms that function according to our physiology. Psychology is biology shaped by genetics and experience. Seeing conflict and communication in terms of their neural underpinnings provides a conceptual framework that can help us better understand the behavior of people in relationship and some of the impediments that must be overcome in working through conflict to resolution. As Louis Cozolino puts it in *The Neuroscience of Human Relationships*, "Brain evolution also provides us with a window to our own functioning and dysfunction, including some of the conflicts we experience in society and within ourselves" (2014, p. 16).

To the degree that this premise is accurate, the more we understand how our body functions, the better able we will be to understand, manage, and regulate our behaviors and to help others do the same. Without that understanding, we are liable to be working in the dark to some degree, to miss opportunities, or to intervene in unhelpful ways. As conflict resolution practitioners, we have tended, understandably, to deal with the observable behaviors of parties and with limited understanding of the roots of those behaviors in internal neural experience. Keeping in mind the neural correlates of conflict behavior, we may be able to expand or adjust our interventions beyond the templates of practice as they have been developed to date.

In the conflict resolution field, we have emphasized that two people will look at the same object or circumstance and see two different things. We've illustrated this fact with various visual analogs (for example, the Necker Cube, the old woman/young woman drawing, the candle stick/dual profile image, the figure on the ground between two antagonists, seen by one as a nine and by the other as a six). The basis of our differences in perception, understanding, and belief is neural. Conflict theorists and practitioners are always trying to better understand the nature of conflict and, therefore, the nature of we humans, we who engage in conflict. This book offers an additional vantage point from which to look at the nature of conflict and another perspective on the experience of those we work with and our own experience as conflict resolution practitioners.

With that, one caveat. Though our consciousness experience is rooted in the physiology of the body, we don't experience ourselves at that level or in those terms. The complex and busy physiological activity of body function that produces cognition and self-experience happens below or outside our awareness. We experience the effects or the products of physiological function, translated into the referential terms of thoughts and feelings. For example, under threat, we don't directly experience the hormonal secretions of the endocrine system. We experience what we call fear or tension. When I look out the window as I sit at my desk, I see trees and fall colors, not the activation of neuronal networks of meaning established by earlier exposure to these elements of the external world. We experience meaning and emotion, not the physiological processes that produce those experiences. Given that this is so, when we try to understand our experience and behavior in terms of their physiological roots, the descriptions are at some remove from what we are familiar with. The science can be explanatory, but can feel unrelated to our regular lived experience. The description of our experience in physiological terms seems to miss something, seems too materialistic, mechanical, and deterministic, the correspondence foreign, maybe seemingly irrelevant, and even possibly threatening. We are biology and chemistry, but we are also our lived experience. In understanding the neural roots of cognition and behavior, we have to continue to work with people at the level of their and our lived experience. We have to maintain a balance between the science and the humanity of life.

Finally, at first glance, this book is addressed to conflict resolution professionals, what I like to call conflict workers. But in truth, the story told here is relevant to all of us since we all are involved in conflicts periodically and all of us wish to improve our own behaviors in the face of disagreements and to help others with whom we are in relationship. In the end, we are all conflict workers seeking to make a better world in the realms in which we live.

ACKNOWLEDGMENTS

The ideas in this book began germinating almost 20 years ago when I woke up in the middle of the night with a simple, but for me at the time profound, realization of the relationship between conflict experience and our reality-construction and identity-formation processes. I shuffled to my desk and wrote the first notes for what became the article *Another Look at Identity-Based Conflict: The Roots of Conflict in the Psychology of Consciousness* (Negotiation Journal, January, 2001). Over time, access to work being done in neuroscience, cognitive neuroscience, and neurophilosophy helped me produce a more solid foundation for my initial thoughts. This book is the result.

Over the years, conversations with and encouragement from colleagues, friends, and students helped me refine my thinking and believe that I wasn't completely off-base. Thanks particularly to Don Tucker, Mark Johnson, Jim Sullivan, Jim Melamed, Mari Fitzduff, Daniel Bowling, Kimberly Rosenfield, Bernie Mayer, Gary Friedman, Carrie Heltzel, Peter Adler, and colleagues in the Accord3.0 network. I'd also like to acknowledge the students in the graduate program at the University of Oregon for their patience and interest as I tested some of my ideas on them. Thanks also to Jane Gordon who made room for me each year to present some of these ideas in their formative stages to the students in her courses. And thanks to Anna Shamble and Kata Bahnsen-Reinhardt, my colleagues and staunch support staff while I was at UO, whose workload increased more often than I care to admit while I delved into early research and writing for this book.

I am deeply grateful to the scientists and philosophers whose work informed and supported my thinking. Browse my reference section to see the list. Their adventurous spirits inspire and lead the way. Among them, I want to particularly mention Don Tucker and Phan Luu whose books *Mind from Body* and *Cognition and Neural Development* are full of insight, wisdom, and beautiful writing.

With his patience, passion, and belief in the work, my editor at Routledge, Paul Dukes, is the reason the book has come to market.

Barbara Kane heard the early glimmerings of the thoughts in this book and encouraged me to carry them forward. Finally, deep gratitude to Grace Bullock, source of light and courage to those around her, who kept reminding me that the brain exists as a part of the whole body. Let it be known that her editing skills far surpass my own and this book would have benefitted greatly had she not been fully occupied writing another one of her own.

Notes

1 The epoch of our appearance is uncertain with periodic new discoveries pushing the period ever earlier. See, for example, article published June 7, 2017 at: https://www.nytimes.com/2017/06/07/science/human-fossils-morocco.html?emc=edit_ta_20170607&nl=top-stories&nlid=51588414&ref=headline
2 See, for example, *Injuries and Violence: The facts*. Geneva, World Health Organization, 2010.
3 Available at: www.mediate.com/articles/mayerfull.cfm
4 Anil Seth (professor of cognitive and computational neuroscience at the University of Sussex, co-director of the Sackler Centre for Consciousness Science, and editor-in-chief of Neuroscience of Consciousness) notes Freud's identification of three major enlightenments for humanity (what he called strikes against the centrality of humanity): the Copernican revolution that recognized that we were not the center of the universe; the Darwinian revolution that demonstrated that we were not separate from the animal world but a part of it; and the third, our current developing understanding of our conscious selves, explaining the nature of consciousness. Seth notes that as we "progressively naturalize our place in the world, we become more a part of the world and less apart from the world." See https://www.theguardian.com/science/2012/mar/01/consciousness-eight-questions-science
5 For a non-technical introduction and overview, see Schwartz, 2015.
6 Available at http://opinionator.blogs.nytimes.com/2016/03/14/the-theater-ofviolence/?emc=edit_ty_20160314&nl=opinion&nlid=51588414
7 See his discussion at https://www.edge.org/conversation/dan_sperber-the-function-of-reason

INTRODUCTION

There is understandable attention being given to the relatively early-stage developments in neuroscience,[1] our study of the functioning of the human nervous system, and to the implications of neurological functioning for all areas of human experience and behavior. This is the new frontier, and we explore it upon the wide-spread and increasingly accepted assumption that we are embodied beings,[2] meaning that our experience of self and world and our behavioral responses and repertoire are determined and constrained by the functional dynamics of our physical bodies and, for the purposes of this book, particularly our nervous system and its central organ, the brain.[3] As Patricia Smith Churchland puts it, "The weight of evidence now implies that it is the *brain*, rather that some nonphysical stuff, that feels, thinks, and decides" (Churchland, 2002, p. 1). In this view, consciousness isn't separate from biology any more than solidity is separate from physics.[4, 5]

In the conflict resolution field, one of the fundamentals we've emphasized is that conflict is an unavoidable part of human social interaction, not a stain on the fabric of relationship but an inherent fiber woven into its fabric. As Jonathan Haidt puts it (with his focus being on conflicts that have to do with over-certainty, moralistic self-righteousness, what he terms "judgementalism," political and religious discord, and general for-and-against antagonisms), conflict behavior in our social relations ". . . is the normal human condition. It is a feature of our evolutionary design, not a bug or error that crept into minds that would otherwise be objective and rational" (Haidt, 2013, p. xx). Conflict is not so much something we do but rather something that we are. We've known this from observation. Sometimes with a sense of resignation, we have been led by history, current events, and our own personal experience to conclude that we can not prevent all conflict, that as human beings interact, conflict will inevitably arise. Conflict resolution professionals have wanted to normalize conflict as we've recognized its pervasive presence in human affairs and appreciated its informative potential for improving relationships and systems.

As theorists and practitioners, we've understood the importance of under-standing the source of a conflict as a necessary diagnostic step preliminary to prevention or treatment. We've asked what it is in the circumstances of living that result in the types of conflicts we see and experience in our engagement with each other and that make many conflicts difficult to resolve?[6] We've tried to answer the question of cause, and not unsuccessfully, by identifying condi-tions that typically lead to conflict. We know, for example, that conflict will often result when there is competition over scarce resources, actual or perceived, or when power differentials are abused or even just present, or when access to data is unequal or the interpretation of data is inconsistent. We've identified that conflict may well erupt in the absence of procedural, relational, or substan-tive satisfaction (Moore, 2014) or in the absence of good communication skills. We've seen that structural elements of context can be a cause of relational con-flict (Duggan, 1996). We know that differences in style and temperament can lead to conflict and that, indeed, diversity of all sorts, cultural and other, can cause friction and misunderstanding. We've described identity-based conflicts. We've been enlightened by relevant social psychological research that demon-strates many perceptual and behavioral tendencies that contribute to conflictual relations. These understandings are based on our observations of behavior and systems. But what is happening within the body and, more specifically, within the brain, the key determinant of our consciousness experience?

Our identification of sources of conflict has been more sociological or anthro-pological than neuroscientific. If we are indeed embodied beings, our conflict behaviors, will be determined by what is happening in the body, at the neural substrate of consciousness (Edelman & Tonni, 2000).[7] As Fuster (2013, p. 58) puts it:

> Cognitive neuroscience is the neuroscience of what we know, which encompasses all our memories and everything we have learned since we were born. It deals with the mechanisms by which our brain acquires, stores, and retrieves knowledge. It deals also with the brain mechanisms that drive cognitive functions – that is, the functions by which we use knowledge in our daily interactions with others and the world around us: attention, perceptions, memory, language, and intelligence. Most impor-tantly, cognitive neuroscience deals with the mechanisms by which our feelings and emotions influence every one of those functions.[8]

Given that we are physical organisms and that it is brain function, rooted in the experience of the entire body in interaction with its environment,[9] that deter-mines our conflict behaviors, it seems reasonable to conclude that advances in our neuroscientific understandings will impact the practice of conflict resolution just as, for example, advances in population genetics are impacting the disciplines of linguistics and anthropology.[10] Speaking about people who work with children, Louis Cozolino, in his *The Neuroscience of Human Relationships* (2014), makes a comment that I think applies equally to conflict workers. He says (p. xviii):

> Parents, educators, and therapists – those of us who should be most concerned with shaping minds – have traditionally paid little attention to the brain. I have heard therapists say that psychotherapy is an art and that the brain is irrelevant to their work. I would respond, as with any art, that a thorough knowledge of our materials and methods can only enhance our skills and capabilities.

How might an understanding of the neural workings of the brain help us work more effectively with parties in conflict? This is the primary question this book asks. Is there a next phase in the development of conflict resolution practice that more explicitly takes into account the neural reality of our human communicational and relational experience? There are reasons to argue that the success of the conflict resolution field has not only been limited but has not achieved its full promise. Some might respond by asking whether the idea of unreached promise is based on an unrealistic vision of what is possible, an idealistic overreach. But given the kinds and level of conflict we see in the world, it is understandable that we ask whether we can be more effective in helping people resolve differences nonviolently and collaboratively at all levels. Certainly we have been able to help individuals and groups meet in safe and well-structured processes to bridge divides, settle disputes, make decisions, and build agreements collaboratively, avoiding less satisfactory power- and rights-based alternatives that would, in many cases, produce less optimal outcomes. That said, for the most part, we work with self-selected parties who already favor, to one degree or another, a collaborative resolution of their dispute. Even within these circumstances, we see parties struggle to deal successfully with their differences, and we see them sometimes fail. Sometimes we see grudging settlements that are perceived as better than the alternatives but that fall short of "transformative" shifts in understanding that seem possible but beyond the parties' reach and our ability, as practitioners, to facilitate. We also see the repeated emergence of unnecessary conflicts. We see parties unable to get to the table in the first place, unable to get sufficiently "outside" their conflict to see the possibility of working things out. We see political and policy differences degenerate into unproductive debate absent constructive joint learning. And we see long-standing, deeply destructive protracted conflicts in which parties are caught up in historical narratives they are unable to escape. If these shortcomings are rooted in the facts of our neurophysiology, are there ways that we can further develop practice to better take into account that reality?

As I mentioned earlier, we are in the early stages of exploration of the notably and exceptionally complex human nervous system,[11] the complexity of which allows for the remarkable fullness and the subtle dimensions of our human experience. Much is being learned about brain chemistry and the role of hormones and neurotransmitters. Mapping of brain region function continues and we delve further into understanding synaptic behavior and cellular activity (Sapolsky, 2017). The project to understand the complexity of distributed neural functioning and dynamic brain structure that produces human cognition remains very much a work in progress, even as we add to our knowledge at an accelerating rate.[12] Though the technical details of our most recent advances in neuroscience lie outside the knowledge sphere of most of us,[13] there is a basic function of the human nervous system that can be described relatively simply and non-technically at a macro and conceptual level. We do know that, whatever the intricate and almost miraculous details, most of which are yet to be discovered and understood, our brains encode our perceptual experience in what Tucker (2007, p. vii) calls "the neural structures of experience" to allow for what we term learning and memory, the very bases of consciousness, cognition, and identity.[14] Our ability to think, understand, know, believe, and, indeed, to have an identity, derives from and depends upon this basic neural function of encoding perceptual experience in neural structures and processes.[15] Our experiences of learning, remembering, knowing, thinking, understanding, believing, and identity are, in this view, identical with the encoding function of the brain, by which abiding neural structures, what might be called neural matrices of meaning, are created in response to perceptual experience.[16] And it is these cognitive processes of thinking, knowing, believing, feeling, understanding, meaning, and identity, embodied in our neural architecture, that are at the core of so much of our conflict relations. Conflict, at the most fundamental level, is based on how we perceive and understand the world external to ourselves, what meanings (stories) we assign or attribute to the objects of our perceptual experience (be they artifacts, individuals, or relational dynamics), what we believe to be true, real, or good in the world, how we think and what we think we know, and whom we experience ourselves and the other to be. At a very basic level, we fight over who we are. Differences involve identity. Identity is embodied.

We are perpetually negotiating our way through the day with each other, engaging, relating, communicating to get agreement on individual or group action, on how we will coordinate our behaviors as individuals influenced by and influencing the other. This is the social dance, whether in a restaurant deciding what to order and talking with the server, with children and spouse coordinating daily activities, in our working relationships, or even when we are just sitting together talking, just hanging out. The backdrop is agreement, negotiated agreement about what we are doing together, how we will be with each other, and what we believe to be true about the world. As soon as disagreement arises that puts into question what we're doing together, how we're doing it, or what we think to be true, conflict arises and we have to figure it out; we have to negotiate the next basis of relational stability. Whatever the manner we negotiate the relationship, whether through the manipulation or imposition of power or collaboratively, the negotiation will be based on our understanding of the world, ourselves, and our relationship with the other. And those understandings exist in the brain's neural networks, the neural structures constructed and established in response to our perceptual experience of the world up to that point in time. Underlying the terms "reality constructs" and "identity formation" are actual neural structures formed in the physicality of our brains. Our stories are embodied, they exist in those structures or, rather, those structures are the stories.

The neural structures and processes of encoded perceptual experience have, as is true of all elements of the physical world, characteristics and limitations that will determine and constrain the experience and the functioning of the human organism of which they are such a critical part.[17] They will determine how we engage with the world and each other; they are the source, at a primary level, of our conflict experiences, and will help to explain why some conflicts are difficult to resolve, more or less, depending on the circumstances.

Certainly, there are other ways to think about, understand, and explain the presence of conflict in human social relations and the difficulties we so often face in resolving some conflicts or preventing their escalation. For example, research suggests that one of the reasons we have liberals and conservatives who battle so vociferously over issues of public policy is the presence of genetic variation in the population in which individuals have different genetic predispositions to be more or less reactive to threats, more or less receptive to change and new experience, and more or less risk averse, three fundamental personality traits that have been found to distinguish liberals and conservatives (Haidt, 2013).[18] Such diversity provides a fitness benefit to the population as a whole, insuring checks and balances and a spectrum of survival strategies and possible responses to environmental challenges, but also results in conflict between the different personality types as they argue over public policy on the basis of their genetically influenced preferences.

While it must be true that, if we are embodied beings, all cognitive experience will be based on the dynamics of neural physiology, our insights into conflict behavior needn't necessarily or always be based on direct reference to the biology of conflict experience. As I mentioned above, we've identified many sources of conflict and have proposed many useful theories on the basis of which we have developed effective ways of working with people in conflict. Further, within the realm of brain science, as we expand the frontier of our knowledge, we continue to learn about the roots of social behavior in the various and complex aspects of the body and brain structure and chemistry.[19] For example, research into the function of the vagus nerve and the entire vagal system is revealing their involvement in social communication, emotional engagement, and sympathetic arousal and modulation.[20] The quest to understand conflict in all its rich variety and to work with it effectively benefits from diverse paths of inquiry into the many features and circumstances of the complex human organism.

To emphasize, my focus here is on the very basic brain function of encoding perceptual experience that is the basis of learning, memory, cognition, and identity and that determines in a fundamental way the relational dynamics of interaction between and among us. Much of what is indicated or suggested by a review of the neural basis of consciousness confirms what we are already familiar with in theory and in informal observation of and social science research into our social behavior and our individual experience. By tying our folk psychology and our social science findings to the organism's neural processes, perhaps we might establish a solid stepping-stone from which to continue our efforts to better prevent, manage, and resolve the conflicts we witness and experience in our lives.[21] I offer the discussion in this book with the hope that it will stimulate some thinking about how an understanding of the neural basis of consciousness experience may lead to more robust and accurate theory development and to more effective practice interventions. As Don Tucker and Phan Luu (2012) put it, "The mind is the brain." How the brain works (informed by and integrated within the experience of the whole body) determines how the mind experiences self and other and how we behave in relationship.

A review of the many journal articles and books that have been written about conflict and conflict resolution reveals many different ways of looking at conflict behavior and how we can understand it in order to more effectively work with people in conflict. This is as it should be. There is not one right conceptual framework, no grand unified field theory that provides the definitive, comprehensive perspective on the dynamics of conflict. My goal is to offer an additional way of thinking about the phenomena of our conflict experience.

To begin with, in Chapter 1, I review some basic aspects of human experience to remind us of what underlies our day-to-day embodied consciousness. I then describe, in Chapter 2, the neural encoding function of the brain that allows for or produces learning and memory that are the bases of cognition and identity, after which I highlight some key characteristics of the encoding function relevant to conflict work (Chapter 3), before looking at how the characteristics of the neural encoding function can help us understand some of the dynamics of communication and relationship (Chapter 4). In Chapter 5, I consider how this theoretical approach applies to various aspects of conflict resolution practice. This is where the rubber meets the road, so to speak. What are the opportunities and limitations that the neural perspective presents to conflict workers? Chapter 6 presents a few ideas on how the theoretical framework might inform conflict resolution training. Finally, I offer some concluding thoughts in Chapter 7.

Notes

1 What Churchland (1996, p. 405) said more than 20 years ago continues to be true, "Although quite a lot is known at the cellular level, the fact remains that how real neural networks work and how their output properties depend on cellular properties still abounds with nontrivial mysteries. Naturally I do not wish to minimize the progress that has been made in neuroscience, but it is prudent to have a cautious assessment of what we really do not yet understand."

2 There is certainly not universal agreement with this perspective. See, as an example, Thomas Nagel's *Mind and Cosmos: Why the materialist neo-Darwinian conception of nature is almost certainly false* (2012). Whether or not there is a "spiritual" essence separate from the body, we do know that neural mechanisms are key and fundamental to cognition and consciousness. We know this from the evidence of the consequences of brain injury and neurological disease to identity, cognition, and consciousness experience. The neural function and characteristics I present in this book don't necessarily preclude or deny the disembodied perspective, nor are the conclusions and implications invalidated by a belief in the existence of a disembodied soul or spirit or self.

3 What Gerald Edelman calls "brain-based epistemology" referring to efforts to ground the theory of knowledge and behavior in an understanding of how the brain works (Edelman, 2006. p. 2), a "theory of consciousness based on brain activity" (Edelman, 2006. p. 9), and what Patricia Churchland calls "naturalized epistemology" (Churchland, 2002), and as Tucker and Luu (2012, p. 208) state it, the "identity of neural structure and cognitive function."

4 To emphasize here, and as will be discussed further on, brains and consciousness do not exist in isolation. As Edelman and Tonini put it, "However, we emphatically do not identify consciousness in its full range as arising solely in the brain, since we believe that higher brain functions require interactions both with the world and with other persons" (2000, p. xii).

5 "Considering the new insights into the neural basis of psychological development, we will suggest that it is now possible to consider a single theory in which mind and brain are studied as the same process" (Tucker et al, 2016, p. 1).

6 As James Crosswhite puts it in his book *Deep Rhetoric*, "What is it about human beings that prevents their gaining satisfactory knowledge, prevents them from reasoning in satisfactory ways? What goes wrong with human thinking in general?" (Crosswhite, 2013, p. 68).

7 "epistemology should be grounded in biology, specifically in neuroscience" (Edelman & Tonini, 2000. p. 207); "Complex psychological functions must arise from bodily structures. There is no other source for them" (Tucker, 2007, p. 218); "To find the mind, we must look to the body" (Tucker, 2007, p. 16); "The structure of a system at any time determines what it *can* experience" (Feldman, 2006, p. 72).

8 Fuster's description here emphasizes the unity of or inseparable connection between thinking and feeling, logic and emotion, in cognition and consciousness. In agreement, I consider what is called "affective neuroscience" to be a subset within cognitive neuroscience, not a separate discipline.

9 "the personality is not a disembodied mental construct, but the individual's unique pattern of brain development. To understand the epigenetic specification of the endophenotype – the individual child – it is necessary to consider not just the genetic coding for traits, but the full context of developmental self-regulation that shapes the growth of the brain and the personality within the complex social and cultural environment" (Tucker et al, 2016, p. 3).

10 For an interesting talk on this subject, see population geneticist David Reich's talk at http://edge.org/conversation/david_reichthe-genomic-ancient-dna-revolution

11 "Many gaps remain and much more must be accomplished in both neuroscience and psychology before a comprehensive picture of thought and knowledge can be glimpsed" (Edelman, 2006. p. ix).

12 "Although some general points can be made about neuronal coding on the basis of available neurobiological data, many, *many* questions remain unresolved . . . Emphasizing this in-progress character of neuroscience is crucial, if a little daunting. At this stage in neuroscience, nothing like a well-established theory of neuronal coding exists" (Churchland, 2002, p. 289).

13 For interesting and accessible discussions of some of the technical perspectives, see Tucker, 2007; Tucker and Luu, 2012; Feldman, 2006; Sapolsky, 2017. There are, of course, many other good sources.

14 "We do not presently understand fully how this categorization is done but . . . we believe it arises through the selection of certain distributed patterns of neural activity as the brain interacts with the body and the environment" (Edelman & Tonini, 2000, p. 48); "underlying any conscious state . . . is a set of neural processes" (Edelman, 2005, p. 116).

15 "The macroscopic properties of mind and language arise . . . from the microscopic properties of neurons" (Feldman, 2006, p. 49); "My notion of personality is pretty simple: it's that your 'self,' the essence of who you are, reflects patterns of interconnectivity between neurons in your brain . . . Most of what the brain does is accomplished by synaptic transmission between neurons, and by calling upon the information encoded by past transmission across synapses" (LeDoux, 2003, p. 2).

16 "the properties of the mind depend fundamentally and in detail on the way the neural networks that are our brains carry out information processing" (Feldman, 2006, p. 58); "ideas are held within brain tissue . . . neural connectivity implies psychological function" (Tucker, 2007, p. v).

17 "Consciousness is a property of neural processes and cannot itself act causally in the world. As a process and an entailed property, consciousness arose during the evolution of complex neural networks with a specific kind of structure and dynamics" (Edelman, 2005, p. 141)

18 Hood (2012, p. 51) reports on research that found generally that one in eight infants are born tending to respond fearfully to new situations (*inhibited*) and one in ten infants are born tending to be less fearful in response to new situations and more able to cope with uncertainty (*disinhibited*). The remaining babies lie somewhere along the continuum between these two polarities. The temperament could be identified as early as four months and was predictive of personality seven years later.

19 Many reviews have already been written of the roots of conflict behavior in brain structures (the hemispheres, prefrontal cortex, amygdala, hypothalamus, etc.) and neurochemicals (oxytocin, dopamine, serotonin, vasopressin, etc.). See, for example, Ken Cloke, *Bringing Oxytocin into the Room: Notes on the neurophysiology of conflict*, available at www.mediate.com/articles/cloke8.cfm; Richard Birke (2010); Lack & Bogacz (2012); Weitz (2011a, 2011b); Fusting (2012); Goldman (2011); and Jill S. Tanz and Martha K. Mcclintock, *The Physiologic Stress Response During Mediation*, available at: https://chicagomediationservices.com/wp-content/uploads/2017/04/The-Physiologic-Stress-Response-Published-Form.pdf

20 See Porges (2011); also Cozolino (2014).

21 "Just as biology cannot be understood except in the light of evolution, psychology cannot be understood except in the light of brain development. Psychology is, indeed, in each moment, brain development" (Tucker and Luu, 2012, p. v).

1

SOME BASICS ABOUT HUMANS AS LIVING ORGANISMS

Before looking more closely at the encoding function of the brain and the implications it has for our relational experiences and for conflict resolution (Chapters 2, 3, and 4), in Chapter 1, I offer a few preliminary observations about the human organism that bear on and are a backdrop to how we experience ourselves and the world and how we behave with each other. I think it is helpful to keep these basic aspects of human experience in mind as we think about the experience of parties engaged in conflict relations. In this chapter, I briefly discuss: that we enter at birth with no experience of self and knowing and proceed to construct those phenomena in response to perceptual experience; that we navigate our environment with the primary motive to survive; that we have only our five senses with which to know the world; that we are concerned with three levels or realms of survival, the physical, psychological, and social; and that we are always in a constant state of environmental assessment, assigning meaning to all perceptual experience, dealing with unknowns, reducing uncertainty, and maintaining the balance between learning new information and adhering to previously learned understandings.

At Birth No Knowing

At birth, there is no conscious experience of self, no self conscious knowing, no conscious thinking, no accessible memory, very little accumulated perceptual experience, no understanding of the world environment into which we enter, and no beliefs about that world. These aspects of human experience develop with life experience.[1] As the saying goes, we have to "learn from experience" and our experience is perceptual. Gradually, we assemble our understanding of the world and develop a self-identity from the sensory impressions we receive as we interact with our environment.[2] Self-experience requires memory, and memory requires encoded perceptual experience. The newborn must accumulate sufficient encoded material to begin the process of making associations among the elements of perceptual experience that begins to build the edifice of meaning that comprises the experience of self. The experience of self arises through the child's interaction with the world as it encodes its perceptual experience of the physical and social environments in which it finds itself.[3]

We Navigate to Survive

Like all living organisms, from single-celled organisms on up the scale of complexity, we navigate our environment to survive and procreate – the evolutionary imperative.[4] Beneath the security of civilization's veneer, the universe is a somewhat hostile environment characterized by entropy and in which we are vulnerable to injury, predators, sickness, and the vicissitudes of food supply and weather conditions. We are able to survive because we are endowed with sensory apparatus sufficient to allow us to successfully navigate our environment.[5] The essential difference between humans and an amoeba or a reptile or one of our fellow mammalian species is the complexity of our nervous system with which we perceive and make sense of our environment.[6] The human brain's complexity allows for greater encoding (learning), storage and retrieval (memory), and associational capacity (creativity), resulting in the variety and richness of our world and identity experiences, the scope of our behavioral abilities, and the dynamics of our interpersonal and intergroup relations.[7] These functions of perception, encoding, retrieval, and association are embodied, are based on the physical functional characteristics of the nervous system, the brain and its extended perceptual apparatus.[8]

Only Our Five Senses

Each living organism navigates its environment with, and only with, its particular perceptual apparatus by which it senses its environment.[9] Humans have only five senses with which to "make sense" of the environment.[10] Our interface with the external world is entirely and exclusively mediated by our five senses.[11] The richness of our consciousness experience, in which the world seems saturated with meaning, obscures the fact that these five senses are our only links with and measures of the environment, and the only basis upon which we construct understanding and meaning. Without these perceptual vectors, there would be no awareness, no knowing. By way of our perceptual experience of the environment, through our limited but sufficient five senses, we construct our understanding of the world and, from that experience, develop what we call our identity, our self-definition that becomes an additional "object" of perception along with the external objects and social dynamics of the physical world. What we know is who we are.[12] Our five senses are all we have to deliver the information with which, in conjunction with our genetic endowment, the brain constructs its understanding of the world and upon which it builds its experience of the self.[13] Ideas, concepts, beliefs, knowledge, understanding are all built from the raw sensory data to which meaning is assigned or with which meaning is constructed. Remove all five senses and we would be completely isolated, drifting in a world of non-experience. We have only light reflecting from the objects around us, human and other, giving us the experience of form and movement; sound emanating from those objects when they vibrate at a level within our hearing range; touch sensation from those elements of the physical world with which we come in direct contact; smells of those objects that release into the air around us sufficient numbers of the molecules that our olfactory sense is able to pick up; and the tastes of chemicals that reach the sensory buds of our tongues. This is all we have of the world external to our bodies, whether through direct perception or aided by technological extension. Language and cultural patterns are significant elements of the perceived external world. From the interaction between internal motives and associations among external stimuli are built meaning, understanding, knowing, and identity.

The elements of the external world have no intrinsic meaning or quality beyond that which we assign to them. The object we call a teacup is a teacup only to us. As we look around, we experience a world saturated with meaning and what is termed "qualia" (the redness of red, the heaviness of weight) but all of that is created after the fact, so to speak, is created internally.[14]

We don't always or necessarily know more about the world than do other animals with less complex nervous systems, nor do we necessarily have a richer experience of the world. For example, a dog knows much more about and has a richer experience of the olfactory environment than do we. Organisms have different understandings of the world depending on their perceptual apparatus and the complexity of their nervous system. The combination of our human perceptual apparatus and the complexity of our nervous system produces our particular knowing of the world, our relational/communicational experience, and our creative abilities. At the fundamental level, we move in our environment as does any living organism, plant or animal, sensing our environment through the sensory apparatus we have, seeking and moving toward that which will nourish us, that which will promote our survival, and moving away from or defending against that which is or appears to be noxious or threatening.[15] This is the process of meaning making for every organism.[16] In this respect, we differ from an amoeba only in kind, not in type.[17]

Three Levels of Survival

Humans are concerned with three levels or realms of survival, three aspects of experience for which we seek security and stability. We act to preserve and promote 1) our physical, 2) our psychological, and 3) our social survival. Do I have enough? Am I someone? Do I belong?

Physical

Our primary survival concern is physical. We are compelled to remain alive and to procreate. We are biological beings and, like all other living organisms, our most fundamental motivation is to continue being alive. The urge to live has been evolutionarily selected for. Over the course of evolution, those individuals with the stronger drive to continue living were more likely to survive and pass along their life-eager genes to the next generation. (We can experience this characteristic by lying down on the floor and trying to die by an act of will. We witness the characteristic in plants, animals, and people, in their determination to continue even in the face of grievous assaults to the body.) This primary motive influences how we function in the social realm. The motivation to physically survive, and the accompanying and ever-present fear associated with this need, the fear that we will not survive, are fundamental drivers of much of our behavior to a degree and in ways that are often, and perhaps most often, not readily apparent to us. As we say about our daily work, our busy commercial and creative activities, they are to "make a living."

In addition to and intimately interrelated with our drive to survive physically, we are motivated to maintain psychological equilibrium and to survive in the social realm. To a significant degree, our physical survival depends upon psychological stability and functional success within a social order. As our physical survival requires sufficient food, water, and protection from the elements, so also our psychological and social survival call for certain provisional, in the sense of providing for, conditions.

Psychological

Psychological survival requires a minimum degree of self-identity stability and a coherent and relatively consistent understanding of the world, of the meaning of things. Along the continuum of psychological health, the brain will do what it can to maintain the coherence and consistency of its conceptual models of self and world even when the match with external reality is poor and the identity construct is less than ideally functional. We can be as vociferous in rejecting ideas and information that contradict and threaten our self-identity and our model of the world as we can be in avoiding or attacking entities that threaten our physical survival. Our attachment to ideas and information that are integral to our identity and world-view can be as firm and committed as our passion for breathing. We see, often with wonder and dismay, how humans will sacrifice their own life or kill others for an idea or a belief.[18]

Social

Social survival requires belonging to and acceptance within a social group. As is commonly noted, we are a social species. Our individual identities, our experience of self-meaning and purpose, and our understanding of the world are, in very large part, grounded in, develop out of, are imparted by our membership within groups – family, workplace, community, political party, religion, etc. Social ostracism or isolation threatens our psychological and our physical survival. We need love, acceptance, and belonging for healthy development and security, both physical and psychological.

These three realms of experience are interlinked, overlapping, and interdependent. We act to maximize success in each of the realms. Threats to our social survival have implications for our psychological and physical survival. Threats to our psychological well-being have implications for our social and physical survival. Each of the three is, to one degree or another, dependent on success with the other two. And, of course, threats to our physical survival threaten our very existence without which there can be no psychological or social survival.

Much of our behavior can be understood as promoting, protecting, or reacting to past deficiencies in the satisfaction of one or more of these survival interests and many of our conflict behaviors are in response to threats, actual or perceived, to our survival in one or more of these domains. Again, we are living organisms like any other in these respects, compelled to survive and procreate. We are able to perceive and react to the elements of our environment, with greater or lesser success depending on the vagaries of chance and the conditions of the moment. But we are also the particular organism we call human, distinctively characterized by capacities beyond any other living organism due to the evolved complexity of our nervous system that allows for a deeply self-reflective identity, an advanced use of language and communication, and a capacity for agency like no other organism.

Constant Process of Environmental Assessment

As living organisms seeking to survive, we are engaged in a constant process of environmental assessment, responsive to incoming stimuli for the purposes of maximizing our survival success.[19] We must understand our environment in order to successfully navigate its physical and social topographies. For this reason, we evaluate all incoming perceptual stimuli to determine whether what is being perceived is conducive or detrimental to our survival, whether it is safe or threatening, to determine if we understand its significance to us, its meaning.[20] The activity of assessment is constant. It is less apparent in the midst of the familiar, in the midst of the already known and learned. But it is less apparent not because the learning function is less active but only because the incoming stimuli confirm what is already known and so our attention is not aroused.[21] As soon as a new stimulus is perceived, or a stimulus challenges or contradicts what has already been encoded, the attentive focus of the organism is aroused and directed at the new stimulus, the new information.[22]

This inquisitive feature, common to all living organisms, is developed to such a degree in humans that our inquiry into the meaning of our surroundings has produced the dimensions of our science and technologies, our artistic endeavors, and drives our persistent philosophical inquiries. There are four aspects of this necessary organism function particularly relevant to relational dynamics involved in conflict and conflict resolution.

Always Assigning Meaning

First, we are always assigning meaning to incoming stimuli[23] (more on the process of assigning meaning later). We cannot process a perceptual experience without evaluating it, naming it, categorizing it, assigning it meaning of one sort or another.[24] You, the reader, are doing this as you read these words, attempting to determine if you agree with them or not, if they make sense within your world understanding, whether they fit within your reality construct, whether they threaten or support, confirm or contradict what you already believe to be true of the world, and whether they matter to you. When we meet someone new,[25] this function of analysis and evaluation is active as we seek to determine the meaning or significance of the individual to our well-being. Are they familiar or foreign, similar to us or different,[26] into which of the established categories in our typology of the world do they belong?[27] The incoming stimuli are "measured against" the encoded matrices of meaning already established by past experience, through processes of neural activation and association (more on these processes later).[28] We are genetically prepared to identify "discrepant and therefore potentially threatening sensory events" (Tucker & Luu, 2012, p. 86). This is one of the reasons we respond to conflict as we do, with heightened alertness, attention, and elevated visceral response. Conflicts convey "discrepant and therefore potentially threatening sensory events" and produce decision uncertainty.

Dislike of Unknowns and Uncertainty

Second, we do not easily tolerate unknowns. We are uncomfortable with uncertainty. We want to name and make sense of all objects of perception.[29] Over the course of evolutionary history, accurate understanding of the environment increased survival fitness. We must find a way to assimilate new information into our already established neural structures, change or elaborate those structures to incorporate (accommodate) new information, or dismiss, deny, or ignore new information as inconsistent with or irrelevant to our understanding of the world.[30]

One way or another, we want a coherent and consistent view of the world. Contradictions, paradoxes, and dilemmas are difficult for us.

Familiar Can Be Ignored

Third, the familiar can be ignored or not paid attention to because we know it already.[31] It is the different, the unfamiliar, the new, the unexpected, or that which contradicts what we already know to be "true" to which our attention is drawn. The significance of the familiar is already established.[32] Not only is the familiar named and cataloged as known but research suggests that, "The brain tags familiar things as good things" (Haidt, 2013, p. 65). This is to say we have a default skepticism about the new or different, particularly if the information contradicts what we already know, and a default preference for the familiar. The familiar feels safer. This is one of the reasons disagreements are disturbing. What is different challenges our understanding of reality and makes us uncomfortable. Among other dimensions, we categorize also along the continuum from familiar to unknown, and show a preference for the former. This is not to say that we are not inquisitive and curious. We most evidently are. Thus the dynamics discussed next.

Mixed Relationship to Learning

Fourth, we have a mixed response to learning opportunities. On the one hand, because we need to know the characteristics of our physical and social environments in order to survive, we are eager and able to learn. We experience internal pleasure reward incentives in the learning experience. On the other hand, we can be resistant to new information that contradicts past learning. (More on this balance when I talk about neural stability/plasticity balance in Chapter 3.)

However we resolve this dilemma, we are compelled to answer all questions that arise, and answers produce an experience of satisfaction. For example, research suggests that both children and adults assume that events have causes (Feldman, 2006, p. 129).[33] This characteristic is one aspect of our incessantly inquisitive, evolutionarily-selected-for need to understand our environment. For every question, we seek an answer. If we can't find one, we'll typically make one up. For every problem, we look for a solution. For every event, we look for a cause or a reason. Because the social world is intangible and its cues subtle, our interpretations of cause and meaning can easily be incorrect. We may wrongly project or misattribute for a variety of reasons. Incoming stimuli may activate previously encoded neural structures that are an inexact or incorrect match with the current external reality. The construction of world meaning is a somewhat precarious venture fraught with possibilities of inaccuracies, inconsistencies, and mistaken biases of various shades.

We become preoccupied with unanswered questions, so much so that our brains work on them as we sleep. That we are inclined to find or propose an answer to all problems or questions that arise is evident in our attraction to puzzles and riddles, the pleasure we experience in solving them, and the pain (experienced as emotional or psychological but that is, at root, physical) we feel when we are unable to solve them.[34] Solutions are satisfying.

All of these characteristics of our human experience involve and are dependent on the capacity to encode perceptual experience in neural structures. Before looking in Chapter 3 at characteristics of the encoding function that are particularly relevant to and have implications for conflict work, I present in the next chapter a macro-level, non-technical review of the basic brain encoding function.

Notes

1 William James (as quoted in Edelman, 2006, p. 4) defined consciousness as a process whose function is knowing.
2 Crosswhite (2013, p. 183) emphasizes the idea that identity is a product of relationship, "a deep rhetorical understanding that beings come to be what they are out of the encounter itself."
3 "learning is invariably directed by motive controls" (Tucker and Luu, 2012, p. 3). By "motive controls," Tucker means the internal motivational survival imperatives and mechanisms for maintaining internal homeostasis that are genetically inherited (adaptive), embedded in the brain stem and lower brain structures, including and especially the limbic system.
4 "natural selection remains a 'struggle for existence' but becomes primarily a struggle with other human beings for control of the resources that support life and allow one to reproduce ... Human behavior, and at an abstract level the behavior of all species, can thus be conceptualized in terms of an evolved motivation to control" (Geary, 2005, p. 3).
5 "the function of brain and mind is to process socially and ecologically salient information and to guide the organism's behavior in ways that result in survival ... or reproductive ... advantages" (Geary, 2005, p. 123); "A brain's job is to support the survival of the creature in which it resides" (Cozolino, 2014, p. 175).
6 "Long before the appearance of vertebrates, *all* the major protein superfamilies had formed. Variations and elaborations within superfamilies were seen thereafter, of course, but no completely original protein superfamilies are found in humans that might account for the cognitive differences between us and our closest relatives, chimpanzees, or even between us and simple worms" (Churchland, 2002, p. 324); "We humans are just mammals that never quite mature. As a result, we retain a kind of embryonic transience throughout life, our neuroanatomy changing (irreversibly) through each experience and behavioral choice" (Tucker and Luu, 2012, p. x).
7 "the wrinkled cortical mantle of the brain has about thirty billion nerve cells or neurons and one million billion connections. The number of possible active pathways of such a structure far exceeds the number of elementary particles in the known universe" (Edelman, 2006, p. 18).
8 "We reason and think (and, I would add, feel, perceive, react) with our brains, but our brains are as they are – hence our cognitive faculties are as *they* are – because our brains are the products of biological evolution. Our cognitive capacities have been shaped by evolutionary pressures and bear the stamp of our long evolutionary history" (Churchland, 2002, p. 40).
9 "we don't have conscious access to reality in a direct sense. We only have access to the mental (and neural) processes of our senses ... we are separated from reality not only by the channels of our sensory systems but also by the biases and inadequacies of our cognitive elaborations of those systems" (Tucker, 2007, p. 70)

10 The question often arises about a sixth sense, what is sometimes referred to as intuition. From the embodied perspective, either that experience is the product of our underappreciated five senses or it is a capacity that derives from perceptual apparatus not yet clearly identified. The essential question is whether we are embodied, whether with five or six senses.

11 "For, no organism, including the human, can surpass the limits imposed by the sensory and motor capabilities it inherits. In other words, that heritage – after critical postnatal periods – limits our sense to light, sound, touch, olfaction, and taste within certain ranges of frequency, intensity, and chemical composition" (Fuster, 2013, p. 51).

12 "The particular patterns of synaptic connections in an individual's brain, and the information encoded by these connections, are the keys to who that person is" (LeDoux, 2003, p. 3).

13 "The world is met at the body surface, at the somatic shell, either through the sense data or the information patterns required for taking concrete action" (Tucker, 2007, p. 211).

14 There is a large and rapidly increasing body of philosophical and neuroscientific literature on the question of how the brain, a physical entity, produces the experience of qualia, an experience that seems to be nonphysical. That discussion is beyond the scope of this book. For our purposes here, it is sufficient to acknowledge that qualia are part of the human experience.

15 In this regard, note the statement by Karl Popper in his collection of essays *In Search of a Better World: Lectures and essays from thirty years* (1995), in which he says, "All things living are in search of a better world. Men, animals, plants, even unicellular organisms are constantly active. They are trying to improve their situation, or at least to avoid its deterioration . . . Every organism is constantly preoccupied with the task of solving problems. These problems arise from its own assessments of its condition and of its environment; conditions which the organism seeks to improve" (as quoted in Brain Pickings at https://www.brainpickings.org/2017/01/26/karl-popper-in-search-of-a-better-world-truth-certainty/?utm_source=Brain+Pickings&utm_campaign=2d27810e3a-EMAIL_CAMPAIGN_2017_03_10&utm_medium=email&utm_term=0_179ffa2629-2d27810e3a-236523045&mc_cid=2d27810e3a&mc_eid=13eb06771e).

16 "Because the human brain is the product of evolution, we can expect to find instructive similarities and continuities between representing in infants and adults, and between representing in human and nonhuman animals. A theory that predicts failure in *any* continuity between humans and other animals in, say spatial or motor or perceptual representation would raise a red flag. A theory that entails a magical origin for complex human representational capacities will raise a red flag. More generally, in science any hypothesis that fills a gap by saying 'and then a miracle happened' is not compelling" (Churchland, 2002, p. 283).

17 Difference in kind but not in type means that humans belong to the same category as do all plants and animals, the category of living organisms, and it is only that we are a different kind of organism. The exceptionalization of humans classifies humans as a different type of being, as did the Christian cosmology of the Middle Ages, for example, with its hierarchy of beings identifying the different types of incarnation, with humans situated between the higher animals and the angels. In that cosmology, humans were seen as qualitatively different than animals, a different type of being, whereas I would say we are only different quantitatively. All organisms, from plants to single-celled organisms and up through the ranks to humans, must have, in order to survive and be alive, the ability to sense and experience their environment. The difference is only in what kind of perceptual capacity. In this way of seeing things, human consciousness is a different kind of consciousness, not a different type of event. Humans are only a further elaboration of a developmental process that began with the first appearance of life.

18 In this regard, Gilligan (1996, pp. 96–97) noted, "people feel incomparably more alarmed by a threat to the psyche or the soul or the self than they are by a threat to the body. The death of the self is of far greater concern than the death of the body. People

will willingly sacrifice their bodies if they perceive it as the only way to avoid 'losing their souls,' 'losing their minds,' or 'losing face.' . . . a perceived threat to the integrity and survival of a person's culture is perceived as a threat to the integrity and survival of the individual's personality or character, and to the viability of one's ethical value system which is a central and essential component of both personality and culture, and is what most intimately links the self and its culture, the culture and its selves. Those are among the reasons why the death of one's culture is tantamount to the death of one's self."

19   "Brains evaluate everything in terms of potential threat or benefit to the self, and then adjust behavior to get more of the good stuff and less of the bad" (Haidt, 2013, p. 64). Of course, this is not to deny the expression of altruistic and cooperative behaviors. See, for example, Dacher Keltner's (2009) *Born to be Good: The science of a meaningful life*, and the work of Frans De Waal.

20   "All living things need to classify their inputs and act on them as best they can. The *neural best-fit matching networks* of our brains are far from perfect; for example, we often initially mistake a stranger for someone we know . . . It is often useful to think of the brain as a system for finding solutions to complex computational problems involving many variables, which themselves are known only approximately" (Feldman, 2006, p. 67).

21   "The model may adapt slightly, but only slightly, because events are largely congruent with it. For the most part, certainty holds . . . significant new learning occurs only when events are discrepant" (Tucker 2007, p. 137).

22   "For example, neurons in the locus coeruleus fire whenever an animal enters a novel environment or something unexpected happens. When they fire, they release a neuromodulator – in this case, noradrenaline – over most, if not all, brain regions" (Edelman & Tononi, 2000, p. 90).

23   There's an inaccuracy in my language here and throughout. It is an inaccuracy of convenience and convention, common in conversation and writing, that is based on our consciousness experience of self rather than on what is actually happening in the body that produces our experience. The inaccuracy is one in which we attribute agency and purposeful action to behavior that is, rather, more receptive and reactive. I have said here, "we are always assigning meaning to incoming stimuli," suggesting that there is an independent self-directed entity that acts to assign meaning. Given what we are learning about the embodied self, what is likely a more accurate description is that external objects and events, in sufficient direct or mediated (through technologies) proximity to be perceived by the organism, stimulate the peripheral nervous system that then carries nerve impulses to the brain that activate previously encoded neural pathways, stimulating a series of neural associations and connections that produce the experience of meaning and trigger subsequent behavior. Such a description has implications (philosophical, ethical, and legal) for our understanding of self and free will that, while both interesting and salient, lie beyond the scope of this book. The organism does act, but not in the way we experience our acting. As Edelman (2004) puts it, "We must confront the difference between the first-person experience and the third-person description of the neural substrate that underlies that experience" (p. 74).

24   "the brain of the conscious verbal individual must close a pattern or 'make sense' at whatever cost" (Edelman, 2006, p. 113).

25   It is a developmental step to learn that others are not the same as we are. For example, "Repacholi & Gopnik found that 14-month old children shared the kind of food they themselves liked rather than the food that the target exhibited preference for. The experimenter made a facial expression of disgust or happiness after tasting either Goldfish crackers or broccoli. Although the 14-month olds consistently shared the crackers (their own preference), the 18 month olds were sensitive to the facial expressions of preference. Repacholi & Gopnik suggest the possibility that although the 14-month olds "were beginning to acquire a psychological conception of desire, it was, nonetheless, egocentric. Thus, although they understood that people request things

because of some underlying desire, they mistakenly believe that everyone's desires are the same" (as reported in Nichols, 2000) To some degree, and not insignificantly, we never entirely lose the egocentric presumption.

26 "We trust and cooperate more readily with people who look and sound like us" (Haidt, 2013, p. 244).

27 "The categorization of knowledge . . . is the essence of all cognitive functions. Perception is the classing of the world into categories. Discrimination is the reclassing and decomposition of sensory information. Attention is the focusing on a class or subclass of sensory or motor information. All our memories are categorized by content, by time, by place, and so on. Reasoning and intelligence are closely dependent on the proper categorization of phenomena, external and internal" (Fuster, 2003, pp. 59–60).

28 "(The amygdala) is an organ of appraisal, and its main purpose has been, and continues to be, to create positive and negative associations (memories) with aspects of the environment to guide and control approach-avoidance behaviour . . . to approach what is life sustaining, avoid what has proved to be dangerous, and ignore things that are irrelevant. It is the amygdala that links our experiences in the present moment with appraisals from the past" (Cozolino, 2014, p. 175).

29 Try to think of something for which you don't have a name.

30 "It is through assimilation and accommodation that an organism interacts physically with external reality" (Tucker, 2007, p. 134).

31 "A decade ago, brain scanning revealed regions in the visual cortex that become flushed when we see an unfamiliar object or scene – a clock, a landscape. Less blood flows to these areas if the same object or scene is viewed a few minutes later. This been-there-done-that effect, or 'repetition suppression,' is a sign of the brain's efficiency and a form of unconscious learning" (Zalewski, 2015).

32 "Through control over these arousal and regulatory systems, the limbic circuits appear to respond to events to provide an initial screening for novelty and familiarity, thus coding the current context as to whether it is appropriate for learning" (Tucker, 2001, p. 9).

33 "System 1 infers and invents causes and intentions. And that, again, is something that happens automatically. Infants have it. We were exposed to that. Infants can recognize intention, and have a system that enables them to divine the intentions of objects that they see on a screen, like one object chasing another. This is something that an infant will recognize. An infant will expect one object that chases another to take the most direct route toward the other, not to follow the other's path, but actually to try to catch up. This is an infant less than 1 year old. Clearly we're equipped, and that is something that we have inherited, we're equipped for the perception of causality" (from talk by Daniel Kahneman at https://www.edge.org/conversation/daniel_kahneman-the-marvels-and-the-flaws-of-intuitive-thinking-edge-master-class-2011).

34 "Research with problem solving in laboratory experiments has shown that people remember the problems they did not complete more than the ones they did" (Tucker, 2007, p. 197).

2

THE NEURAL ENCODING FUNCTION

Within our skulls lives a fleshy organ of almost unimaginable complexity with functional dynamics that range from macro-level morphology to micro-level chemical and electrical activity at the cellular level.[1] Gerald Edelman (2005, p. 16) points out that if you started now counting the synapses (the structures that allow electrochemical signals to pass from one neuron to another and that are involved in establishing networks or webs of neuronal structures) in the brain at a rate of one per second, it would take you 32 million years to count them all.[2] Beyond what we are learning about brain function (for example, the sheer number of synapses,[3] the delicate balance of membrane properties that give neurons their subtle electrical charge, the cellular-level action of neurotransmitters, the molecular binding of neurotransmitters to post-synaptic receptors, the distributed and interconnected activity among different brain regions with different neurotransmitters and chemicals whose properties change the timing, amplitude, and sequences of neuronal firing, the reciprocal connections between different brain structures that provide what are called reentrant processes that seem to be key to consciousness and self-awareness (Edelman, 1992, 2006; Edelman and Tononi, 2000; Tucker, 2007; Tucker and Luu, 2012; Fuster, 2013)), there remains so much that we don't know, and very much more than we do know. What we do know remains disjointed and not unified, parts of a puzzle not all of which yet fit together. The vocabulary of neural structures, networks, matrices, circuits, etc. is to some degree only metaphorically representative of an organic reality that is much more complex and dynamic than we can easily visualize. The brain is in a constant hum of activity with millions of synapses firing simultaneously in a vast array of inter-related and overlapping patterns beyond our capacity to map at this point.

Neuroscience is in its relative infancy or perhaps its early adolescence, active, adventurous, and full of new discoveries and understandings. There are competing theories of how learning and memory work (for a review, see LeDoux, 2003), different frames of focus and emphasis (for example, Dehaene, 2001), and, as is true of all scientific frontiers, cumulative research is exploring dead ends and making course corrections as it constructs a reliable map of this new territory. Our tools, though increasingly powerful and able to provide access to finer detail, remain relatively blunt. Researchers are eager for the next generation of technology.[4] Moreover, different researchers work on different areas of the territory, from different perspectives, with different guiding premises and areas of focus,[5] make different interpretations of the evidence we have been able to decipher thus far, using different metaphors and terminology to describe brain function, the nature of consciousness, the self, and the interrelationship between conscious and unconscious activity. Somewhere in the neighborhood of 30,000 brain researchers gather each year for the Society of Neuroscience conference. As the accumulative research project progresses, there is some disagreement among the attendees about how the brain works and what is suggested about who and how we are. We are too early in our exploration for there to be a grand, universally agreed upon, coherent theory of brain function. We are like the proverbial blind men describing the elephant. The brain is a very complex elephant.

Until our more recent advances in neuroscience, human behavior has been described and understood without reference to the underlying physical determinants of those behaviors and often with recourse to explanations that assume a disembodied consciousness,[6] though some early theorists, including William James and Sigmund Freud, understood that there was very likely a neural basis to human consciousness experience and behavior. Tucker and Luu (2012, p. 4) note that:

> The neurologist and neuroanatomist Sigmund Freud had attempted to explain learning and memory within a model of self-organizing connections within neuronal networks . . . In his *Project for a Scientific Psychology*, Freud proposed that memory could be explained as a strengthening of neural connections through use . . . As the process of learning modifies neuronal connections, Freud recognized that neuronal networks face an inherent dilemma of maintaining stability or allowing plasticity.

In the face of the inadequate technology of the time, Freud abandoned his anatomical experimental approach to pursue his psychological theory-building and therapeutic practice.[7]

Though how the system of encoding, storage, recall, and connectivity works is not fully understood and theories are being built upon limited but advancing empirical evidence[8] (see, for example, Barsalou, 1999; Gallese, 2011; Tucker, 2001, 2007; Damasio, 1994, 1999, 2010; Edelman, 2005, 2006; Seung, 2012; Fuster, 2003, 2013; Kandel, 2006), there is growing consensus that we are embodied beings and the functional characteristics of the body will explain and determine the nature of our consciousness experience and behavior.[9]

Without going into the precise and intricate details of what we currently know of the biology, we can speak at the conceptual and non-technical level about the developmental process that encodes perceptual experience in neural networks (learning)[10] that are preserved and accessible (memory)[11] in a dynamic[12] structure within which novel connections can be made (creativity). This is the fundamental brain activity that allows for consciousness, cognition, and identity.[13] The process is ever-active as present experience combines with past experience to create the new and ever-evolving individual identity.[14] It's interesting and notable that we use the term "belief system" in an unintended reference to the fact that beliefs exist as a physical system of neural structures. We speak also of being "shaped" by our experience and of "formative" experiences. These metaphors apply literally. It is the body that is shaped and formed by experience, and particularly the neural structures of the brain. The "we" we speak of is our body.

The activity taking place within the organism as, for example, our head turns to follow an object or as we track the behaviors of two individuals with whom we are speaking, the vast amount of visual and auditory information we absorb and process in a constantly changing context against the backdrop of our previous experience in life, with processing happening at the microsecond scale and with no interruption in the assimilation, accommodation, and categorization processes taking place, boggles the mind (so to speak!). We remain unaware of the almost inconceivably complex internal events, active every moment, that determine our conscious and unconscious experience and our behavior.[15] We don't directly observe the physical processes that produce our lived experience, and until recently, our science, has not provided much of a view into those processes.[16] As a consequence, we have not tended to understand our behavior and experience in terms of the basic brain function of encoding perceptual experience in neural structures.

The neural encoding process begins at the very earliest stages of our development and continues throughout our lives. As Fuster (2003, pp. 35 and 37) puts it:

> At every step of development, the expression of (the) genetic plan, the structural phenotype of the neocortex, is subject to a wide variety of internal and external influences. These influences create the necessary and permissive conditions for the normal development of the neocortex and its neuronal networks. Among the essential factors is the interaction of the organism with its environment. Through sensory and motor interactions with the environment, the afferent, efferent, and association fibers of the neocortex will develop and form the networks that are to serve cognitive functions [and] Because the potential functional connections between neuronal assemblies and networks are practically infinite, there is no such thing as the complete cognitive development of the cortex. Networks and knowledge are open-ended. Never in the life of the individual do they cease to grow or be otherwise modified.

Prenatal Beginnings

As fetal development advances, the nervous system takes shape, from brain stem to mid-brain to cortex along with the extended peripheral nervous system. As the neural anatomy and perceptual systems develop, the establishment of neural matrices that encode proprioceptive and perceptual experience becomes possible.[17] We do not enter the world as a blank slate. Our genetic endowment prepares us with the capacity to engage with the world and we meet the world with given internal motives that are the survival imperatives of the lower and midbrain structures, brain stem and limbic system (Tucker, 2007).[18] That is to say, how we engage with the physical reality that is accessible to our senses is conditioned by our unconscious and preconscious survival motives. Genetic inheritance provides the structural capacity for consciousness, learning, and memory. Endowed with that structure, the individual is then shaped (literally) by experience.[19] Each individual interacts with the environment with her or his genetic inheritance and temperamental predisposition.[20] Perceptual experience is not, by itself, determinative of outcome. But whatever the composition of nature and nurture, the mix is encoded in neural structures that are relatively stable.[21]

As the fetus's perceptual apparatus begins to function, its brain is able to begin the process of learning, encoding perceptual and proprioceptive experience[22] in neural structures or networks or pathways or matrices or webs[23] that are established by the nerve signals triggered by perceived stimuli arriving from the peripheral nervous system as it interacts with the external world, the uterine environment to begin with.[24] Random spasmodic movement by the fetus begins to wire neural connections as the organism begins to discover and learn about itself and its surroundings, begins to experience its body in relation to the space around it.[25] The physical sensations of movement and touch begin to define identity.[26] These early experiences are stored in developing neural structures.[27] Without such storage, there would be no continuity, no accumulation of knowledge, and no development of self. The process of learning and memory accumulation begins in these early pre-birth stages and then accelerates upon birth when the infant is exposed to the myriad stimuli of the world into which it enters.[28] Thus begins the learning process and the formation of the structures that will subsequently allow and produce cognition and identity.[29] The processes that begin encoding perceptual experience and organizing corticolimbic networks through embryonic activity-dependent formation continue from birth throughout life, structuring the brain, with the canvas of knowledge increasingly busy with the neural structures formed from experience in the world.[30] The organizational process shaping the network anatomy is motivated by the organism's survival imperatives as they interact with the contextual conditions of the environment moment to moment (Tucker and Luu, 2012).[31]

As a side note, but significantly, the embryonic brain produces many more potential synaptic connections among neurons than are ultimately used. Those that are used remain. Those that are not are eliminated[32] in a "use it or lose it" winnowing process of subtractive elimination.[33] This process of activity-dependent pruning continues after birth.[34] It is known that the newborn arrives with a surplus of synaptic capacity (what Tucker and Luu (2012) refer to as "exuberant synaptogenesis") that provides a broad canvas of learning potential.[35]

Birth and the Beginning of Meaning Making

Very much over-simplifying the complex and not-yet-fully understood neuro-physiology, we can say that the newborn begins to "make sense" of the flood of stimuli to which it is exposed by linking one encoded perceptual experience with another.[36] We can describe this process in a kind of diagrammatic or analogic illustration of the actual global and integrated developmental experience of an individual. In actual life, no perceptual learning element is isolated from or independent of the full, multi-modal "world flow" consciousness experience of the individual moving through time and space. But a simplified description will remind us of, and allow us to talk about, the basic function of neural encoding and structural elaboration that is learning and memory formation.[37] So, for example, we can say that the physical sensation of mother's breast, experienced and encoded by the newborn, is linked with the neurally encoded experience of warmth and the sensation of hunger-satisfying nourishment, and later linked with the encoded perceptual experience of the mother's face to create matrices of meaning. Step by step, experience by experience, in interaction with its immediate physical surroundings to begin with, then its family, and, ultimately, its culture,[38] a world of meaning is constructed within the brain of the developing individual via encoding and associative linking of one perceptual experience with another, the basis of understanding, meaning, cognition, and self.[39] Fuster (2003, p. 112) notes, "knowledge, memory, and perception share the same neural substrate: an immense array of cortical networks or cognits that contain in their structural mesh the informational content of all three."

As another discrete example to illustrate the global process, an infant learns a new word by associating the sound, a nonsense syllable to begin with, with another perceptual experience.[40] The nonsense syllable "tree" is associated with the visible object (or the tactile perception for a blind child) that the culture, by convention, has named "tree," along with any additional perceptual impressions that are encoded with the first experience of a tree, particular scents or the moist greenery of spring, for example.[41] With repeated exposure, the nonsense sound is encoded as is the perceptual experience with which the sound is associated and the two are linked neurally, thereby creating meaning for each in their relationship.[42] When the sound is encountered again, parts of that neural structure are activated to produce the experience of knowledge, in this case knowledge of the word-sound and the naming of the object so called. Until there is something with which the nonsense syllable can be associated, there can be no meaning; the nonsense syllable will remain just that. This is why nonsense syllables are nonsense. They don't yet correspond to another perceptual experience established in a neural structure. As soon as a nonsense syllable is associated with a phenomenon, it takes on meaning and becomes a word. Assigned meaning through association is the process of language acquisition.[43] The ability to learn a language is the ability to encode and then match sounds with elements of experience (creating meaningful words) and to learn patterns of arrangements among categories of those sounds (grammar).[44]

Gradually, additional perceptual experiences are connected to the initial elementary neural structure.[45] Subsequent perceptual experiences having to do with trees build a complex, nuanced, and varied experience of "tree" encoded in extended, dynamic neural networks. Exposure to variations of case form the category,[46] and additional experiences of and with trees, climbing trees, falling from a tree, chopping down a tree, becoming lost in a forest, squirrels, birds, and other animals nesting in trees, picnicking or making love beneath a tree, as well as the link with arbitrary shapes on a page or computer screen that are the letters of a written language that have themselves been associated with particular verbal sounds to give them meaning, elaborate a vast neural matrix of associations having to do with trees and the individual's related experience over time – camp, car accident, lumber and building, deforestation, national forest management regimes, global respiration and atmospheric composition, climate change, concepts of growth and seasonality, fire cycles, etc.[47] There accumulates ever-more-complex and extensive neural circuits or networks, nets of networks, networks within networks (Fuster, 2013), systems of circuits (Damasio, 1999).[48] Meaning becomes elaborated in nets of associations.[49] These are the structures of understanding and the basis of cognition and identity.

The correspondence can be between a word-sound and an external object or an internal experience. When we are first exposed to the distinction between, for example, passive and active vocabulary, we can link the words "passive" and "active" to our internal experience of words used and words understood but not used. In that linkage, we learn something new. Prior to hearing these word-sounds linked to our internal experience, we had not known of these categories applied to language use. And we are able to make the connection between the words "passive" and "active" in this unfamiliar usage context because we had previously learned the meaning of the word-sounds "passive" and "active" in other contexts. So is constructed the edifice of knowledge day-by-day, moment-by-moment as we are exposed to new experience that we make meaning of by relating the new to the already known. As Bruce Hood puts it in his book *The Self Illusion* (2012, p. 8):

> These spreading patterns of electrical activity are the language of mental life. They are our thoughts. Whether they are triggered from the outside environment or arise from the depths of our mental world, all thoughts are patters of activation in the matrix that is our mind.

The mind arises from the patterns of neural connections in the network architecture in a state of constant associational activity (Tucker, 2007).

The encoded information is what we call knowing and is the structure of our identity.[50] We experience the patterns of activation as colors, objects, thoughts, meaning, recognition, emotions, self, etc., but what is actually happening is the firing of neuronal circuits. When we say we "know," really what we are saying is that we are experiencing the activation of neural structures that are configured through associative, combinatorial processes incorporating elements of various neural matrices previously established either as a result of perceptual experience or internal experience or both. In the act of perception, the continual interplay between perceived object and organism, dynamic and continuous, changes the organism, or at least changes the state of the organism. The degree of change depends on the nature of the relationship between organism and object and the significance or meaning of the object to the organism (Dehaene, 2001, p. 139). As Tucker and Luu (2012, p. 209) put it:

> Each cognitive process is a developmental event, an act of the historical self. Furthermore, each cognitive process is a transformational event; as the representation is consolidated, the self is then changed. The degree of change depends on the negotiation between assimilation and accommodation, effecting the consolidation of cognition . . . Thought shapes the literal anatomical structure of the brain, and the self.

Without an internal referent for a new perceptual experience, there can be no understanding and a new set of knowings must be developed, a new set of neural matrices established that will extend or link in one way or another to the matrices of meaning already existing.[51] We can imagine a flying pig only if we are already familiar with pigs and with flying.[52] We all have had the experience of trying to learn a new word-sound for which we have no easily identified referents. It might have been "heuristic" or "ouster," for example. Trying to learn the word, we might have asked ourselves whether heuristic was a noun or an adjective. Was ouster a noun or a verb? And if a noun, did it identify a person or an act? We might have had trouble finding associative links by which to give meaning to the word-sound. Perhaps you remember when you were young trying to "get" the meaning of words like irony or metaphor or cynic or euphemism, or the difference between paradox and dilemma. These words were more difficult to learn because it was more difficult to connect them with something we already knew, to make associations with previously encoded experience, or to attach them to any object of physical perception. This is the source of the problem that adult learners of English have with prepositions, a problem of referent, having the right association between word-sound and meaning. On this point, there was an interesting story in a *New York Times* article (Fuller, 2015) on a problem being faced in Myanmar as it opens to the rest of the world after 50 years of isolation.

The native language has no words for many of the objects and ideas that are standard and essential currency in global political, economic, commercial, and technical conversations. Not only are there no native words for racism, federal, globalization, institution, or privacy, for example, but the concepts don't exist so that even when an English word is imported or a new Burmese word-sound is created, speakers have no neural structure referent to which to associate the word-sound.[53]

We begin language use with words for physical objects and basic action, nouns and verbs (and in single syllables), because of the tangible accessibility of the word-sound's perceptual referent, allowing neural structures of meaning to be more directly and easily established. "See Spot run," not "See Spot hesitate," or "See Spot contemplate," or "Consider Spot's running." Many words take some time and repeated exposure to learn and understand. The capacity for abstract thought requires a number of years to develop.

From these elementary though complex beginnings, the elaborate construction of world-knowledge and self-identity are built.[54] To repeat, what we call "learning" is the process of encoding perceptual experience.[55] What we call "knowing" is the activation of embodied perceptual experience in networks of encoded neural structures and associations. Memory, the requisite for self-identity, is the activation of encoded neural structures.[56] Thinking and creativity are the linking of encoded neural matrices of meaning. The elaborations and extensions of neural structures in response to successive perceptual experience[57] and the dynamic, variable linkages among them, continue in cascading nets of associations of decreasing salience from strong to faint, and from conscious to unconscious, depending on the circumstances of the moment.[58] Each new perceptual experience builds on what has already been encoded,[59] connecting in multiple ways to different parts of the complex network with varying degrees of strength.[60] Meaning is always and only created by association.[61] As Mark Johnson (2007, p. 10) puts it, "Meaning is relational." The process is cumulative and elaborative. We are constantly adding to our definition and experience of self and our understanding of the world, familiar experiences reinforcing and confirming already established structures and the unfamiliar presenting the brain with the challenge whether to incorporate the new information within, add to, or change its already established neural structures.[62]

In this way, the "you" as you are today is formed from the moment of your conception in the joining of sperm and egg to the fullness of your current experience of a complex self in a world rich with meaning. One's formative experiences will be more or less salutary. As we know, adverse childhood experiences and deleterious cultural identity messages will be as impactful as will be more positive self-definition messages, contributing to the fundamental architecture of the developing brain and having lasting effects on learning, relational responses, and resiliency.[63]

Each moment's new experience will either confirm or complement past experience, add new information, or contradict past experience.[64] Whatever the case, each moment's information must be addressed in one way or another and must be related to the neural structures already established, building a coherent and consistent understanding of the world. Confirming information will strengthen or reinforce previously established neural pathways. New information will add to the complex networks of encoded understanding. New information will always be measured against already established neural structures. The ease with which and how new information is incorporated into the elaborating structures will depend on many factors. Contradictory information has to be dealt with, either held in parallel with the previously encoded experience with which it is contradictory or replacing or revising some parts of the neural networks.[65]

The system is in a constant state of change and development. As Jerome Feldman (2006, p. 72) puts it:

> It is now clear that learning and permanent memory in animals come about through the strengthening of neural connections (synapses) . . .When the strength of connections between neurons is modified, we have a fundamental structural change. The neural network is now different and will respond differently to new experience. That is, *learning does not add knowledge to an unchanging system − it changes the system.*

The architecture of dynamic wiring among neural connections allows for novel associations, subtleties of meaning, variations of response to the same stimuli in different contexts, and the richness of meaning that characterizes the human consciousness experience.

The encoding of perceptual experience is not an exact recording, not a one-to-one mapping.[66] The tracings are partial and inexact, dynamic, variably persistent, malleable, often more impressionistic than a precise or exact representation of the mind-independent reality, though there is a good deal of precision, accuracy, and durability involved, sufficient, in most cases, to successfully, to one degree or another, navigate our physical and social environments.[67]

The networks that develop in response to perceptual experience are formed through changes in the strengths of the synaptic connections between neurons.[68] Repeated firing strengthens connections. Neurons that fire together, wire together.[69] Thus the impressive, in both senses of the word, impact of culture's repeated and pervasive messaging on individual identity.

Thinking is a process of accessing and linking encoded material.[70] The linking and combining of elements in the vast neural web is always happening, awake or asleep, as long as we are alive, in response to the stimuli of lived experience. The buzz of consciousness, the busyness of mind chatter, and the phantasms of dreams are the activity of neural firing· the hum of connections and associations being made.[71] There is a selection process involved that has to do with survival salience.[72] The sets of associations and linkages are determined by the conditions of the moment. The conscious aspect is what we are aware of. The unconscious portion allows functional activity without flooding conscious awareness. Much is unconscious because there is not need for attention in the moment. That said, the unconscious associations influence behavior as much as, if not more than, our conscious associations (Haidt, 2013; Churchland, 2002).[73]

The complexity, subtlety, and scope of our thinking seems mysterious and impressive to us only when we forget that thinking is no more than the elaboration of associations or connections among previously encoded perceptual experience made complex because of the vast storage, retrieval, and associational capacities of the human nervous system.[74] Certainly, our thinking capacity is impressive, but it is built only upon the associational process of linking one item with another. The thinking process begins with the relatively simple and basic associations the infant makes among early-encoded neural structures, word-sound "hot" and the physical sensation of heat, for example. What we call "abstract" thought is thought like any other, built up of the elementary encoded elements of perceptual experience, composed of more or less complex and innovative neural nets of associations.[75] Thoughts, call them abstract or not, are a form of creativity, the novel linkage of neural structures. If no perceptual experience, then no encoded neural trace (learning) and no access to storage (memory) because nothing has been stored to access, and therefore no thought. From the infant's germinal experiences, gradually more complex thinking is elaborated. Learning to think is a bit like learning to juggle. We begin with two balls and work up from there. The difference is in the physical limits to the number of balls we are capable of keeping in the air, with juggling somewhere in the neighborhood of 12 or 13, with thinking many more by many orders of magnitude.

As is suggested by this account of learning and knowing, there are features of the system of neural encoding and storage that are particularly relevant to the presence of conflict in our social relations and to the challenges we face in preventing or resolving conflicts. In the next chapter, I consider seven of those characteristics.

Notes

1 "In the 50 million years of primate evolution ...the relative size of the neocortex accelerates; it grows disproportionately to such a degree that it seems legitimate to speak of a 'neocortical explosion'" (Fuster, 2003, p. 19).
2 Some estimate that there may be in the neighborhood of 10,000 distinct types or classes of neurons in the brain.
3 Even speaking of synapses is a kind of coarse generalization that hides the complexity of the physical reality. As Michael Hendricks describes them, "Synapses are the physical contacts between neurons where a special form of chemoelectric signaling – neurotransmission – occurs, and they come in many varieties. They are complex molecular machines made of thousands of proteins and specialized lipid structures. It is the precise molecular composition of synapses and the membranes they are embedded in that confers their properties ...The features of your neurons (and other cells) and synapses that make you 'you' are not generic. The vast array of subtle chemical modifications, states of gene

regulation, and subcellular distributions of molecular complexes are all part of the dynamic flux of a living brain. These things are not details that average out in a large nervous system; rather, they are the very things that engrams (the physical constituents of memories) are made of" (September 15, 2015, www.technologyreview.com/view/541311/ the-false-science-of-cryonics/?utm_campaign=newsletters&utm_source=newsletter-daily-all&utm_medium=email&utm_content=20150916).

4 One of the newest technologies is called optogenetics, invented by scientists at Stanford University and first described in 2005. With this technology, scientists are able to insert a genetically modified light-sensitive gene into specific neurons and then activate or turn off the neuron with a hair-thin fiber-optic thread inserted into that brain cell, thereby determining specific neural involvement in brain function and behavior. For example, with the manipulation of particular neurons, the behavior of a mouse can be changed from violently aggressive to tranquil in an instant. This technology offers specificity beyond that of other technologies like fMRI and dense-array EEG to further our understanding of neural function. As another example, a new chemical treatment allows researchers to directly see nerve fibers in mammalian brains. Newly developed sophisticated computer programs let researchers match nerve cells and fibers in micro-thin brain slices to create a three-dimensional map of the connections. Another technique, called Clarity, immobilizes biomolecules such as protein and DNA in a plastic-like mesh in a postmortem brain, after which, the fats in the brain tissue are dissolved to expose the three-dimensional wiring pattern to view (as reported in https://www.technologyreview.com/s/528226/neurosciences-new-toolbox).

5 "Figuring out how the brain works is a daunting task. For that reason, neuroscientists usually work only on pieces of the puzzle – like aspects of cognition, emotion, or motivation – rather than on the whole organ and its systems at once" (LeDoux , 2003, p. 301).

6 "We believe that this convergence between neurobiology and phenomenology is not a mere coincidence. On the contrary, it can yield valuable insights into the kinds of neural processes that can account for the corresponding properties of conscious experience" (Edelman and Tononi, 2000, pp. 111–112).

7 More than 30 years later, in *Beyond the Pleasure Principle*, Freud wrote, "Biology is truly a land of unlimited possibilities. We may expect it to give us the most surprising information, and we cannot guess what answers it will return in a few dozen years to the questions we have put to it. They may be a kind that will blow away the whole of our artificial structure of hypotheses" (as quoted in Schwartz, 2015, pp. vii–viii).

8 "We do not know exactly, of course, how functional patterns are distributed across the corticolimbic networks. Judging from the way memories are activated, these network patterns often seem to resonate and recruit new patterns, as if forming complex waves of meaning" (Tucker, 2007, p. 183).

9 "Mental activity is brain activity" (Churchland, 2002, p. 30); "We also know that the mind arises from the brain and that all psychiatric illnesses involve organic processes" (Cozolino, 2014, p. 77).

10 "At the core of cognition is adaptive memory consolidation, through which learning produces structural changes in the brain and the self" (Tucker and Luu, 2012, p. vi).

11 "An innate capacity for synapses to record and store information is what allows (brain) systems to encode experiences. If the synapses of a particular brain system cannot change, this system will not have the ability to be modified by experience and to maintain the modified state. As a result, the organism will not be able to learn and remember through the functioning of that system" (LeDoux, 2003, p. 9).

12 "in each brain, the consequences of both a developmental history and an experiential history are uniquely marked. For example, from one day to the next, some synaptic connections in the same brain are likely not to remain exactly the same; certain cells will have retracted their processes, others will have extended new ones, and certain others will have died, all depending on the particular history of that brain" (Edelman and Tononi, 2000, p. 47).

13 "the mind must be achieved by the connectional architecture of the brain" (Tucker, 2007, p. 179).

14 "the phenomena of mind are due to the ongoing developmental changes in neuroanatomical differentiation. Every thought reorganizes the tissue" (Tucker and Luu, 2012, p. v).

15 "We do not presently understand fully how this categorization (neural mapping) is done but . . . we believe it arises through the selection of certain distributed patterns of neural activity as the brain interacts with the body and the environment" (Edelman and Tononi, 2000, p. 48).

16 "we can never be conscious of the inner workings of our cerebral processes, but only of their outputs" (Dehaene, 2001, p. 16).

17 "At the physical level, there must be mechanisms that encode the data of experience within neural networks" (Tucker, 2007, p. 94).

18 "To be adaptive, memory and cognition must be motivated" (Tucker and Luu, 2012, p. 70).

19 "the gross connectivity of the brain's networks and the structure of the brain are controlled by genetics, but the fine connectivity is achieved through experience. Functional differentiation is experience dependent" (Tucker, 2007, pp. 160–161).

20 "Nature and nurture become one during development, and the line between organic and functional dissolves into what is now called *experience-dependent plasticity*. This term denotes that our brains are structured and restructured by interactions with our social and natural environments" (Cozolino, 2014, pp. 77–78).

21 "According to the now most plausible network models, knowledge and memory are contained in an immense array of overlapping, interactive, and widely distributed networks of interconnected neurons of the cerebral cortex. The networks are formed by life experience and constitute the substrate of all cognitive functions" (Fuster, 2013, p. 62).

22 "it may even be that a spontaneously moving fetus in late development distinguishes between brain inputs arising from self-generated bodily movements and those inputs generated by motions induced from without. There is enough evidence to make the case that input from value systems [Edelman's term for neural systems responsible for releasing survival-related neurochemicals] and proprioceptive systems can combine with modal sensory inputs to yield some of the earliest conscious experiences. It is likely that such fundamental adaptive systems remain central for the rest of an individual's conscious life, whatever the additional qualia may be that develop with ongoing experience" (Edelman, 2005, p. 133).

23 Pick your terminology: Edelman (2006) calls them neuronal groups, neural circuits, and even at one point meshworks (Edelman and Tononi, 2000); Damasio (1999) calls them variously neural pathways, neural patterns, neural ensembles, neural maps, neural circuits, and neural networks; Feldman (2006) calls them neural clusters; Tucker (2007) calls them neural networks; Dehaene (2001) use the term workspace; Fuster (2013) uses the terms cognitive networks, neuron assemblies, or cognits; and Freud (1990) used the term associative paths.

24 "every one of your sense organs contains neurons that are activated by some type of physical stimulus. Sensory neurons kick off the journey along neural pathways from stimulus to response . . . It is clear that these pathways exist; if they didn't, you wouldn't be able to respond to stimuli" (Seung, 2012, p. 52).

25 "the mind evolved from the brain's mechanisms of bodily control" (Tucker, 2007, p. 12).

26 "The embryo's own spontaneous, spasmodic actions become the motive vehicle for the early stages of neural self-organization" (Tucker, 2007, p. 281).

27 "the control of neural development, through regulating the spatiotemporal organization of neural activity, is a process of self-organization. Initially, it proceeds under general embryological guidelines, but even in the early intrauterine phases it is self-organizing, in that the fetus's own spontaneous actions shape its experiential activity-dependent plasticity. In childhood, the primary motive vectors of approach (hedonic expectancies) and avoidance (anxiety and discrepancy) appear to continue the embryological activity controls of habituation and redundancy" (Tucker and Luu, 2012, p. 137).

28 "Through continued neural ontogenesis, mammals continue to grow and differentiate their neural networks throughout life. Neural growth is continuous . . . Learning is then a literal neurodevelopmental process . . . Just as cognition must be understood as a neurodevelopmental process, mammalian brain development must be understood as a cognitive process" (Tucker and Luu, 2012, p. vii).

29 "This discrimination (the notion of self) may actually originate in utero during the late fetal stages, but certainly occurs during early postnatal development. It provides a reference for distinguishing self from nonself through kinesthetic inputs that may act in addition to, and separately from, explicit sensory contributions to qualia space" (Edelman 2004, p. 129).

30 "Because of the practically infinite combinatorial power of the 10 to 20 billion neurons or brain cells in our cerebral cortex, the breadth and specificity of our individual memories and knowledge are potentially infinite" (Fuster, 2013, p. 15).

31 "As the mind operates, it reflects the ongoing neurodevelopmental process, continuing the self-organization of neural connections that began in the embryonic differentiation of the neural tube and that continues throughout life" (Tucker and Luu, 2012, p. v).

32 "The specification of the fine structure of neural connections is activity-dependent, meaning that only synapses that are engaged by ongoing brain activity are retained" (Tucker and Luu, 2012, p. 2).

33 "The brain's infantile architecture is woven from an overly dense pattern of neural connectivity, and the functional networks are sculpted through Darwinian subtractive elimination – the death of unused connections" (Tucker, 2007, p. 281); "The maturation process of the memory substrate, however, consists not only of a gradual increment of elementary structure, but also of the pruning of that structure. Neurons, Axons, and synapses that are not used are eliminated from an early exuberance of them. That attrition results from the selection of those elements that the growing organism utilizes at the expense of those that it does not" (Fuster, 2013, p. 74).

34 "The activity-dependent sculpting of neural connectivity in embryonic differentiation is now only the beginning of a momentum of adaptive information structure that continues throughout life. As it continues, activity-dependent sculpting forms the fine architecture of cortical anatomy to encode the distributed representation of memory" (Tucker, 2007, p. 162).

35 "In humans, this sculpting of cortical anatomy by experience occurs not just for a few months or years as in most mammals, but over a decade or more. If there is a single biological fact that allowed language to evolve from prelinguistic cognition, it was probably not a unique gyrus of the brain, nor a particular segment of the vocal tract. Rather, it was the radical neoteny that allows culture rather than the genome to specify the connectional anatomy of the human brain" (Tucker, 2001, p. 3).

36 An infant, once able to perceive and recognize discrete objects and people, is at first surprised and intrigued when one disappears and reappears from behind an object. The disappearance is complete and utter until the baby begins to "learn," encoding perceptual experience that says the other doesn't disappear when he or she is not seen.

37 "Learning is neural morphogenesis, continued into postnatal development . . . Learning is then the continuation of neural differentiation throughout development" (Tucker and Luu, 2012, p. 1).

38 Our perceptual focus begins with the physical world, the world of objects, their edges, dimensions, movement, texture, solidity, taste (note how the infant brings physical objects to its mouth to learn about them) and their salience to our survival needs (food, water, shelter, warmth, etc.) and secondarily, though no less importantly, moves to the social world, the dynamics of the other humans in our environment. (Note our tendency, both in our projections and our attachments, to anthropomorphize animals that are neither inanimate objects nor human beings.)

39 "By considering these questions, we will see how it may be possible to relate the mind's psychological structures to the brain's physical architecture. This is an architecture formed by the pattern of connections among neurons" (Tucker, 2007, p. 31) and "the structures of intelligence are achieved through neural connections, such that the pattern of those connections implies the pattern of mind" (Tucker, 2007, p. 92).

40 Tucker and Luu emphasize that the intention of the speaker contributes significant content in the information exchange that produces meaning. "Studies of infants learning new words in a naturalistic context of interaction with the mother have shown that infants attend carefully to the mother's intention in speaking a new word, and use the context of her gaze or actions in interpreting the significance and meaning of the word . . . A word is not learned out of the context, such as if the mother speaks it randomly. The meaning of the word is then literally 'what Mom means'. The child then internalizes this as her own meaning. The brain's representations, and the implicit self assembled from them, are residuals of the social context. Self-regulation then continues to be built on the templates of internalized social transactions" (Tucker and Luu, 2012, p. 137).

41 "As Freud wrote in his monograph on aphasia, a word 'acquires its meaning by being linked to an "object-presentation" . . . The object-presentation itself is . . . a complex of associations made up of the greatest variety of visual, acoustic, tactile, kinaesthetic, and other presentations' (1915, Appendix C, p. 213)" (Gallese, 2011, p. 198).

42 "The image we see is based on changes which occurred in our organism – including the part of the organism called brain – when the physical structure of the object interacts with the body. The signaling devices located throughout our body structure – in the skin, in the muscles, in the retina, and so on – help construct neural patterns which map the organism's *interaction* with the object. The neural patterns are constructed according to the brain's own conventions" (Damasio, 1999, p. 320).

43 "*information is relational*. The information that achieves such interesting functions in the parallel-distributed networks is formed through the *patterns* of relations among elements, not the content of elements themselves . . . Information is formed by connecting elements" (Tucker, 2007, p. 99).

44 Theories of language acquisition remain under debate and offer another example of our incomplete understanding of brain function.

45 "With learning and experience, cognits grow and connect with one another, sharing notes that represent common feature. Consequently, in the cerebral cortex, cognits interconnect and overlap profusely, whereby a neuron or group of neurons practically anywhere in the cortex can be part of many memories or items of knowledge. The strength of the synapses within and between cognits varies widely, depending on such factors as selective attention, saliency, repeated experience, rehearsal, and emotional impact . . . Cognits originate and evolve in the course of life. Some expand as new memory or knowledge is acquired and synaptic connections are strengthened with it. Others shrink and weaken from lack of use or aging, each factor accompanied by attrition of synaptic contacts" (Fuster, 2013, p. 14).

46 This movement continues to the development of concept and the use of metaphor. See, as one source of discussion of conceptual thought, Johnson (2007).

47 I recall realizing at one moment in my late teens that a tree is a large plant. I had always seen trees, known trees, as a separate category. I had not included trees in the category of plants. Plants were defined in my mind as smaller than trees. The category of plants was limited by a size parameter and a quality parameter different than what had defined trees for me. Suddenly, I looked at trees differently. They were big plants. It was a bit of a "mind-bending" experience.

48 "Take, for instance, the memory of a hammer. There is no single place in our brain where we will find an entry with the word *hammer* followed by a neat dictionary

definition of what a hammer is. Instead, as current evidence suggests, there are a number of records in our brain that correspond to the different aspects of our past interaction with hammers . . . These records are dormant, dispositional, and implicit, and they are based on separate neural sites located in separate high-order cortices" (Damasio, 1999, p. 220).

49 "Information implies relation" (Tucker, 2007, p. 227).

50 "Psychologically, the self is the coherent system of concepts, memories, and regulatory capacities for attention and intention that operate to maintain internal consistency, as well as consistency in interpersonal relations. For the embryo and fetus, the self is the biological process of organizing internal consistency . . . For the child and adolescent, the same neurodevelopmental process of maintaining internal consistency continues, but now achieved within the social context to create the integrated psychological patterns of a coherent self, or when dysfunctional, the fragmented self of psychopathology" (Tucker et al, 2016, p. 39).

51 "With learning and experience, cognits (Fuster's word for neural matrices or networks) grow and connect with one another, sharing nodes that represent common features. Consequently, in the cerebral cortex, cognits interconnect and overlap profusely, whereby a neuron or group of neurons practically anywhere in the cortex can be part of many memories or items of knowledge" (Fuster, 2013, p. 14).

52 "Everything the child learns must be based on what she or he already understands" (Feldman, 2006, p. 199).

53 In a similar vein, we can understand the common confusion about the use of some of the grammatical forms of "effect" and "affect." The neural wirings of association get crossed or confused because the terms are so similar in sound.

54 Introspective experience becomes more sophisticated with the development of identity, of the sense of self, but it begins in the infant with the basic internal experiences of hunger, pleasure, attachment, desire, intention, etc.

55 "Millions of individual neurons link up to form neural networks that perform the many functions of the nervous system. In turn, neural networks can interconnect, allowing for the evolution and development of increasingly complex skills, abilities, and abstract functions. The specific combination of activated neurons involved in a particular function is known as its *instantiation*. Instantiations encode all our abilities, emotions, and memories and are sculpted and modified by experience. Once neural patterns are established, new learning relies on the modification of established instantiations patterns" (Cozolino, 2014, p. 31).

56 "It seems . . . probable that memories are stored as patterns of many connections." (Seung, 2012, p. 80); "In a complex brain, memory results from the selective matching that occurs between ongoing, distributed neural activity and various signals coming from the world, the body, and the brain itself" (Edelman, 2000, p. 94).

57 "a child learns about a dog and then a short while later is excited to point out another dog – only this one is a cow. The attentive parent helps with the differentiation process by explaining the difference between dogs and cows. The increasing complexity in the child's intelligence is achieved through increasing structural differentiation, that is, the separation of finer distinctions among the increasing variety of conceptual elements" (Tucker, 2007, p. 101).

58 "Brain maps are not static like those of classical cartography. Brain maps are mercurial, changing from moment to moment to reflect the changes that are happening in the neurons that feed them, which in turn reflect changes in the interior of our body and in the world around us" (Damasio, 2010, p. 66).

59 "synapses are changed every time our brain records an experience" (LeDoux, 2003, p. 68).

60 "Neural systems appear to acquire knowledge in two ways, weight change (change in the synapses) and structural recruitment (the strengthening of a previously latent connection between active neural clusters)" (Feldman, 2006, p. 38).

61 "the human brain constructs the information of mind through linked patterns of meaning, patterns woven across the hierarchy of each hemisphere's corticolimbic (core to shell) networks. Each concept is then linked across these distributed network representations through waves of meaning recursively engaging each network in turn. Meaning is thus formed by neural network patterns traversing both the visceral (personal significance) and somatic (reality interface) structures of experience" (Tucker, 2007, p. 16).

62 The neurodevelopmental process of cognition is both cumulative and ongoing. It organizes experience within the fine connectional architecture of the brain's networks" (Tucker and Luu, 2012, p. 25).

63 See for example, Franks and Turner (2013).

64 "Cognits [again, Fuster's term for neural matrices of meaning] originate and evolve in the course of life. Some expand as new memory or knowledge is acquired and synaptic connections are strengthened with it. Others shrink and weaken from lack of use or aging, each factor accompanied by attrition of synaptic contacts" (Fuster, 2013, p. 14).

65 Analogy, simile, metaphor are associative processes. The dynamic nature of associative linkages is what allows for creativity, originality, invention, imagination, intuition, deva vu, problem-solving, reasoning, abstract thinking, misunderstanding, confusion, synesthesia, and many other experiences of consciousness.

66 "Brain-based epistemology contends that our knowledge is neither a direct copy of our experience nor a direct transfer from our memorial states" (Edelman, 2006, p. 152).

67 "Our memories are *prejudiced*, in the full sense of the term, by our past history and beliefs. Perfectly faithful memory is a myth . . . The brain holds a memory of what went on during an interaction, and the interaction importantly includes our own past, and often the past of our biological species and of our culture" (Damasio, 2010, p. 133).

68 "Repetition of a pattern of successful firing also triggers additional intra-cellular changes that lead, in time, to an increased number of receptor channels associated with successful synapses – the requisite structural change for long-term memory" (Feldman, 2006, p. 80).

69 This phrase is derived from the ground-breaking and ahead-of-its-time work of Donald Hebb. See Tucker (2007); Tucker and Luu (2012); Edelman (2004); LeDoux (2003); Seung (2012); Feldman (2006).

70 "Thought is structured neural activity" (Feldman, 2006, p. 3) and "a thought is embodied as a pattern of synaptic transmission within a network of brain cells" (LeDoux, 2003, p. 319).

71 Meditation practice is a kind of mind technology to still neural activity for consciousness-health benefits.

72 "cognition is not comprised of isolated mental skills, but rather emerges from the neural networks that evolved for motivational control of sensation and action, negotiating between both visceral and somatic constraints" (Tucker and Luu, 2012, p. 91).

73 "Non-conscious perception of emotional stimuli is generally associated with more rapid and intense responses in terms of physiological changes and facial expressions (in the observer) than conscious perception of emotional stimuli. This suggests an inverse relationship between stimulus awareness and its impact on behavioural and neurophysiological reactions" (Tamietto and de Gelder, 2010, p. 704).

74 "Every human brain has billions of neurons that together make trillions of synaptic connections among one another . . . At any one moment, billions of synapses are active" (LeDoux, 2003, p. 49).

75 "Abstract thought grows out of concrete embodied experiences, typically sensory-motor experiences. Much of abstract thought makes use of reasoning based on the underlying embodied experience" (Feldman, 2006, p. 7).

3

SOME KEY CHARACTERISTICS OF THE NEURAL ENCODING SYSTEM

In this chapter, I discuss seven key characteristics of the basic neural encoding function that bear on the incidence of conflict and on our work to prevent, reduce, or resolve conflict. The seven characteristics are: the brain's internal connectivity; the neural stability/plasticity balance; neural activation; the delay between stimulus and response; expectancy; the dorsal and ventral systems of attention and motivation; and memory. In the chapter following this, I discuss in more explicit terms some of the relational implications of the functional characteristics of embodied cognition and consciousness.

Connectivity, Coherence, and Consistency

Over the past 150 years, much has been written and proposed about how the brain is structured to accomplish what it does and how its structure explains its function. How is the brain] divided? What are its structural components? Which parts are responsible for which aspects of cognition and behavior? How are the different parts inter-related? Are there modules independently responsible for elements of cognitive function and, if so, how are they delineated? Is there an independent homunculus that is the self? Many earlier theories have been abandoned,[1] the concept of a homunculus most prominently among them (Damasio, 1999; Dehaene, 2001, 2014; Edelman, 1992). There is no question that there are differentiated regions playing different roles in the organization of the whole, the most obvious being the two hemispheres, but disagreements remain or, short of disagreement, evidential interpretation continues as we try to map the structural and functional terrain.[2]

The picture is complex because we know, on the one hand, that there are defined brain structures and neuronal groupings that play different roles in cognition, memory, and consciousness, but on the other hand, we have also come to recognize the integrated nature of the whole brain.[3] The consensus seems to be that the brain is massively connected[4] and that consciousness experience and memory are not compartmentalized.[5] Cognition and behavior involve all levels and areas of the brain from cortex to brain stem[6] in a complex, distributed, and circumstantially dependent recipe.[7] The different parts of the brain don't function in isolation or independently. A striking demonstration of the connectivity of brain function is seen in the experience reported by neurosurgeon Mark Rayport during an operation in which he was stimulating the olfactory bulb, the region of the brain that produces the experience of smell. When asked to remember a happy time in his life, the patient, conscious during the operation, reported the sensation of smelling roses when the region was stimulated. When then asked to think about a difficult time in his life, stimulation of the same cluster of neurons produced the sensation of rotten eggs (reported in Hood, 2012, pp. 233–234). The story illustrates the dynamic interconnectivity of the brain and its functional coherence.

There are a number of implications relevant to our purposes here that follow from this aspect of brain function.

First, concepts of logical or rational thinking divorced from emotional content and survival motives are incorrect.[8] There is no cognition that does not, by definition, include emotional and motivational content.[9] The separation of thinking from emotion or reason from motivation is artificial, contrived, and inaccurate (Haidt, 2013; Tucker and Luu, 2012; Feldman, 2006; Damasio, 1999, 2010; Johnson, 2007). Just as there is no separation between mind and body, so also is there no separation between thinking and feeling, between reason and emotion.[10] We make the distinction in our language for the sake of being able to speak about aspects of our experience. We make the mistake of concluding that because we can speak about these aspects separately, they are separate. The brain is an integrated and interconnected whole. Cognition is a mix of reasoning capacity and emotional response. Incoming stimuli will activate a range of responses among which there will always be an emotional component, more or less prominent depending on the circumstances.

The collection of structures most closely and intricately involved with emotion, motivation, long-term memory, and behavior comprises the more ancient area of the cortex typically referred to as the limbic system. This system is positioned at the center of hemispheric traffic and includes the most densely structured bundle of neural pathways with connections to the rest of the brain.[11] As Tucker and Luu (2012, p. 121) emphasize:

> Even though each level of the cortex (limbic, heteromodal association, unimodal association, primary sensory and motor) engages differing degrees of limbic charge, the effective control of cognition requires engaging the limbic base . . . Although it has been traditional in neurophsychology to consider the cortex in an opponent balance with subcortical and limbic influences, exerting inhibitory control over them . . . the modern anatomical evidence on network organization implies that the cortex must integrate four levels.

Additionally and likewise, though we can experience them distinctly, there is no separation between our physical and cognitive experience.[12] The whole organism is affected by incoming stimuli or internal activations. The whole organism responds to any life experience.[13] This is why the old adage that only sticks and stones will break our bones is false. Words go deep into the body. Research suggests that verbal abuse is as harmful and damaging as physical abuse, if not more so, and will prompt short and long-term physical responses. Input to one part of the system will involve other parts of the system.[14] Physical stimuli will affect psychological experience. Psychological experience will produce physical responses. For this reason, in conflict resolution work, settings and surroundings matter.[15] In conflict resolution work, we are always dealing with emotions as we deal with technical, monetary, and other issues that require rational analysis. And parties will respond viscerally and emotionally to the intellectual issues.

Second, the necessary coherence that characterizes our experience and understanding of the world suggests integrated, multi-level, and multi-modal brain function.[16] Without such seamless coherence, we would not successfully navigate our environment. The myriad elements of our perceptual experience must fit into a somewhat coherent (though not necessarily accurate or correct) narrative of understanding.[17] As a consequence, we perceive and experience other people not only with a full range of perceptual, emotional, and motivational input but also within the context of our integrated and coherent world view into which they must fit, one way or another.[18] So also will parties require that any proposed settlement of their dispute fit into their world story, must make sense within that narrative.[19]

Finally, the integrated whole brain involvement in perceptual response means that we can hold only one point of view or understanding or picture of the world at a time.[20] We have only one system, and the various elements of the system do not operate independently. This is not to deny nuanced understanding and our ability to see multiple sides of an issue, but there must be a kind of internal consensus, so to speak.[21] Our experience may vacillate between or among different perspectives, with more or less willingness, ability, or tendency, depending on circumstances. But at any given moment, we will see things one way or another.[22] The duration of and level of commitment to a particular point of view will vary. The constraint applies also to our understanding of the meaning conveyed by language. A word or words will mean one thing or another to us, but not both at once. If I have heard your words as critical of me, it may be difficult for me to perceive them, and therefore you, otherwise. In other words, it may be difficult to establish different neural pathways as I attempt to understand what you really mean (and therefore, what you mean to me).[23]

This feature of cognition is easily demonstrated in object perception with optical illusions like the Necker Cube, the Rubin vase, or the well-known old woman/young woman drawing. It is more than likely that this characteristic of perception is an evolutionarily selected fitness factor. Simultaneous contradictory perceptions of the same stimulus would result in confusion, making it difficult to respond effectively to environmental cues. We must be committed to one view or another, and then act on that basis. Errors will happen and from those we will learn as long as the error hasn't resulted in the organism's death.

Another demonstration of the phenomenon is a subject's experience of binocular rivalry in research lab conditions in which the subject's two eyes are presented with incongruent and independent stimuli in a split visual field. The subject sees one view and then the other, the images switching back and forth beyond his or her volition. A corresponding psychological reality is the phenomenon of cognitive dissonance in which we feel the discomfort of two contradictory understandings when we must see the situation one way or another. Cognitive dissonance can be triggered when we experience our behavior to be at odds with an ethical belief that we hold. It can also be triggered by, for example, an experience that leads one to feel favorably toward a member of an "enemy" group. In fact, the two circumstances are analogous. In the latter, favorable feeling towards a member of an outgroup corresponds to a behavior and the perception of the other group as "enemy" corresponds to an ethical belief. The mind has a difficult time holding the two contradictory understandings simultaneously. We prefer a consistent and coherent view of the world, a story of the world that accounts for and explains every aspect of our perceptual and cognitive experience.

Neural Stability and Plasticity

As mentioned earlier, we are drawn to learn, we are excited to learn, we experience pleasure in learning; to be a living organism requires that we are eager and able to learn. Our inquisitive nature is not a superficial personality preference but a deeply rooted, evolutionarily selected behavioral trait conveying powerful fitness benefits. But as well being able to learn new things, effective navigation of the environment requires that we retain and can rely upon what we have already learned.[24] We are genetically prepared to learn the characteristics of a new environment that is inconstant and not always predictable[25] and also to depend on our learned assessment of a contextual reality that we expect to be relatively stable. Openness to new information and secure attachment to previously encoded information exist in a dynamic tension, a necessary balance of receptivity and skepticism that can be adjusted, hopefully judiciously, as circumstances change.[26] The degree of and propensity toward stability or plasticity is not fixed. Neural structures are variable according to the survival salience (physical, psychological, social) of the perceived circumstantial conditions of the moment.[27]

Once something is learned, there exists a kind of inertia[28] to the information, an inherent and necessary neural resistance to replacing previous learning with new information, especially if that information counters or makes irrelevant a previous learning.[29] Survival was not easy as our species developed, and we depended as much on how well we retained what was learned as we did on how able we were to learn new things.[30] What is learned becomes a part of our self-definition, not easily relinquished. Abandoning previous learning is not a casual or cavalier act. As we construct our neural edifice of world understanding, we want the bricks already put in place to remain, if possible. New bricks that don't fit or that don't confirm by their addition require effortful reconstruction. As Tucker and Luu (2012, p. 8) put it:

> The *stability-plasticity dilemma* faced by neural networks in the presence of new input is a fundamental principle that underscores the importance of regulating learning, not only to add new information, but to protect the old. Change is thus not inevitable in development; it has a cost that must be managed through explicit mechanisms that assign value to stability versus plasticity . . . When development is understood as structural organization, the balance in neural as well as psychological structural development may therefore require negotiation between *assimilation*, adapting new input that is consistent with the internal structure, and *accommodation*, adapting the internal structure to the new input.

Tucker (2007, p. 139) notes Thomas Kuhn's observations about the nature of change in scientific paradigms as a real-world demonstration of the stability/plasticity dilemma and the difficulty an individual faces in accommodating new information that counters or contradicts what is already known, believed, or understood on the basis of past experience:

> Kuhn learned that a major change in the ideas of a field is typically resisted by most of the people in that field. This resistance remains strong even when the evidence for the change has been gathered and widely disseminated yet logically conflicts with the established theory.

When assimilation fails and denial is no longer possible, accommodation brings about a new order.[31] It is obvious that conflict resolution work must take this characteristic into account since in conflict resolution we are involved in a change process.

Additionally, and as I mentioned earlier, the integrity or survival of the self-identity, on the one hand an enduring construct and, on the other, a dynamic and mutable structure, requires a threshold degree of consistency and durability.[32] Given that what we know is who we are, changing what we know (or believe) means changing who we are, to one degree or another. Given that our knowing, and therefore our self-identity, is embodied, learning new information requires change that is not abstract but physical.[33] When we ask someone to change her or his mind, we are speaking not only figuratively but also literally.[34] Depending on the circumstances, change will be more or less easy to allow, and particularly less easy if the new information contradicts what is already known and if the change required involves "deeply held beliefs" (note the metaphor) and values that underpin core personal identity.[35]

Under conditions of threat, actual or perceived, or of uncertainty, reliance on previously learned "knowledge," upon which the organism has depended in the past, increases in order to maintain security. The well-documented freeze, flight, and fight responses to threat, whether physical or psychodynamic, are attempts to preserve and protect the internal status quo from the perceived external threat. In such circumstances, greater effort is required to overcome resistance to change.

There is an analog in the cultural realm to the neuronal stability/plasticity balance within an individual.[36] At the macro level, culture carries a significant degree of stability (c.f. Kuhn's work on paradigm shifts, mentioned above), but at the micro level of individuals within the culture, behavior is variable, introducing plasticity into a system that tends to endure. It is at the micro level that change happens over time within the macro system. Styles of music or dress or cooking evolve as individuals experiment with variations to cultural norms. Language evolves. Belief systems that are part of the cultural structure shift over time, occasionally with a massive, generalized, and relatively quick shift, but more often gradually and incrementally. A society's culture is resistant to radical change just as an individual is resistant to dramatic shifts in belief and identity structures. Revolution risks destruction. Evolution accomplishes change while maintaining stability. In conflict resolution, we are asking people to see the issues, the other, and potential solutions in new ways, to see them differently. But at a certain point, innovation becomes destabilizing. In resolving conflicts, change happens one step at a time. Some steps are too big to take in one stretch, in which case, if change is to be accomplished, the step must be broken down into smaller steps, or the perception of the step must shift in order for it to be achieved.

As we age, the tendency is that neural structures will become more resistant to change. They have fired together longer and so are wired together more firmly.[37] So also, the longer the history of a conflict, the more difficult it can be to change. As the saying goes, old habits die hard. That said, though resistance may increase with time, change is always possible.[38] Experienced events lie on a continuum of significance to the construction of self; they vary in terms of how much they "matter" to us. We say of some experiences, they are "life changing."[39] And though children are generally more neurally labile, they are also susceptible to rigid commitment to a particular understanding, as they attempt to establish secure markers in their world- and self-constructions. We may hear in the sandbox bold categorical statements of "'Tis not! . . . 'Tis so!" So it is also with some "young" conflicts. They can be vehement and clamorous as they erupt in the moment, though they have a relatively recent history.

Neural Activation

As previously discussed, the newborn begins its learning experience almost from scratch. Neural structures are established with each new perceptual experience, building the ever-more-complex web of knowing that continues to develop throughout the life of the individual. Everything is new when we first arrive. As we gather experience, the world becomes increasingly familiar, that is, we develop (we become) a more extensive network of neural structures based on our more extensive exposure to the world environment.

We move within that environment in a constant state of perceptual inter-action, some of which is within our conscious awareness and much of which is incorporated unconsciously (Haidt, 2013; Bergen, 2012; Fuster, 2013).[40] In either case, each additional incoming stimulus "enters" into the already estab-lished web of previously encoded experience, either adding new dimension to the network or reinforcing pathways already established. With more experi-ence, we more frequently have the experience of "recognizing" (to know again) incoming stimuli. We know more of our world. Functionally, the incoming nerve impulses generated by perceptual experience of external phenomenon activate portions of the neural network already established by past experience, creating an internal resonance.[41] When you see something that looks like a feather lying in the path on which you are strolling, the image activates those linked neural pathways of associations established by your previous experiences of feathers. When you see the object more clearly and "realize" (real-ize) that it is not a feather, your activated feather associations quiet and the knowledge matrices associated with the new perception come into play. When someone throws you a ball, the matrices of meaning established by your past experience having to do with the behavior of physical objects approaching in an arc of flight are activated, allowing a response to the external event that will include mov-ing your body to catch or defend yourself from the arriving object. Additional matrices of meaning associated with the perceptual experience of the thrown ball may also be activated, perhaps having to do with past experience with father, sibling, or friend, or with experiences related to performance, achievement, and associated anxieties, along with any associations that have been established in response to your past relational experiences with the thrower of this particular ball, distant or more recent, positive or negative.[42]

Similarly, when we meet someone, the visual perceptual experience of their presence activates particular neural structures. There is a match with a neural structure already established. We have met this person before, therefore we "know" them, we recognize them. Or the perceptual stimulus activates links with other similar previous perceptual experiences. In the past, we have met someone or people like this person. They remind (re-mind) us of someone we have known previously, or perhaps of a type of person. The reminding may be informative or misleading. Our understanding of the present circumstance may be somewhat accurate or inaccurate. In any case, we don't see the person before us objectively as they are but rather we experience those parts of whom we are that are activated by the perception of their presence in the moment.[43] You may have had the experience of meeting someone about whom you would say, "I've never met someone quite like her before." You certainly know she is human and female and Caucasian or Asian with recognizable features, etc. But there is a quality that doesn't correspond to any past experience you've had, for which you have no neural structures to be activated. In this case, new neural structures are established in response to that previously unknown quality, neural structures that would be activated should you meet someone subsequently with the same or similar characteristic.

It is in this way that all our experience of the external world is subjective. Each of us experiences a different world, one dependent on what our experience, encoded in our neural structures, has been to that point in time. We don't neutrally or objectively perceive the external world. In fact, we don't see the external world as it is. We experience our internal responses activated by the perceptual stimuli arriving from the external world. The correspondence between our internal activated matrices of meaning and the external stimulus will be more or less consonant. There is much room for misunderstanding. Our impressions of the other will be more or less accurate. Any two people will experience the same stimulus differently, to one degree or another. Note, as one example, the dramatic variation in perceptions of the president of the United States giving the State of the Union Address. Much of the time, any discrepancy between our activated internal experience and the object of perception is immaterial. Sometimes it is significant, as in cases of the activation of an inaccurate stereotype.

Activation of established neural networks explains the variation in our relationships with others even though we are, in one way of looking at it, the same person in each relationship we have. Not only are our relationships with others different because each individual with whom we are in relationship is different one from the other, but our relationships with others are different also because we are experienced by each person differently. We are a different person for each of them because we, as a perceptual stimulus, activate neural matrices of meaning specific to each of them, based on their individual histories.

What gets activated within an individual in any given moment will depend on the external circumstances and the state of the perceiver in that moment.[44] Thus, the same stimulus, what someone says, for example, may have different internal results at different times for the same recipient of the message. Circumstances can make for different stimulus salience, resulting in different meaning in the moment and, therefore, in a different behavioral response. What might be a relatively innocuous expression in one circumstance might be triggering (perceived perhaps as offensive, hurtful, or belittling) in another.[45] Not only is the aphorism true that "every bit that you add to the pot makes the soup taste different than if you had not," but also any bit added to the pot will taste different depending on the soup that's in the pot.

Only what has previously been experienced can be activated by new experience. If we are confronted with something with which we have had no previous experience, "we don't know what to think," as the saying goes. New neural structures must be established on the basis of the new experience and tied into the network that already exists.

As previously discussed, language *acquisition* is based on encoding of word-sound and referent and linking the neural structures. Language *expression* and *comprehension* are based on the activation function.[46] When I speak (leaving aside questions of the self's internal roving "searchlight of selective attention" (Tucker and Luu, 2012) and the question of free will[47]), neural structures within my brain are activated that allow me to vocalize the words that then traverse, as sound waves, the physical space between me and my listener. The sound waves perceived by my conversational partner carry no meaning with them but activate neural matrices of meaning associated with those sounds within the listener. Hopefully, there will be sufficient correspondence between the meaning structures we each have associated with the word-sounds to result in effective communication and mutual understanding. More on the dynamics of this exchange when we discuss communication in a later section.

For discussion's sake, we can speak of the activation of a neural structure by a particular perceptual stimulus, but in actual experience, our neural networks exist as a complex, interconnected, and dynamically variable web, and contextual circumstances are multi-modal and multi-dimensional. Any given stimulus or set of stimuli will set in motion a cascading sequence of neural events ranging from centrally salient and prominent to increasingly peripheral and fainter, the network of associations becoming signal-weaker the further from the center of activation, depending on the cues and the circumstances of the moment, in a process of spreading activation.[48] As an example of spreading activation, experimental research has shown that the outcome of moral decision-making can be affected when subjects are exposed to a bad taste or smell during or immediately prior to their decision-making. The unpleasant stimulus activates circuits that affect other circuits in a kind of priming effect that results in a decision different than what would have been arrived at without the unpleasant sensory stimulus.[49]

In all cases, what is activated will depend on the significance (physical, psychological, and/or social) of the stimulus to the individual, the state of the individual in the moment (the sum, in a complex and somewhat mysterious calculation, of all the individual's past experience to the present moment, including relevant factors of genetic inheritance), and the contextual circumstances of the moment. The dynamics of interaction between individual and environment happens quickly[50] and in the context of non-stop, multi-modal input. We are activated by and respond to a symphony of sensory input in every instant, responding consciously and unconsciously to the composite and streaming experience. Not only do we tend to respond quickly but research[51] suggests that our micro-second response to a given stimulus will include a positive or negative feeling state before we are conscious of our thinking or emotional response, what Zajonc terms affective primacy, a preferential bias associated with the stimulus almost immediately in the process of perceptual activation. Once again, we see that we are not neutral in our response to our perceptions. Biases are activated in the very act of perception.[52]

Our survival, relational effectiveness, and well-being depend upon our responses to our perceptual experience. One of the characteristics that distinguish humans from other living organisms is the ability to delay, in some circumstances and to some degree, our response to a stimulus, permitting behavioral choice among a repertoire of options that bears obviously on conflict management.

Delay between Stimulus and Response

At the unconscious level, we respond in micro-seconds to stimuli, including, most importantly, the people and the social dynamics in our surrounding environment. We are not able to avoid these activated responses. They are an inherent part of our perceptual experience. However, at the level of conscious experience, part of our psychosocial developmental process is the cultivation of the ability to replace the natural impulsiveness of infancy and childhood with some degree of response management.[53] Unlike amoebas or reptiles, for example, our nervous system structure includes the functional adaptation that allows delaying, in some circumstances, behavioral response to stimuli.[54] As Tucker and Luu (2012, p. 120) put it:

> The general process for developmental self-regulation, through the viscero-somatic mechanisms of memory consolidation, is a process of negotiating concepts that mediate between internal visceral needs and the complex demands of organizing a self in an interpersonal context. Although both these boundaries, visceral and social, provide essential constraints, cognition is the primary arena for human self-regulation. Extending the mammalian trend, humans do not interface with the world through simple stimulus-response reflexes operating in immediate negotiations between the world and the internal biological milieu. Rather, we operate through cognition.

There are limits and exceptions to our ability to delay response to perceptual stimuli. We are unable, for example, to interrupt the patellar (knee jerk) reflex. Behavioral interruption of the startle response requires significant effort (or uncommon calmness[55]) that is susceptible to the individual's emotional state.[56] Threats to physical safety or integrity will likely result in an immediate and uncontrollable response (for example, our quick retraction from a damagingly hot object or our physical response to tripping). We've all experienced how difficult it can be in an emotional relationship quarrel to manage or control our responses (freeze, fight, flight) in the face of consciously or unconsciously perceived psychological/emotional threat. Stage fright is an example of a response to stimuli that is largely outside of the individual's control while it is in full bloom.

The gap between stimulus and response tends to be reduced in conditions of heightened threat and greater insecurity, whether the threat is to physical, psychological, or social well-being and whether actual or perceived.[57] Conflict, by definition, presents threat of one sort or another to the individuals involved and, consequently, parties in conflict will have more difficulty exercising their ability to delay visceral and emotional responses in their conflict interactions. Yet this is exactly what we are asking them to do in conflict resolution processes.

Our capacity to delay response allows us to reflect before acting, to consider and weigh options, to problem-solve and, presumably, to determine adaptive behavior most conducive to well-being. However, as Tucker and Luu (2012, p. 3) note, "Because simply being slower to respond is not adaptive, the mechanisms of mammalian memory became *expectant*, preparing the animal to respond rapidly to future events." That is, slower is not necessarily better. Balance is key, knowing when to delay and consider and when to react quickly. Typically, we apply insufficient delay to our responses in conflict circumstances. Mediation is meant, in part, to assist parties in moderating their reactive responses.

Not only do our neural mechanisms allow us to delay response to immediate stimuli, but they provide an internal experience, largely unconscious, that has a predictive quality based on past experience, what Tucker (2007) and Tucker and Luu (2012) term expectancy, inherent "assumptions" about what will or should happen in the immediate future based on personal history.

Expectancy

As I have been describing, we arrive at each new moment embodying the neural structures established by the sum of our past experience to that point, a dynamic identity of knowing ready for and exposed to the next moment of lived experience.[58] We expect the next moment to confirm our experience of the world to date, or to differ or contradict in predictable ways.[59] As Tucker and Luu (2012, p. 120) put it, "Through cognition, past experience is consolidated into integrated values, beliefs, and attitudes, in order to anticipate future events through motivated (worrisome, hopeful, playful) expectancies." This applies even to the degree to which we may expect something different to happen, that expectancy also, necessarily, based on past experience. As new moments arrive (speaking about time is always a metaphorical endeavor), we meet them knowing only what we have experienced to that moment, encoded in our neural structures. The next moment is a mystery; the future doesn't yet exist. We base our behavioral decisions on the conditions of the moments as they arrive, informed by past experience.[60] Tucker (2007) and Tucker and Luu (2012) use the term "expectancy" to name the state of an organism that presumes, in any given moment, continuity, consistency, and confirmation of past experience.[61] We cannot meet the next moment free of our expectancies. Only the newborn comes in completely open, so to speak.

As Patricia Churchland (2002, p. 40) puts it:

> If . . . the main business of nervous systems is to allow the organism to move so as to facilitate feeding, avoid predators, and in general survive long enough to reproduce, then an important job of cognition is to make *predictions* that guide decisions. The better the predictive capacities, the better, *other things being equal*, the organism's chance of survival. In a population of organisms, those who are predictively adroit do better than those who are predictively clumsy, other things being equal.[62]

Our internal experience of predicting, planning, and imagining the future conveys a feeling almost as if the future exists, as if we can reach into it with our prediction and move pieces of that world around, an experience of creating scenarios not so much *of* the future but *in* the future. But the experience is an illusion of consciousness. In actual fact, a prediction and the experience of anticipation are the activation in the present of some set of previously encoded neural matrices the selection of which is dependent on motive (internal) feedforward and contextual (external) feedback selection pressures. What is experienced as anticipating future states is actually reviewing past states, based on present circumstances.[63] It can't be any other way, of course, since the future doesn't exist, but our internal experience gives the impression of a different relationship to and conception of the future and a different character or quality to the experience of prediction.[64]

Expectancies are an hypothesis about what the future will be, allowing the individual "to determine appropriate actions under conditions of uncertainty" (Tucker and Luu, 2012, p. 96). Given that the future is always, to one degree or another and by definition, uncertain, expectancies are always in a state of active readjustment as we evaluate what to do next based on the addition of our most recent experience to our past experience. Any assessment of the likelihood of a particular outcome in the future will be based on a calculation of factors from past experience, leading often, as we know, to mistaken predictions.[65] Planning is the activation of encoded past experience with the inclusion of useful, creative, anticipatory associations that take into account contingencies and reveal innovative, potentially successful strategies. The "imagination" of contingencies is experienced as a projection into the future but is, in fact, the activation in the present of what is already known, assembled in novel ways. In fact, we can't imagine what we haven't experienced, though we can mix various elements of our past experience in creative ways to construct options of possibility. It can seem that we invent beyond what we already know, but invention is always and only based on novel connections among what is already encoded. The human organism has a great capacity for making "outside the box" connections because of the vast complexity of our nervous system that allows for lots of dynamic encoding, storage, and retrieval associations.[66] Nevertheless, and again, we can only imagine flying pigs if we have had previous experience of pigs and flying.[67]

For the most part, we are not aware of our state of expectancy, experiencing the circumstances of the present moment as if directly, immediately, and accurately. Below our conscious awareness, we are in a constant state of expectancy, the active patterning of our neural networks imposed upon the newly arriving perceptual stimuli.[68] Our past experiences color or filter or contribute to our perceptual experience of the present. As Tucker (2007, p. 132) puts it:

> With the historical self as the embedding context for consciousness, we are aware not so much of the world as it is but rather of what we want it to be – or, depending on the extent of personal trauma, of what we fear it will be.

We don't meet each new moment fresh and innocent, so to speak. Our perception of present circumstances is influenced and often distorted by our past experience,[69] an "expectancy bias" (Tucker, 2007) that blends past and present.[70] This is another way of talking about the perceptual bias I spoke of in the earlier section on activation in which I noted that our perception of the other is not of them as they are but rather is the experience of those aspects of ourselves that are activated by the perceptual stimuli of the other's presence. But the expectancy phenomenon is proposed to be more than the condition of receptive response of previously encoded neural structures to new stimuli (Tucker, 2007; Tucker and Luu, 2012).[71] Expectancy is seen to have a more active or non-neutral dimension driven by the internal motive impulses of the lower brain.[72] As Tucker and Luu (2012, p. 59) put it, "learning is fundamentally prospective and goal-oriented, as need states prime expectancies for desired outcomes, and as those expectancies then organize working memory to shape successful and well-organized action plans." Action plans must be based on past experience, however creatively constructed. To shift behavior, expectancies must change. Expectancies change with experience that differs from past experience, creating new expectancy maps, within stability/plasticity limits.

The Dorsal and Ventral Systems and their Balance

The neural structures of the brain are organized along three primary dimensions: left/right (lateral hemispheric specialization); front/back (anterior/action and posterior/perception); and inside/outside (visceral limbic core addressing internal bodily homeostasis and survival motives/somatic sensorimotor shell interfacing the nervous system with the external world) (Tucker, 2007). For our purposes, the last of these is particularly relevant, what Tucker (2007) terms the ventral and dorsal corticolimbic divisions of the neocortex and limbic systems, the inside to outside (dorsal) and the outside to inside (ventral) systems.

Integrated with the process of receptive perception of external stimuli, there exists a concurrent system of motive expression, including motives genetically programed to maintain internal homeostasis and psychophysical survival. The consolidation of learning and memory,[73] the development and activities of cognition,[74] the formation of identity, and behavioral expression and action regulation are the product of the blending of the neural dynamics of these two systems, the integration of perceptual experience in relation to its motivational significance (Tucker and Luu, 2012).[75]

The two systems can be seen as self-to-world (the dorsal system, the expression of internal motives, egocentric) and world-to-self (ventral system, the processing of incoming stimuli, allocentric). As Tucker and Luu (2012, p. 57) put it:

> There are two directions for the consolidation process. One runs from the core visceral self toward the somatic interface with the world, and the other runs in the opposite (limbipetal) direction, from the realities of the sensorimotor context to constrain the operations of the core.

It is in these two systems that we see the critical balance of action and constraint, intention and attention. Again, as Tucker and Luu (2012, pp. 96 and vii) put it:

> In the context of frontopolar control over thalamic mechanisms . . . the dorsal frontoparietal network is important to *intentional* control whereas the ventral frontoparietal network is involved in *attentional* control. Conceptually, intention and attention could be seen to emphasize internality and externality, respectively, as vectors of control. Understanding these vectors of orientation, shifting between egocentric intentions versus attentional differentiation of external information, may be important for characterizing the different modes of cognitive control [and] Within the mammalian brain, memory consolidation negotiates between two boundaries: the interface with the environment, as represented by the *somatic* (sensory and motor) nervous system, and the interface with the internal requirements for adaptive homeostasis, as represented by the *visceral* (internal milieu) nervous system. The somatic nervous system has its basis of representation in sensory and motor cortices. The visceral nervous system has its basis of representation in limbic cortices.

Just as the dynamic response of neural structure to perceptual experience must balance stability and plasticity, the organism must balance internal, goal-driven behavior and context-driven behavioral constraint, a balance of self-emphasis and other-emphasis, of motive arousal and experiential reactivity (Tucker et al, 2016), of self-absorption and consciousness of the other. With too much of the former, we will be like the bull in the china shop, exhibiting narcissistic disregard of others. With too much of the latter, creative expression is inhibited by over-dependence on the approval of others.[76] At the level of psychopathologies, symptoms of anxiety, depression, obsessive-compulsive behavior, and paranoid disorders (internalizing disorders) are associated with an imbalance towards ventral system activity, an over-reliance on and concern with external evaluation and contextual stimuli. Conversely, symptoms of histrionic and impulsive behaviors and narcissistic and psychopathic personalities (externalizing disorders) reflect an imbalanced reliance on internal motivational action expression (Tucker and Luu, 2012, p. 110). In the distorted or imbalanced state, dominance of dorsal motive-driven urges degrade to the operations of a narcissistic self, and dominance of ventral attention to external stimuli degrade to exaggerated anxiety and hostility, an alienation of self from world, and a descent into anxious obsessions and paranoid fixations (Tucker and Luu, 2012, p. 206).

All activations of neural networks are determined or influenced, to one degree or another, by our base survival motives that are conveyed via the dorsal corticolimbic system.[77] The encoding of perceptual experience is controlled in part by the lower brain survival and homeostasis motives of the organism.[78] One aspect of the neural system seeks hedonic satisfaction of internal survival motives (dorsal) while another is engaged in determining when to adjust understanding and behavior in response to external circumstances that are survival salient or that contradict previous understanding (ventral).[79] An extensive review of studies that measured brain activity in subjects involved in learning tasks, probability tracking tasks, social economic game exercises, internal–external action control exercises, and trust games, demonstrated the predominance of one system over the other in actions that were based on external information and those in which internal motive control was paramount (Tucker and Luu, 2012, p. 97ff).

In any given moment, each individual is involved, largely unconsciously, in the calculus of this balance,[80] determining to what degree external conditions demand attention and to what degree it is safe or necessary to act on the basis of internal motives. How much will the internal motive impulses dominate behavior and how much will the individual be receptive to external input?[81] This dynamic is at the core of social life and cooperation[82] as we seek to blend our assertive motive drives with new information received from the environment in the present moment.[83]

> The elementary organization of action thus involves dual and opposite control processes. One is impulsive and projectional. The other is constrained and reactive . . . the projectional mode is well suited to support the hedonic expectant cognition underlying approach learning, whereas the feedback mode is well suited to support the focused learning and vigilance required when events are discrepant with the ongoing context model . . . the dorsal projectional mode motivates goal-oriented intention. The ventral reactive mode motivates differentiated, critical attention . . . the dorsal projectional mode is egocentric; the ventral mode is inherently responsive to actions of others.
>
> *(Tucker and Luu, 2012, p. 90)*

Learning and cognition depend on the coordination between these two "motive biases," dorsal limbic feedforward and ventral limbic feedback (Tucker and Luu, 2012, p. 104).

When we feel threatened by conflict, our tendency will likely be to act on the basis of our internal motivational experience and we may have difficulty attending to and taking into account the external needs and expressions of the other. With assistance, we can apply our capacity to delay response in order to create a better balance between these two cognitive systems. This is one of the goals of mediation, to help parties both actively speak and actively listen, to express their own needs and experience, and to attend to the needs and experience of the other.

Memory

Memory is the word we use for the neural traces of experience that remain encoded for some amount of time and to which we have access, under the right conditions, whether we're speaking about the mechanisms of short- or long-term memory.[84] Without memory, we have no learning and no identity. The workings of memory remain far from being fully understood. The language we use to speak about memory is self-referential, reflexive, and inexact, in the sense that we are our memories. There is much more to be said about memory than I will discuss here, including the different types of memory (for example, categorical subsets such as somatic, semantic, emotional, procedural, and episodic designations). Exactly how memory is stored and retrieved remains not fully understood. We hold a vast store of memories most of which are outside of our conscious recall at any given moment. A memory may be activated to conscious awareness that we haven't thought about in years and which seemed, to all intents and purposes, to have been entirely forgotten. But there it is, newly available like a forgotten item found in a treasure chest hidden in the attic of our unconscious mind.

The encoding of perceptual experience takes place first in what we term working or short-term memory, the capacity to hold aspects of experience, thoughts, ideas, "in one's mind" moment to moment. Working memory is, for example, the capacity to remember a telephone number we have read or heard, to read a menu and remember the parts of it that appeal, to read a book and keep track of the unfolding plot as we read, to remember what we have just very recently seen or experienced, or to remember a dream upon first awakening. Working memory allows us to carry on a conversation, think through a subject, plan, and problem-solve. The process of memory consolidation shifting the elements of short-term working memory to long-term retention, what becomes what we know, is based in significant part on "motivational significance" (Tucker and Luu, 2012, p. 56), that is, how salient are incoming stimuli to internal survival-interest motivations.

Whatever record is converted from short-term memory to long-term storage along the continuum extending from relatively brief retention to very long-term recall, will not be fixed as a permanent, immutable record.[85] Rather, it is dynamic, malleable, "recategorical" as Edelman (2006) puts it, subject to shifting and change, somewhat like a sand dune. The sand dune remains, but its form is shaped by the winds of time and the circumstances of ongoing experience. Memory is constantly being remolded; the pathways that store past experiences are in constant interaction with the brain's ongoing activities. The past is a bit of a moveable feast as its meaning shifts according to present circumstances and the accumulation of additional experience. In the healthy state, there is some overall consistency, coherence, and some degree of durability, but the interconnections among the complex, interdependent neural matrices are in constant dynamic engagement. Thus, for example, we can have a different experience of self in conditions of pain or illness during which the meaning of things can shift, or our mood can be changed with the arrival of a sunny day after days of grey skies. Or our mental constructs can be changed with the introduction of a new piece of information when we might respond, "Oh, I didn't know that. That changes everything." Meanings shift; the extensive webs of understanding are interconnected and pull on each other.

More than we recognize, memory is subject to revision and alteration. Personal history, like academic global history, is an interpretive and story-telling venture based on selected and incomplete data and subject to the distortions of socio-cultural and personal psychological lenses altered by the pressures and dynamics of the moment. In this regard, it appears that the very process of accessing a memory subjects the memory to change. Tucker (2007, p. 192) observes:

> An interesting and unexpected effect of the consolidation process is that a memory that is re-activated, even after being integrated into storage, may become more susceptible to interference than one that is not . . . The unintuitive result is that things that normally strengthen the memory (because they make it active at the time) also make it more vulnerable to disruption by anything that interferes with the consolidation process . . . when a memory is activated, such as through being cued or recalled, it may become more susceptible to interference by new, similar material than if it had not been recalled at all. These findings have practical implications for understanding memory recall. When a person is questioned about an event, such as a crime, we assume, within the naïve view, that the person's memory is a veridical record of the event, like a video that can be played back. Instead, the memory is a reconstruction, and the distributed cybernetics of the memory representation cause it to be susceptible to interference by correlated data, such as alternative interpretations that an investigator may suggest. Each recall, each access of the memory, is thus an intervention. Memory seems to be altered by each effort to address it, not unlike the elementary particles of quantum physics.

Each time a memory is recalled, it becomes what is termed "labile," subject to being changed or lost as it requires, upon recall, additional protein synthesis in order for it to be reconsolidated for future retrieval.[86]

The process of new memory creation in response to current experience, whether external perceptual experience or internal associational experience (what we call thinking) is not independent from the neural structures already established by past experience. The two are in constant dynamic interaction, each affecting the other.[87] We are a dynamic system in which present circumstances affect long-term memories and long-term memories affect the perception and retention of present circumstances.[88] As Fuster (2013, p. 81) puts it, "We not only remember what we perceive, but also perceive what we remember." This is another way to talk about expectancies referred to earlier. Our perception of current circumstances is influenced or distorted by past experience. Further:

> Memory, it now appears, has not evolved to record things as they actually were, but to be able to predict things better in the future, should certain similarities in observed events occur, and to provide a script should such similarities arise.
>
> *(Lack and Bogacz, 2012, p. 40).*

Short-term memory is converted to long-term memory (consolidation) through repetition, attention, and through meaningful association. Highly charged events, significant, emotionally laden, survival-threatening or survival-positive events, and events with strong connection to other significant neural matrices of meaning will tend to convert to long-term memory. Synaptic activity is affected by neurochemicals. Neurochemicals are released or not depending on a number of factors among which are the significance to the organism of its experiences in the moment. For example, norepinephrine is involved in the enhancement of memory and is present in greater quantity in the event of an emotionally significant experience (LeDoux, 2003, p. 313). In the absence of that kind of immediately apparent salience, repetition, repeated exposure, rehearsal, and focused attention are necessary.

Culture is a prominent example of repetition. The repeated and pervasive messages of culture wire individuals in that culture. We are born into a narrative that becomes a part of our own personal narrative as we absorb the immersive information of our cultural environment. Cultural, religious, and national narratives are persistent and difficult to change because they are so deeply and intricately woven into our neural structures. This is why so-called identity conflicts pose such challenges and why they are so called to begin with. We say of them that they are "deep-rooted," that the issues involved are "close to the bone."[89]

There is a limit to what can be held in short-term memory, commonly understood to be in the range of seven distinct items or "chunks" of items. New input will crowd out or "overwrite" previous input. Some elements of experience will be stored only briefly in working memory, to fade and disappear within a short time so that working memory can be devoted to new input that requires attention. Some elements of experience will be converted from working (short-term) memory to long-term storage, available for later recall. The duration or persistence of the contents of long-term memory isn't fixed but rather exists on a continuum.

In our experience of the external world, we do not take in all of the available information. Not only do we each perceive the world around us differently according to our past history, but the elements of the perceptual field will vary in their salience to us. What is retained or activated within our neural systems will differ, person to person; therefore two people will have different memories of the same past event.[90] We see evidence of this phenomenon when two people in a conflict argue about what happened in the past.

It is only when content moves from short-term working memory to long-term storage that it becomes part of our identity, our understanding of the world and ourselves, more or less significantly. It is only at that point, when new learning is incorporated and endures, that we are changed, more or less profoundly.

One of the distinctions made in parsing the complexities of memory is that between *implicit* and *explicit* memory. Much can be said in defining the two types but for our purposes here, the salient difference is that implicit memories are largely unconscious whereas explicit memories tend to be conscious or available for conscious recall. To illustrate, the remembered details of our autobiography are examples of explicit memory, whereas the general impacts of parental style on us as children are examples of implicit memory. Our understanding of the rules of tennis is based on explicit memory, but our learned ability to hit a tennis ball well is based on implicit memory. The content of explicit memory is made up of discrete facts and events that require access and awareness in order for us to navigate and function in the world. Explicit memory allows us to remember faces, the rules that apply to social circumstances, the language and stories of our culture. Explicit memory is organized in time sequence whereas implicit memory is not related to time measurement or placement. Explicit memory is contextualized and the contents of explicit memory are tied to known source events, whereas implicit memory is context-free and has no source attributions. The first forms of implicit memory develop prenatally. The first contents of explicit memory are not retained until some time after birth.

It appears that a vast majority of memory is implicit, and this makes sense when you think about it because we are influenced by our environment constantly from the moment of our conception and in ways that we are most often not aware or conscious of. Key to our discussion here is that the contents of implicit memory "shape our emotional experiences, self-image, and relationships" (Cozolino, 2014, p. 133). Parties' response to each other and to the conflict situation will be colored or influenced by the implicit memories accumulated through the course of their lives as well as by the explicit memories that are directly associated with their experience of each other and the conflict circumstance. The elements of parties' implicit memory that affect their behavior in a conflict resolution process will be invisible to us and will be difficult to uncover. But we will often see the results of that influence when, for example, what might be termed an "overreaction" might be "attributable to an enhanced sensitivity based on prior learning" (Cozolino, 2014, p. 135). Implicit bias is a subset of or one example of implicit memory.

Notes

1 "But anatomy teaches us that these cognitive capacities are not isolated 'modules' in some psycholinguistic space, but rather linked networks in a bounded corticolimbic hierarchy" (Tucker, 2001, p. 16).
2 "Predictably, quasi-phrenologies . . . have been lately on the wane. It is not the case, however, that modules do not enter cognition at some point. To the contrary, they are essential in the lower cortical stages of cognition – namely, in primary sensory and motor cortices. In the higher stages, however, as in the cortex of association, modules 'dissolve' into networks by virtue of the essentially associative nature of cognitive information in that cortex" (Fuster, 2013, p. 61).
3 "Consciousness is . . . not the prerogative of any one brain area; instead its neural substrates are widely dispersed throughout the so-called thalamocortical system and associated regions" (Edelman and Tononi, 2000, p. 36) and "the process of consciousness is a dynamic accomplishment of the distributed activities of populations of neurons in many different areas of the brain" (Edelman, 2005, p. 6).
4 "Any thought or action involves a significant fraction of the billions of neurons (in the brain) – the computation is massively parallel" (Feldman, 2006, p. 5); "the architecture of the brain also comprises a distributed neural system or 'workspace' with long-distance connectivity that can potentially interconnect multiple specialized brain areas in a coordinated, though variable manner" (Dehaene, 2001, p. 13).
5 "memory is not localized in one site. Rather, once it is laid down in tissue, a memory is widely distributed across the networks of the neocortex of the cerebral hemispheres" (Tucker, 2007, p. 171); "memories – the base substance of mind – are stored not in any privileged location but distributed throughout the networks. Conceptual elements or representations must then be assumed to follow the stacked structure of the corticolimbic connectional pattern" (Tucker, 2007, p. 179). Evidence suggests that, "conscious perception involves global connectivity in the brain, whereas unconscious perception is restricted to a smaller region" (Churchland, 2013, p. 243).
6 "All levels of the neuraxis, from the primitive circuits of the brain stem to the cortex of the telencephalon, must be coordinated in the control of neural activation" (Tucker, 2007, p. 149) and "The corebrain motivational networks provide integrative and evaluative controls, whether establishing the needs of the self or resonating with those of another. In both cases, significant experience is organismic, engaging the entire vertical hierarchy of the organism's neuraxis rather than modular or isolated into discrete mental faculties" (Tucker, 2007, p. 199).
7 "This realization of the evolutionary history in the morphogenesis of each individual brain means that behavior, including language, must be achieved through vertical integration of all levels of the evolved neuraxis . . . The most complex functions of the frontal lobe (telencephalon), for example, require the recruitment of attentional regulatory influences from the thalamus, motivational influences from the hypothalamus (both in the diencephalon), and elementary arousal controls from brainstem reticular (mesencephalic) arousal systems" (Tucker, 2001, p. 6).

8 "With the modern evidence on cortical connectivity organized around the limbic base, we can also see how the mind must frame even abstract concepts in relation to their visceral significance" (Tucker and Luu, 2012, pp. 32–33).

9 "it is not the case that intellectual function is without emotion. Indeed, emotional and motive mechanisms may be essential to the most subtle and abstract concepts we can achieve . . . the mind's operations require contributions from all of the levels of the evolved neuraxis" (Tucker, 2007, p. 273).

10 "Perhaps the most important lesson from the brain's corticolimbic architecture is the implication that concepts (especially abstract ones) cannot be captured at one level of network representation. Rather, they must be organized through linked structures spanning the full corticolimbic hierarchy" (Tucker, 2007, p. 219).

11 "In the mammalian cortex, the greatest connection density occurs within the limbic . . . networks at the hemispheric core" (Tucker, 2007, p. 208).

12 "Even when . . . pain does not come from the internal organs but is limited entirely to the somatosensory domain (e.g., in the skin), it is not only the somatic representation that is important to the functional experience of pain. The visceral networks of the limbic system are also integral to evaluating the emotional significance (and thus understanding the meaning) of somatosensory pain" (Tucker, 2007, p. 256).

13 "The connectivity of limbic networks allows not only the integration of widespread cortical regions, but the recruitment of subcortical motivational systems. A cognitive representation, such as supports the understanding of a word, is thus multileveled, with four or five discrete network levels in the pathway linking limbic (visceral) with neocortical (sensorimotor articulation) representations" (Tucker, 2001, p. 2).

14 "Any perturbation in one part of the meshwork may be felt rapidly everywhere else" (Edelman and Tononi, 2000, p. 45).

15 "circuitry across brain regions links modalities, infusing each with properties of others. The sensory-motor system of the brain is thus 'multimodal' rather than modular. Accordingly, language is inherently multimodal in this sense, that is, it uses many modalities linked together – sight, hearing, touch, motor actions, and so on. Language exploits the pre-existing multimodal character of the sensory-motor system" (Lakoff and Gallese, 2005, p. 2).

16 "The learning of multiple elements of an experience (its sights, sounds, and smells, its emotional and motivational significance, its movement patterns, and so on) is facilitated, allowing the whole experience to be stored at once, albeit across multiple systems" (LeDoux, 2003, pp. 314–315).

17 "What is particularly striking about the operations of the conscious human brain is the necessity for integration, for a unitary picture, for construction, and for closure . . . The conscious brain in health and disease will integrate what can be integrated and resists a fractured or shattered view of 'reality'" (Edelman, 2005, p. 136).

18 "It neglects ambiguity and suppresses doubt and, as mentioned, exaggerates coherence. I've mentioned associative coherence, and in large part that's where marvels turn into flaws. We see a world that is vastly more coherent than the world actually is. That's because of this coherence-creating mechanism that we have. We have a sense-making organ in our heads, and we tend to see things that are emotionally coherent, and that are associatively coherent, so all these are doings of System 1" (from talk by Daniel Kahneman at https://www.edge.org/conversation/daniel_kahneman-the-marvels-and-the-flaws-of-intuitive-thinking-edge-master-class-2011).

19 "Now, coherence has its cost. Coherence means that you're going to adopt one interpretation in general. Ambiguity tends to be suppressed. This is part of the mechanism that you have here that ideas activate other ideas and the more coherent they are, the more likely they are to activate to each other. Other things that don't fit fall by the wayside. We're enforcing coherent interpretation. We see the world as much more coherent than it is" (Grossberg, 1999, p. 33).

20 "we cannot be aware of two mutually incoherent scenes or objects at the same time because our conscious states are not only unified, but are internally coherent in the sense that the occurrence of a certain perceptual state precludes the simultaneous occurrence of another one ...The need to make a coherent, conscious scene out of seemingly disparate elements is seen at all levels and in all modalities of consciousness" (Edelman and Tononi, 2000, pp. 25–26).

21 "The inevitable result of this holism is that new information ... disrupts the prior information (the stability of existing knowledge) ...The mind is not neatly modular, with components or faculties of specific cognitions. Rather, it is of a piece, such that new learning disrupts old knowledge.This is a dialectical balance in which information is not free. It requires transformation. In order to find a new and improved self, one must sacrifice one's old self" (Tucker, 2007, p. 22).

22 "the occurrence of a certain perceptual state precludes the occurrence of another one" (Edelman and Tononi, 2000, p. 147).

23 Paranoia is an extreme case demonstrating faulty connections that are difficult to rewire.

24 "In the general sense, the problem of maintaining old learning in the process of acquiring new learning is described as the *stability-plasticity dilemma* ... as modifying weights for new learning leads to disruption not just of individual weights, but also of the distributed patterns of old learning" (Tucker and Luu, 2012, p. 26); in general, *neural plasticity* involves changes in brain wiring as a function of experience, wherein inputs, either from the neuronal milieu or external world, influence the functional synaptic architecture (Tucker et al, 2016, p. 8).

25 "Plasticity in brain and cognitive systems is important because it is one outcome predicted to result from an evolutionary history of having to cope with variation in social and ecological conditions" (Geary, 2005, p. 8).

26 "Neural connections are material structures ... stable enough to remain the same for long periods of time, but they are also plastic enough to change" (Seung, 2012, p. 77).

27 For a fascinating and amusing demonstration of a predominance of the neural stability factor in some circumstances, see the short video at https://www.youtube.com/watch?v=MFzDaBzBlL0

28 "learning engages an unconscious struggle with the inertia of the self, the relational mass of personal information.And when it is done, we are transformed and cannot remember being otherwise.When we are children, the self is light, and we are fully transformed by each instance of reality ...When we grow old, the self becomes increasingly crystallized and ever more massive with accumulated wisdom.As a result, with increasing age we incorporate progressively less information – unless, that is, we are able to tolerate what must become the price of the unrestricted learning that is now available in the Information Age: a continually labile and childlike identity" (Tucker, 2007, p. 133).

29 "There is evidence that the recognition of discrepancy and the focusing of attention that are required to support new learning are carried out specifically in the frontal networks of the mammalian brain. This shift toward accommodation, of changing the internal representation to incorporate the necessary new learning, seems to reflect a separate strategic learning mechanism, one that is geared to maintain the focus of attention sufficiently to overcome the connectional inertia of the mammalian cortex" (Tucker, 2007, pp. 137–138).

30 "I have called the problem whereby the brain learns quickly and stably without catastrophically forgetting its past knowledge the stability – plasticity dilemma. The stability – plasticity dilemma must be solved by every brain system that needs to rapidly and adaptively respond to the flood of signals that subserves even the most ordinary experiences" (Grossberg, 1999, p.2).

31 Neuromodulators (serotonin, dopamine, norepinephrine, epinephrine, acetylcholine) play a significant role in providing for brain structure plasticity (learning) by modulating synaptic behavior through either inhibition or excitation (LeDoux, 2003).

32 "the self . . . must possess a remarkable degree of structural invariance so that it can dispense continuity of reference across long periods of time . . . Relative stability supports continuity of reference and is thus a requisite for the self" (Damasio, 1999, p. 135).

33 "Modern neuroscience research is providing new insights into the mechanisms of human neural plasticity that allow each child to self-organize, to respond to patterns of environmental information with adaptive changes in patterns of neural representation" (Tucker 2001, p. 3).

34 Crosswhite (2013, p. 63) speaks of "The capability to change one's mind – and one's life – when the experience of argumentative transcendence calls for it."

35 "Stability is the steady state, when expectancies match reality. Of course, the more complex your expectations are, the more they are prepared for disconfirmation by some element of ongoing reality. When a discrepancy is encountered, then you face the stability-plasticity dilemma. You can stay the same (choose stability), in which case you are uninformed, but at least you preserve the historical self. You can change (choose plasticity) and become informed, but in the process you have to give up the old self and confront the painful novelty of a new identity" (Tucker, 2007, p. 133).

36 Thanks to social and cognitive scientist Dan Sperber and his talk at https://www.edge.org/conversation/dan_sperber-an-epidemiology-of-representations for stimulating this line of thinking.

37 "If cognition is an ongoing neurodevelopmental process, then each developmental phase (and each idea) is fully constrained by prior phases of the ontogenetic process . . . The stability-plasticity dilemma of distributed networks causes the capacity of new learning to be constrained by prior learning" (Tucker and Luu, 2012, p. 209).

38 "Although plasticity is reduced after the critical period, it remains in some form to support learning and reorganization of function in the adult brain . . . Neural plasticity thus first appears as a neurodevelopmental mechanism, serving to organize the brain's connectivity in the process of embryological differentiation. It then remains as a neurodevelopmental mechanism after birth, during the critical periods in which environmental interaction adapts the brain's networks to the information in the unique environment that the organism discovers. Finally, neural plasticity continues to support the brain's functional differentiation throughout life, in the general process of learning and adaptation of behavior and cognition to environmental demands" (Tucker et al, 2016, p. 8).

39 "The negotiation between stability and plasticity is dynamic, meaning that earlier patterns of cognition and behavior may be modified by significant new experiences, and by significant operations of self-regulation" (Tucker and Luu, 2012, p. 192).

40 "Ninety-nine percent – to give it a number – of what we perceive in our daily life is unconscious . . . We transit through the world unconsciously 'testing hypotheses' – that is, expectations – about that world. Only if those hypotheses are disproved do we become aware of them and of their falsity . . . Then, the new or unexpected suddenly captures our conscious attention" (Fuster, 2013, p. 20).

41 This is the basis of what we call triggering and of posttraumatic stress (PTSD) reactivity.

42 Activation by perceptual stimuli does not require awareness. For example, when a subject exposed to a series of words flashed on a computer screen so rapidly that they are only consciously perceived as a letters and patterns flashing by is asked for a word that comes to mind, typically the subject will share what he or she experiences as a random thought that is, indeed, one of the words in the flashed sequence. (See, for example, Dehaene, 2001, pp. 107–108 and p. 115ff.)

43 "The stability-plasticity dilemma of distributed networks causes the capacity for new learning to be constrained by prior learning . . . Freud described the embedding of new cognition within the frame of prior experience as *transference*, reflecting the transfer of latent unconscious mental contents into the current mental process (Freud, 1953). Because of transference, the psychoanalyst could understand fundamental developmental

issues through observing the patient's behavior in the present moment" (Tucker and Luu, 2007, p. 209). Of course, we are always doing this, not only with our therapist. All new incoming stimuli activate elements of past experience, including latent unconscious material that produces the process we call projection.

44 In 1999, the psychologists John Bargh and Tanya Chartrand published a paper, "The Unbearable Automaticity of Being," arguing that our default state is reacting to the latest stimuli. We adopt the roles that our immediate environment provokes (as reported by Daniel Zalewski, *New Yorker Magazine*, March 30, 2015).

45 "Neural computation involves *continuously finding a best match* between the inputs and current brain state, including our goals" (Feldman, 2006, p. 5).

46 For the complexities of language activation see, for example, Lakoff and Gallese (2005).

47 As a side note, Spinoza's comment on free will is interesting. "Men are mistaken in thinking themselves free; their opinion is made up of consciousness of their own actions, and ignorance of the causes by which they are determined" (as quoted in Hood, 2012, p. 122).

48 "Through many such tests, experimental psychologists have determined that the spread of meaning – from an idea to its close associates and then to more remote ones – happens over time in a regular and predictable gradient of relatedness. They have called this process 'spreading activation.' The implications of this term are that concepts are related in memory in coherent networks of meaning and that regions of these networks can be activated through use" (Tucker, 2007, p. 106) and "When you hear or read (or see, or taste, or smell) something new, your brain's spreading activation mechanisms automatically connect it to related information" (Feldman, 2006, p. 235).

49 "Because the brain is richly connected and profusely activated, there is no such thing as an isolated or purely abstract thought. One idea automatically activates others . . . connected concepts are neurally connected" (Feldman, 2006, pp. 37–38).

50 "a wide range of experiments agree that people react to stimuli in around 100 milliseconds, or a tenth of a second" (Feldman, 2006, p. 55).

51 By Robert Zajonc, reported in Haidt, 2013, pp. 65–66.

52 See, for example, the research on implicit bias. More on implicit bias in the following chapter's section on perception.

53 "A general principle in the evolution of intelligence may be that there is increasing delay interposed between stimulus and response" (Tucker and Luu, 2012, p. 3); "Rather than reflexes producing actions from fixed stimulus patterns, higher mammals are able to mediate their actions with increasing evaluation of environmental data . . . (this) is achieved not just in mental space but also in the physical space of the brain's networks" (Tucker, 2007, p. 161); "In fact, inhibiting our impulsive thoughts and behaviors is one of the main changes over the course of a lifetime that contributes to the development of the self. When these regulatory systems fail, then the integrity of the self is compromised" (Hood, 2012, p. 15).

54 "A general principle in the evolution of neural control systems is that simpler organisms respond with specific reflexes. A significant stimulus is linked by a reflex arc to an appropriate response. In contrast, more complex and highly evolved organisms show increasingly elaborate delays between stimulus and response" (Tucker, 2007, p. 63); "It is in the evolution of mammals that we find the first appearance of the massive ordered reticulum – the networks of billions of neatly structured neurons – in the cortex of the telencephalon. This radical architecture seems to have brought the capacity for increasing delays between stimulus and response" (Tucker, 2007, p. 137); "Unlike nearly all other species, most humans have the crucial ability to inhibit heuristic-based responses . . . and thus the ability to make decisions and draw inferences on the basis of explicit processes" (Geary, 2005, p. 195).

55 Experimental studies with long-time meditators, Buddhist monks, demonstrate a much reduced and briefer startle response to an applied startle sound and much attenuated

residual response to the stimulus exposure than is the case with non-meditators (as reported in www.gq.com/story/happiest-man-in-the-world-matthieu-ricard?utm_source=pocket&utm_medium=email&utm_campaign=pockethits and see also http://psycnet.apa.org/journals/emo/12/3/650/).

56 One of the symptoms or indicators of PTSD is an active or over-active startle response.

57 "There has been enormous evolutionary pressure toward brains that can respond fast and effectively in complex situations" (Feldman, 2006, p. 5).

58 "Through understanding principles of distributed representation, we can appreciate that personal history is indeed implicit in current cognition . . . new learning is invariably embedded within an existing representational network" (Tucker and Luu, 2012, p. 209).

59 "Starting with their motivated expectancies, mammals respond to information that signals discrepancies from their predictions in order to adapt their world models to the realities they face. This is the way they learn" (Tucker, 2007, p. 21).

60 "the cognitive process involves a kind of negotiation between expected patterns held by the brain's memory systems and the incoming patterns in sensory networks mirroring the sensory data. An adaptive resonance is then established by the coincidence of motivated expectancy with actualized sensation. In the case of a mismatch, control signals are engaged that trigger and support the continued search for a match" (Tucker and Luu, 2012, p. 41).

61 "Expectancy may be the neurodevelopmental algorithm for bridging assimilation and accommodation, through preparing the internal representational structure for significant (and possibly disruptive) new information" (Tucker, 2007, p. 8).

62 Our experience of expectation and prediction reflects a "belief" that there will be a future, a next moment, a belief founded not on any evidence but only on the fact of our experience of past moments. We proceed as if there will be a future (a new present) because our experience has taught us that another moment has followed on the previous thus far. In fact, we have only the present with no guarantee of another and we exist only in the evolving present.

63 This is demonstrated in the case of D.B. as reported by Klein and Nichols (2012, p. 681), "Following cardiac arrest and presumed hypoxic brain damage, D.B. had knowledge of his own traits, and yet he was 'unaware that he had a past and unable to imagine what his experiences might be like in the future.'" Without access to encoded past experience (memory), there can be no imagination of a future.

64 The infant cannot, for the most part, plan or predict and has no experience of future, not having had sufficient experience of time passing to formulate the concept. Even in those early stages, however, expectancies have begun to develop on the basis of recent and new perceptual experience.

65 We see a reflection of this characteristic of expectancy in a baby's surprise at seeing us reappear from behind a barrier to their vision of us.

66 "expectancies are the natural extension of the increasing memory capacity of mammalian brains" (Tucker, 2007, p. 140).

67 "To the extent that they incorporate the residuals of experience that are encoded within our representational networks (our concepts), the interpretive structures of consciousness must be historical, the developmental products of personal life histories" (Tucker, 2007, p. 132).

68 "As a result of experience, expectancies are held in the most embedding limbic networks. These are valued expectancies, predictive models for how the world should be – how it should feel. Through resonance with the environmental data patterns in sensory networks, perceptions are continually arbitrated between the internal (visceral) and external (somatic) interfaces" (Tucker, 2007, p. 181).

69 "Thus, expectancies arise from memory to shape the processing of perceptual detail. In Shepard's terms, perception is 'hallucination constrained by the sensory data'" (Tucker and Luu, 2012, p. 33).

70 "We are biased to expect regularities in the world, such as the interaction patterns of our childhood social and emotional relationships. We expect these implicitly and unconsciously. When people act otherwise, we are confused. Experience, in its conscious as well as unconscious forms, is a function of the historical self" (Tucker, 2007, p. 132).

71 "As Kant realized, the mind/brain is not just a passive canvas on which reality paints. The brain organizes, structures, extracts, and also creates. Reality is always grasped through the lens of stacks upon dynamical stacks of neural networks. There is no apprehending the nature of reality except via brains and the theories and artifacts that brains devise and interpret" (Churchland, 2002, p. 368).

72 "expectancies are the base of perception . . . these are motivated by internal needs, and . . . information itself is formed only when data resonates with personal significance" (Tucker, 2007, p. 247).

73 "The networks of the cortex are constrained by the anatomical structure and physiological data at the dual boundaries (of the dorsal and ventral systems), marked by the visceral limbic function at the core of the hemisphere and the somatic networks of primary sensory and motor cortices mapping the interface with the world. Cognition and the memory consolidation that underlies it, must arise through the continuing and dynamic arbitration of these constraints" (Tucker and Luu, 2012, p. 77).

74 "Thus the embodiment of human cognition can be understood in relation to the physical functions of the neural networks that affect cognition. There are *visceral* constraints at the limbic core . . . providing motivational control. There are *somatic* constraints at the sensory and motor cortices, providing a kind of reality testing as concepts are mapped to the environmental requirements for perceptions or actions . . . As a result, memory consolidation must arbitrate between the sensory and motor requirements at the somatic shell and the emotional and motivational requirements at the visceral core" (Tucker and Luu, 2012, p. 29).

75 "Although normal human self-regulation is organized through a kind of tensile balance of the impetus and the artus (dorsal self-to-world and ventral world-to-self systems), children may develop a reliance on one mode or the other as a function of complex patterns of genetic bias interacting with the exigencies of environmental challenges presented by their specific family contexts" (Tucker and Luu, 2012, p. 124).

76 "The dynamic modulation of cognition by motive activation and arousal are best seen in the exaggerated cognition associated with strong mood states . . . The phasic arousal dimension, experienced as Positive Affect or elation, expands the scope of working memory, and thereby facilitates holistic concepts . . . In strong states of elation, such as clinical mania, this broad scope and inherent optimistic affective bias lead to grandiosity, which is not only broad in scope . . . but also reflects the inherent egocentrism of dorsal corticolimbic processing . . . In contrast, the same individual, when depressed, shows a deflation not only of affective arousal, but of felt importance of self" (Tucker and Luu, 2012, pp. 124–125).

77 "human cognition is always motivated" (Tucker, 2007, p. 112).

78 "Motives are the organizing forces, operating across the vertical levels of the neuraxis and providing the neural excitement that allows the sculpting of information patterns. Experience is thereby consolidated into personal patterns of neural connectivity" (Tucker, 2007, p. 162).

79 "One form of expectant cognition is biased toward maintaining a context representation with hedonic goals. Another form engages sustained attention to modify the model in the face of aversive or discrepant events" (Tucker and Luu, 2012, p. 58).

80 "Self-regulation requires a balance of motivational control with socially sensitive inhibitory control in the ongoing behavioral process" (Tucker and Luu, 2012, p. 78).

81 "The most complex and abstract constructions of the mind must emerge from the confluence of personal motivation with the data of the world" (Tucker, 2007, p. 231).

82 "these elemental, opponent and complementary, neural control mechanisms can be understood to shape broad domains of human psychological function, from elementary learning to abstract cognition to complex challenges of social relations" (Tucker and Luu, 2012, p. 91).

83 "Human self-regulation then negotiates the impulse for hedonic gratification and the constraint required for social propriety" (Tucker and Luu, 2012, p. 110).

84 "memories exist as modifications to the connectivity of neuron in the brain. Memories come into existence when brain cells – neurons – change how they connect to other neurons by sprouting new structure and pruning back old structure. This changes how one neuron connects to other neurons. Information about events in my life and about what makes me *me* is stored in patterns of connections between living brain cells – neurons. Memories ... all exist in the way neurons connect to each other" (Churchland, 2013, p. 12).

85 Seung (2012, p.91) mentions the "dual-trace" theory of memory in which, "Persistent (neural) spiking is the trace of short-term memory, while persistent connections are the trace of long-term memory. To store information for long periods, the brain transfers it from activity to connections. To recall the information, the brain transfers it back from connections to activity."

86 See, for example, "Fear Memories Require Protein Synthesis in the Amygdala for Reconsolidation After Retrieval" at www.nature.com/nature/journal/v406/n6797/pdf/406722a0.pdf

87 "The short-term memory that is fundamental to primary consciousness reflects previous categorical and conceptual experiences. The interaction of the memory system with current perception occurs over periods of fractions of a second in a kind of bootstrapping: What is new perceptually can be incorporated in short order into memory that arose from previous categorizations" (Edelman and Tononi, 2000, p. 109) and "The mind is a function of the whole of personal history. The mechanisms of memory consolidate the ongoing representation of events, not in isolation of a static present but in the dynamic context of an unfolding life" (Tucker, 2007, p. 187).

88 "The information in your working memory is what you are currently thinking about or paying attention to. And because working memory is temporary, its contents have to be constantly updated. But working memory is not a pure product of the here and now. It also depends on what we know and what kinds of experiences we've had in the past. In other words, it depends on long-term memory" (LeDoux, 2003, p. 176).

89 This is the challenge people face in psychological therapeutic efforts to revise harmful self-stories that were encoded early in life and that comprise a significant portion of the individual's identity.

90 "memories are necessarily associative and are never identical. Nevertheless, under various constraints they can be sufficiently effective in yielding the same output" (Edelman, 2005, p. 53) and, "memory is a system property reflecting the effects of context and the associations of the various degenerate circuits capable of yielding a similar output. Thus each event of memory is dynamic and context-sensitive ... it does not replicate an original experience exactly ... Such interactions allow a non-identical 'reliving' of a set of prior acts and events, yet there is often the illusion that one is recalling an event exactly as it happened" (Edelman, 2005, p. 52).

4
IMPLICATIONS FOR CONFLICT AND ITS RESOLUTION

In the characteristics of the brain's neural encoding function, we can see root causes of some of the conflict behaviors we are familiar with observationally. Whole brain connectivity means that activating any part of the vast net of inter-related neural structures will implicate many other parts. This is what makes value conflicts so difficult to resolve. They are not discrete problems to be settled, an insurance or contractual dispute, for example, but involve and infiltrate large realms of the neural network. So also for what we call identity-based conflicts in which we may be dealing with almost the whole set, to one degree or another, of neural structures that make up the person's understanding of self and world. Because we are dealing with an extensive and interconnected network of mean-ing when working with value- or identity-based conflicts, proposed shifts in understanding in a conflict resolution effort may be experienced as too radical an alteration of neural structure and will be met with resistance. Managing a suc-cessful change of understanding in conflicts that involve values and identity will often require attention to pace and degree of narrative revision. The more deeply involved a conflict is with values and identity, the more we will have to take into account cognitive biases (confirmation bias, for example) that influence party understanding and analysis of issues and information.

The balance between the dual propensities towards stability of previous learn-ing and new-learning plasticity presents both opportunities and challenges to the practice of helping parties in conflict situations shift their narratives. Attachment to old narratives and counter-productive activation of previously established matrices of meaning are more likely in conflict conditions.[1] We become slightly paranoid, in the non-clinical sense, or move towards that end of the trust/safety continuum in circumstances of conflict and perceived threat, whether acute or chronic. We tend to become more suspicious, skeptical, and distrusting. We are said to be, and experience ourselves to be defensive, feeling the need to protect what we know and believe to be true. That said, the potential for transformation is ever-present in our capacity for learning, for seeing the world anew, when the conditions are conducive.

Anxiety is a product of or part of the threat experience. In the anxious state, it is more difficult for us to delay visceral responses to our experience of the other in a conflict. Our reactivity is heightened. We are on a "short fuse." We see, in conflict, shortening to the point of disappearance the time between stimulus and response. We are less able to reflect and consider new information. This reinforces how important it is, when trying to help people find their way through the thickets of a conflict, that we create contexts perceived as safe in which they will be less likely to be immediately or uncontrollably reactive.

The almost constant state of readiness to react in conflict situations is conditioned by hyper-vigilant expectancies that can distort the perception of present circumstances. In conditions of conflict and threat, we experience egocentric separation of self from other, heightened perception of the other as different, foreign, strange, and threatening as the conflict stimulates reactive dorsal pathways of action control and fight, flight, freeze responses (Tucker and Luu, 2012). The longer the history of the conflict, the more "ingrained" are the neural structures of enmity, like a riverbed deeply channeled by the historical flow of the conflict. The dorsal/ventral "balance of egocentric motives versus fidelity to the constraints of perceptual reality" (Tucker and Luu, 2012, p. 77) can be upset in conflict. On the one hand, too much motive drive will overwhelm the ability to be receptive to external information. On the other, excessive preoccupation with contextual cues will hamper the ability to attend to internal needs.

Because neural structures are dynamic and variable according to circumstances, with different elements becoming more or less activated and prominent and more or less labile according to the salience of current stimuli, change is not just an on/off switch. Parties may adjust their narrative in the mediation setting, establishing new meaning matrices, but find that subsequent exposure to the pre-mediation environment re-stimulates the conflict narrative. A shift in perceptions and narrative that struggling business partners may achieve in mediation or Israeli Jews and West Bank Palestinians may experience during sports relationship-building or in citizen-to-citizen dialogue may not hold upon returning to their home community where other stimuli activate the old narratives.

In complicated ways, either when a conflict has been longstanding or when a new conflict links with neural structures established in earlier relationships, the conflict dynamic itself, beyond the substance of the conflict, can become part of one's identity and part of the relationship definition. The conflictual behavior patterns become habit. "This is how we do things. This is who and how we are together. This is what this relationship is. This is its reality. This is how it works." In this circumstance, to break the conflict logjam, we must work on the relationship dynamic itself as well as on the substance of the disagreement. Not only are the parties in dispute about the issues but the structure of their relationship is broken, its patterns distorted. The parties' perception of, and therefore their behavior within their relationship must be shifted or reconstructed. New patterns of understanding and behavior must be formulated and practiced.

We can see that the characteristics of neural function have implications for social engagement that can lead to conflict and that can make conflict difficult to resolve when it does arise. In the following sections, I look further at some of the implications for our understanding of: communication; perception (including the perceptual biases of in-group/out-group identification, stereotyping, projection, attribution and attribution bias, the fundamental attribution error, implicit bias, confirmation bias, naïve realism, and reactive devaluation); identity; relationship; recovery from trust, betrayal, and trauma; priming, mirroring, and affect contagion; and knowing, learning, and change.

Communication

Though we are not always thinking about our lives in these terms, we face the existential reality of isolation. Each of us is alone within the consciousness experience of our own bodies. Connection with others, so important for our physical and psychological well-being, must take place across the gap between us. Our methods for bridging that gap are limited. We do not have telepathic capacity (though technological advances may conceivably provide that ability in time). Of our methods, language, along with physical behavior and touch, is primary. The commonality of human experience along with certain cognitive capacities (for example, theory of mind, empathy, neuronal mirroring, and perspective taking) allow us to develop agreement about what given word-sounds signify. But the use of language for communication is not simple, exact, or dependably successful. We tend to take language communication for granted, expecting that our speech acts will be understood as we mean them to be, and don't think much about what is actually happening in the physical exchange. But the premise of embodied cognition carries with it some important insights.

Communication through spoken language is a more intimate act than we often acknowledge. My spoken words are vibrational entities generated by my body and transmitted across the gap between us to enter into your body, activating neural structures within you.[2] When I speak with or at you, my words enter your body and engage with the neural matrices that are the very structure of your identity, threatening or seeking or offering or requesting to change or contribute to the physical architecture of who (what) you are.[3] This is not an insignificant or incidental matter. As a consequence, you will receive my word-sounds into your body more or less welcomingly, more or less willingly.[4] In some sense, you will make more or less "space" available for my words within you. In our common parlance, you will be more or less "open" to what I am saying, more or less willing to allow my words to change you. We, as organisms, have some ability to modulate access to our internal structure. We defend against information we perceive to be harmful or threatening just as we will defend against physical violence.

To whatever degree you are receptive to my words, the receptivity is a neural phenomenon and my words will affect your body in one way or another, like pebbles thrown into a pond.[5] It is therefore not surprising that we may be cautious or resistant when listening to the other, in allowing another's words to enter into and affect us. Issues of trust, permission, and the potential for violence are involved. Words are powerful. We are vulnerable.[6] There is a deep intimacy involved in our exchanges.

In communicating, we are always dancing with the dynamics of power and control, not at a theoretical but at the physical level. To communicate is to influence, in one way or another and to one degree or another.[7] To influence is to change that which we influence. As we speak together, we are involved in a process neural change, of mutual neural sculpting in the best of circumstances and a kind of self-protective defensive or assertive and aggressive verbal jousting in more difficult conditions. In any communicational interaction, we face the prospect that we will change the other and we will be changed by the other. We have some control, more or less depending on circumstances, over how much and in what ways we will change. In circumstances of collaboration, trust, and safety, we build neural structures together, open to being changed by each other, engaged creatively and playfully. In circumstances of conflict or disagreement, we use our words to wrestle with each other, we wield them as weapons, as swords and shields, we resist the influence of the other on our neural structures and exert force, pressing with our words, in our attempt to change their neural structures. The greater the conflict, the deeper the distrust, antipathy, anger, hate, or perception of threat, the more resistant we are to change in response to the other's presence and expressions.

There is a sense in conversation that we are always on the verge of disagreement as we protect our neural structures of understanding and identity in the face of incoming words that have the potential to alter those structures, and more so in relationships of low trust or low security.[8] As you read these words, you are involved in a constant process of evaluation, ready to disagree the moment what I say does not conform to a closely held belief or understanding. Whether we are seen, by ourselves or the other, as wrong or right is of great significance, the former threatening the stability of our neural structures and the latter reinforcing those structures. Our structures of knowing will be more or less secure to begin with. We may defend weak structures beyond what they warrant, even in the face of contradictory information. When working with parties in conflict, attention to stability and confidence issues will help us consider what a party might need in order to set aside defenses.

All things considered, communication with language works remarkably well, but communication remains a challenge even with those very similar to us, with whom we share a common background, with whom we feel "on the same team," on the same side, with whom we feel close. Even around friendly tables, we can clash and joust, competing to be right, to assert power, or seek control. We argue. We differ. We even beg to differ. We are different. We see things differently. We try to convince or persuade, to impose or cajole. Whether you agree or disagree with me is of great and primal importance; when you agree with me, I like you; you confirm my neural structures and thereby you reassure, and make of you and me an "us," a tribal affiliation.[9] When we agree, communication becomes easier. We feel that we are experiencing the same territory, that we live in the same world.[10] And indeed, we are experiencing similar neural sensations. When you disagree with me, you challenge my understanding of the world and, therefore, my identity. The space in which we engage with each other is neural, not a disembodied conceptual realm.

Given the intimacy of communication in which our words enter into another's body, there exists always the possibility of abuse of power, the potential for violence. We can injure with the words we choose and how we deliver them, with what pitch, tonal dynamics, volume, and accompanying facial expressions and body postures and movements that are part of the speech act. We see this harmful potential most plainly demonstrated in verbal abuse directed at children whose neural structures of meaning about the world and themselves are in formative, and therefore more vulnerable, stages, disproving the old adage that words are less harmful than sticks and stones. The more significant the other in the child's identity construct, the more harm done; verbal abuse from a parent is more destructive than verbal abuse from a stranger, for example. Similarly, we see the power of words in instances of "brainwashing" (better called "brain-soiling" or "brain-saturating" or "brain-invading") and propaganda in which words are used in an attempt to mold neural structures against the will of the target.

Because words, and the ideas carried by words, can be coercive and manipulative in their capacity to shift the neural architecture of the listener, we carry a burden of ethical responsibility as speakers.[11] As listeners, we have a responsibility to cultivate a sufficiently secure identity to protect against assault while, at the same time, being "open" to hearing contradictory, differing, or emotionally laden messages. Intention is therefore a critical part of communication as we send our words to and into the other. Coercion, the manipulative use of power, and violence are often just a thin line away. Crosswhite (2013, p. 134) addresses the dangers and the dilemma inherent in communication in his discussion of rhetoric (the discipline devoted to the use of language to communicate effectively, responsibly, constructively, influentially, and nonviolently) when he observes, on the one hand, "This is the promise of reason – to settle conflicts without violence, to settle them through reasoning that properly appreciates and evaluates the different perspectives that have come into conflict" and, on the other hand, "in order to be an alternative to violence, rhetoric must in some way resemble it." By this he means that even the peaceful speaker seeks to change the other, and in this way shares an objective similar to that held by the violent communicator. As he wrestles with the dilemma, Crosswhite makes it a point to emphasize the importance of recognizing also "the difference between consent and coercion" and, therefore, between the communication practices of rhetoric and communication practices that are violent. But the point is made that words are powerful, and that with power comes danger, risk, and responsibility; the greater the power, the greater the responsibility.

Tracking the mechanics of language production, transmission, and reception, we can see why understanding can sometimes be difficult to achieve and misunderstanding can so easily result. As the speaker, I activate word-sounds (or, word-sounds are activated within me, ignoring again the question of what the self is) that are associated with a web of neural meaning matrices that have been established over the course of my experience in the world.[12] When I produce these word-sounds and send them across the gap between us, they are delivered to you only as sounds, not carrying with them the meaning I associate with those sounds.[13] When the sounds enter your body, they activate the neural matrices of meaning you have established in association with those sounds on the basis of your experience in the world, which has been different, to a greater or lesser extent, than my experience in the world.[14] To one degree or another, the neural matrices of meaning that we each associate with a particular word-sound will differ.[15] Much of the time, the difference between our meaning associations will be inconsequential, the correspondence close enough to not interfere with our communicative understanding. But sometimes the meaning structures within me associated with a word-sound will be sufficiently different from those activated by my word-sound within you that there will result a mismatch between my intended meaning and your internal experience. We will have a misunderstanding. Hasson et al (2012, p. 2), in speaking about what they call "brain coupling" in the communicational interaction, put it this way:

> Seeing or hearing the actions, sensations or emotions of an agent trigger cortical representations in the perceiver (so called vicarious activations). If the agent has a similar brain and body, vicarious activations in the perceiver will approximate those of the agent, and the neural responses will become coupled. If the agent, however, has a brain and body that are fundamentally different from those of the witness, this vicarious activation pattern will look fundamentally different from that in the agent and the brain responses will not be coupled.

In either case, whether the difference between our neural structures is inconsequential or consequential, we may not perceive the difference without further communication to sort out the differences in our understandings of the words we are using. Because the differences in meaning associations are not immediately perceptible, it can happen that we are unaware of a misunderstanding as it is taking place. I may expect and believe that my words are activating in you a meaning experience closely similar to the meaning experience activated within me in producing the words, but my assumption may be incorrect. And you may believe that the neural matrices of meaning activated within you by my words are what I intended to activate within you, what I meant, and your assumption may be incorrect. We may think we are talking about the same thing when we are, in fact, referencing two considerably different sets of meaning structures. The greater the difference in our backgrounds, in our lived experience, the greater the chances of misunderstanding. As we know, communicating across cultural differences is difficult even with a lot of effort, partly because we don't share the same referents and partly because it's difficult to perceive where and when differences exist.[16] In a conversation about gun control, the associations a gun ownership proponent has with the word "freedom" may be different than those experienced by a gun control advocate. Even in circumstances in which we are convinced that we share the same meaning, for example as members of a group, a religion, a club, or a nation, we will have different inner experiences of the words, issues, and topics, with no immediate way to know what and how great the variations in our meanings.

Another complication that can arise as we communicate with each other is that I, as the speaker, may set in motion unintended "triggering" sets of associations in you the listener. My words may activate neural matrices of meaning in you that I had no idea existed and that are distinct from the associations with those words that exist within me. We so often speak with an egocentric, almost narcissistic focus on the meanings that our words have for us, expecting that our words will activate the same associations in our listeners. Being unfamiliar with parts of their history, we will not know that a word or set of words is, for the other, inflammatory, trauma-triggering, or threatens or activates neural constructs that are key parts of the their identity scaffolding. So also with the expressive cultural accouterments of dress, hygiene habits, hairstyles, beard, make-up, body decoration, postural norms, etc., that may activate associations different than intended or expected.[17]

This is not to say that the speaker is unable to take into account the listener's meaning associations and to speak in such a way as to more likely activate neural structures of meaning in the other that more closely correspond to the speaker's intention and communication goals. But because we are isolated entities with different and unique histories,[18] we must devote attention to actively revealing the differences in our world understandings if they are not to trip us up. Especially in circumstances of conflict and disagreement, the work to discover our different meanings in order to not add the fuel of misunderstanding to the fire of conflict will be more critical. Similarly, it becomes more necessary in conflict that we be aware that our words may activate in the other neural structures of one sort or another that will be unhelpful to understanding and resolution.

Interestingly, there is neurobiological evidence that supports the theory that language production is inhibited in highly stressful circumstances (Cozolino, 2014, p. 21). The theory suggests that in our evolutionary roots, under conditions of threat, the fright/flight/freeze response likely included avoiding the creation of sound that would give away our location to predators. Recent research indicates decreased activation of neural circuits responsible for language production in states of high stress arousal, particularly in individuals experiencing posttraumatic stress (PTSD). Given that we depend to such a great degree on language in conflict resolution processes and that conflict can be highly stressful, these findings underscore the importance of paying attention to the possibility that a party may be having difficulty participating effectively in a negotiation or conflict resolution process.

We have known observationally the dangers, pitfalls, and requirements of communication. We've recognized that there are words we can say that will improve the chances of successful communication in circumstances of conflict. "Is this a good time to talk?" "I'd like to have a conversation about . . . Are you willing?" "I really want to understand what you mean when you say . . ." "What is it that you heard when I said . . .?" "Can you help me understand what came up for you when I said . . .?" "What I'm understanding you to be saying is . . . Is that correct?" "What does . . . mean to you?" All of these approaches and others are efforts to address characteristics of communicational experience.[19] Recognizing and acknowledging the neurophysiological reality of embodied cognition can help us to more purposefully adopt and more firmly anchor better practices to prevent or deal with disagreements and misunderstandings.

Perception

Through folk observation and the evidence of experimental social psychology, we are familiar with the relational patterns of projection, attribution and interpretation, the fundamental attribution error, reactive devaluation, naïve realism, implicit bias, confirmation bias, and so on. Each of these perceptual tendencies reflect our commitment, sometimes irrational and counter to the facts, to our own previously established neural structures that are our understanding of the world.[20]

As I discussed earlier, the organism must make sense of its environment, must assign meaning to incoming stimuli, one way or another.[21] When presented with a photograph of people engaged in a nondescript activity, the observer will unavoidably make up a story of what is happening.[22] Perception of the images in the photograph will activate aspects of the observer's encoded past experience triggering assignment of meaning to the images. We do this without volition. If asked, we will tell a story about what we believe is happening in the photographic image, on very little information. So also when we meet a new person. We speak of "first impressions," conveying the underlying reality that the incoming stimuli physically impress themselves upon the neural substrate, activating related meaning associations. Cozolino (2014, p. 138) reports:

> Research has found that, although it takes our brain 400–500 milliseconds to bring sensations to conscious awareness, it takes only 14 milliseconds to implicitly react to, and categorize, visual information . . . A study of

first impressions found that exposures of just 100 milliseconds were long enough to make judgments about attractiveness, likeability, trustworthiness, competence, and aggression that did not change with increases in exposure time. The amygdala processes social information faster than the blink of an eye.

It is difficult, if not impossible, to suspend judgment entirely.

As also discussed earlier, our understanding of the other is a blend of current circumstances and the activation of elements of our past experience by the perception of the other's physical characteristics and behavior. This is the basis of what we call projection and bias.[23] Our interpretation will be a more or less accurate match with what is actually happening mind-independently, depending on a number of factors including how familiar we are with the individual. There is great latitude for misperception and misunderstanding as is seen, for example, in the phenomenon of implicit bias. The biases involved in implicit bias are neural meaning structures that have been encoded in response to past stimuli exposure, most commonly the messages of a culture that deliver persistent meaning messages about, for example, particular groups of people, blacks, whites, heavy people, women, blond women, Hispanics, police people, corporate CEOs, etc. Inaccurate understandings will confuse and complicate relationship. Implicit biases are not restricted only to our perception of others. We carry implicit biases about ourselves as well, what we call self-image or self-esteem biases that are the neural residue of messages we received about ourselves during our more formative years.

We see similar dynamics in the phenomena of transference and countertransference in which the neurally encoded experience of a past figure is inappropriately associated with a current figure in ways that are not apparent but that can lead to conflict. The perception of the current figure activates neural network associations with the past figure and the two perceptual experiences become confused or conflated.[24] Transference terminology is another way of speaking about the neural phenomena of activation and expectancies.

The perceptual process is bidirectional, so to speak.[25] We receive incoming stimuli in the present moment but our expectancies (including our implicit biases) determine, to some degree, what we perceive. The extent to which past experience colors present perception will vary according to circumstance. As Fuster (2003, p. 84) puts it:

> Perception is not only under the influence of memory but is itself memory or, more precisely, the updating of memory. We perceive what we remember as well as remember what we perceive. Every percept is a historical event, a categorization of current sensory impressions that is entirely determined by previously established memory . . . Perception can thus be viewed as the interpretation of new experiences based on assumptions from prior experience.

The fundamental attribution error, naïve realism, and reactive devaluation reflect the egocentric nature of perceptual experience. In each case, we discount the experience of the other and elevate our own experience as the arbiter of truth and value. Our tendency or default premise is to find our neural experience more reliable than the other's experience as he or she reports it. In disagreement about a subject or situation, we attribute the reasons for the other's analysis (mistaken, as far as we are concerned) to flaws in their character or deficiencies in their perceptual capacities, and our own assessment of the subject or situation to our accurate perception of external reality (the fundamental attribution error). Our tendency is to believe that we perceive the world accurately and relatively objectively whereas the other who disagrees with us is uninformed, biased, irrational, stupid, obstructionist, perverse, or otherwise mistaken (naïve realism). This bias is universal; we apply it to one degree or another to all our perceptual experience. The effect is heightened in conflict circumstances.

Reactive devaluation, by which we discount a suggestion or offer made by our adversary for the resolution of a conflict, might be said to follow from our experience of naïve realism.[26] In addition to possible issues of control and distrust, to accept your proposed settlement offer in a negotiation requires "letting go" of my understanding of the situation and accepting your evaluation. I must discount your offer in order not to discount my assessment. Without sufficient incentive to overcome my attachment to my "realism," I will filter information to sustain my established neural structures, favoring and recalling information that confirms or supports those structures, discounting or ignoring information that contradicts those structures (confirmation bias).

These perceptual characteristics do not necessarily rule the roost but they are strong tendencies, counterbalanced by the phenomena of empathy, perspective taking, and theory of mind that are also rooted in neural structure activation. We are typically enthralled by our own perception of the world, that is, by what is activated within us in response to incoming stimuli. It is the only experience we have and on it we feel we must rely. Our default response is full commitment to what we believe we see, to assume we see "the truth," that our perception of reality is accurate. We also tend to assume that others see the world as do we. The assumption is only partially correct.

Mercier and Sperber (2011, 2017) have come up with an interesting theoretical perspective on reasoning (the Argumentative Theory) to explain why we argue and why disagreement is an important component of our efforts to achieve an accurate understanding of external reality upon which we can depend and act. Commenting on the Argumentative Theory, Jonathan Haidt says, "Reasoning was not designed to pursue the truth. Reasoning was designed by evolution to help us win arguments."[27] In this view, human reasoning evolved in order to test our own and the others' reality assessments in an uncertain world in order to minimize the chances of proceeding on the basis of incorrect information, as a check and balance mechanism to counterbalance naïve realism. We depend on others to challenge our reasoning, to "keep us honest." In collaboration, we seek to co-create understanding, to counter the impulse to win and be right. But successful collaboration must be able to manage a healthy amount of disagreement as the parties zero in on a common understanding. As Haidt puts it:

> Science works very well as a social process, when we can come together and find flaws in each other's reasoning. We can't find the problems in our own reasoning very well. But, that's what other people are for, is to criticize us. And together, we hope the truth comes out.[28]

And as Hugo Mercier explains it:

> If you tell me something that disagrees with what I already believe, my first reaction is going to be to reject what you're telling me, because otherwise I could be vulnerable. But then you have a problem. If you tell me something that I disagree with, and I just reject your opinion, then maybe actually you were right and maybe I was wrong, and you have to find a way to convince me. This is where reasoning kicks in. You have an incentive to convince me, so you're going to start using reasons, and I'm going to have to evaluate these reasons. That's why we think reasoning evolved.[29]

Within the view of the Argumentative Theory, confirmation bias is seen as a necessary and important part of reality testing. Again, as Hugo Mercier puts it:

> Psychologists have shown that people have a very, very strong, robust confirmation bias. What this means is that when they have an idea, and they start to reason about that idea, they are going to mostly find arguments for their own idea. They're going to come up with reasons why they're right, they're going to come up with justifications for their decisions. They're not going to challenge themselves . . . And it's weird, when you think of it, that humans should be endowed with a confirmation bias. If the goal of reasoning were to help us arrive at better beliefs and make better decisions, then there should be no bias. The confirmation bias should really not exist at all . . . But if you take the point of view of the argumentative theory, having a confirmation bias makes complete sense. When you're trying to convince someone, you don't want to find arguments for the other side, you want to find arguments for your side. And that's what the confirmation bias helps you do.

Reasoning doesn't necessarily lead to good outcomes not because reasoning is essentially flawed but because its purpose is to systematically strive for arguments that justify our beliefs or our actions in order to reality test the beliefs and actions of others. In this way, reasoning contributes to the production of sound group decisions in the face of individual variation, making sense of confirmation bias, motivated reasoning, and reason-based choice (Mercier and Sperber, 2011, p. 60).

The solution to the problem of these perceptual biases is to engage in consultative or collaborative exchanges in which mistaken perceptions can be revised in a process of joint consensus-building. Once again, as Hugo Mercier puts it in discussing the Argumentative Theory:

> People mostly have a problem with the confirmation bias when they reason on their own, when no one is there to argue against their point of view. What has been observed is that often times, when people reason on their own, they're unable to arrive at a good solution, at a good belief, or to make a good decision because they will only confirm their initial intuition . . . On the other hand, when people are able to discuss their ideas with other people who disagree with them, then the confirmation biases of the different participants will balance each other out, and the group will be able to focus on the best solution. Thus, reasoning works much better in groups. When people reason on their own, it's very likely that they are going to go down a wrong path. But when they're actually able to reason together, they are much more likely to reach a correct solution.

For conflict resolution practitioners, the key is helping people argue or disagree in a constructive way, not abusing power, not trying to dominate, but meeting with inquiring minds and with the goal not to be right but to find right.

The perceptual distinction we make between in-group and out-group members, stereotyping that is a subset of the more general categorization function, and the behaviors that tend to result also reflect dynamics of the neural basis of experience.[30] In addition to our more deeply patterned in-group affiliations (the result of the evolutionarily selected need to belong for identity construction and physical survival purposes), new in-group identification can happen very quickly, as we see, for example, when we join an organization as a new employee, or newly attend a school. Similarly, there exists a continuum of stereotyping emphasis. To one degree or another, we stereotype everyone we meet as a way to understand external reality.[31] Our brains are wired to seek and make patterns among the elements of our perceptual field, and to place the elements of perceptual experience into categories that help us keep track of and make sense of the world. Every perceptual experience will activate elements of our past experience and will require the brain to place the stimulus within our categorization structures of knowing.[32] When we see a chair, we will likely be unconscious of the categorization process. When we see a person, the results of neural categorization may become more evident to us, whether the stereotyping is positive or negative. In-group members share characteristics. This is comforting. We prefer the familiar. They confirm and reinforce our neural structures, our reality constructs. We favor all objects of perception that confirm previously encoded neural structures, whether they be objects, people, social dynamics, or ideas.[33]

The eager process of perceptual understanding is demonstrated in experiments described by Bergen (2012) in which eye movement was tracked while subjects listened to words as they looked at images that either corresponded directly, partially, or not at all to the words they were hearing. The eye tracking revealed that the subjects began to look at the images according to what was suggested by the initial phonemic sounds of the words, measured in micro-seconds. With images before them of a beaker, a beetle, an electronic speaker, and a carriage and the word "beaker" spoken, participants' eyes began looking at the beaker and beetle as soon as the first syllable was perceived and then stopped looking at the beetle as soon as the "k" in "beaker" was heard. As Bergen (2012, p. 137) puts it, "That means that they're making guesses as soon as they start hearing a word about what in the environment it could possibly refer to." Making guesses is a poetic or euphemistic way of saying it. More accurately, the aural stimuli activated related neural structures of meaning that corresponded to the images being perceived. We do this all the time, making guesses, and very rapidly, about what incoming stimuli mean, making those guesses based on our past experience. In the experimental cases reported by Bergen, the subjects' guesses are confirmed by the unequivocal data of the completed word and the concrete images on the page or screen. In our experience of social life, perceptual data will often remain unclear or uncertain and the interpretation (activations) may be inaccurate and with no immediate or direct way of determining accuracy. A related aspect of perception is "the remarkable tendency of brains to seek out closure and avoid gaps" (Edelman, 2005, p. 37). This is most obviously demonstrated in visual illusions like the Kanizsa triangle but is also seen in our interpretive assumptions about people's behavior. Again, we will make up stories in the absence of information.[34]

The transmission of cultural norms forms our perceptual understanding of in-group and out-group members. The meaning of a given perceptual stimulus may vary by culture. For example, all humans ravenously monitor faces, along with bodily movement generally, for information about safety and danger, approval and dismissal, agreement and disagreement, acceptance and rejection. But the meaning of, for example, eye gaze will vary according to the norms established by a given culture, those norms encoded in each individual during the processes of socialization. A diverted gaze will appear within one culture as a sign of deceit or lack of attention but will be a sign of respect in another culture. An intent direct gaze will be experienced as an insult or sign of aggression in one culture and as an indication of honesty, openness to relationship, or attentive engagement in another. So it is with other aspects of body posture, movement, and proximity. Again, to remind and emphasize, the norms exist as physical structures in neural networks, subject to the stability/plasticity balance required for knowing and learning.

Identity

The experience of self is at the core of our conscious experience. What the self is has preoccupied inquiring minds for several millennia. We have speculated with the only tools we had available, the tools largely of introspection and philosophy. But the explanation of self is not a philosophical matter but rather a neuroscientific matter, though, certainly, philosophical questions remain. The question has appeared to be the former because we've not produced sufficient knowledge with the latter. If the self is embodied, the answer is in the body and we won't have the answer until we understand the body.[35] We are only now beginning to understand that part of the body most primarily involved in the experience of self, the brain, and extended nervous system. We have been similarly fascinated by and have speculated about the stars in the night sky. Without today's tools, over the course of the millennia and within our different cultures, we proposed many interesting theories about what we saw in the sky. It might be fair to say that, at this point, our tools for understanding the stars are more advanced than our tools for understanding the workings of our nervous system. In any case, we do have an experience of self and my assumption here is that self-identity is intimately bound, if not identical with what we know, and what we know is a blend of genetic inheritance and the accumulation of perceptual experience more or less precisely preserved in dynamic neural structures. The syllogism then suggests that the self is an emergent experience arising from integrated reciprocal links among those neural structures.[36]

As I noted earlier, preservation of self-identity is one of our three survival motives. The structure of the self is not rigid but neither is it unconditionally flexible or pliable. In this regard, it is like the rest of the body, supple to an extent and within limits.[37] For most of us, our experience of self is relatively stable, but it is never rock solid. As we meet each other and engage in social relations, we are, at some level, involved in a dialogue of identity, a negotiation of information about the world upon which or of which our identity is built, a balancing act in which we seek to maintain our identity structure as we engage with the other, a dynamic that can seem, in conflict situations, whether mild or severe, a bit reminiscent of pillow fights on a balance beam. In conflict with others, we are concerned about maintaining the stability and integrity of our identity structure. In the healthy and secure state, worldview and self-identity are amenable to change, to development and growth, to further elaboration. Feeling safe and secure, we can be open to the other's input. But as differences and disagreements, which in one way or another will be perceived as threats, arise in a social relationship, dynamics of dominance and control can become evident. We may become more resistant to external influence. Maintaining the integrity of our internal neural identity structures becomes our primary concern. Our experience is physical, though the neural processes are outside our awareness.[38] That said, we may notice a tightening of our body, a reflection of the underlying neural experience. As I've been emphasizing, disagreements involve the very structure of our body.

As I discussed earlier, our communicational interactions will change us, more or less depending on the circumstances.[39] Note some of the metaphors we use: how "attached" or not we are to our point of view; how "tight the bonds;" how "flexible" or how "rigid" we will be; the "disintegration" of identity; to "lose our bearings;" to be "anchored" in our point of view; information or experience that is "life-changing," meaning, in fact, body-changing, self-changing.[40]

Our self-identity is a kind of meaning. As I discussed earlier, meaning arises from associations between and among percepts, the relationship between the notes, not so much the notes themselves.[41] Self arises out of and is made up of meaning associations, and becomes itself an object of perception. The meaning associations compose a story of ourselves, of the world, and our place in the world. One of the characteristics of our story-telling about the world and ourselves is that we want to be a positive character in the story we tell. We want to feel well of ourselves. One of the challenges we face in conflict resolution is that parties are often struggling with questions of being right or wrong, good or bad in the conflict narrative. We face the prospect that we may have been wrong or might have transgressed in some way in the conflict history, and it is not untypical that each party is proclaiming the other wrong or bad, yet we are motivated to maintain a positive self-story. Settling a conflict will be furthered by creating and maintaining a positive self-narrative for each of the parties in the conflict story as the narrative is shifted to incorporate the elements of a settlement agreement.

We are partly defined by those with whom we are in relationship. A change in any of the elements of our experience, including a change in the structure or definition of our relationship with another, or our understanding of the other, will, to one degree or another, change our self-identity.[42] This is one of the reasons that divorce presents parties with painful challenges. The forced change in perception of the spouse and of the relationship requires a change in the parties' understanding of themselves. This can be a very difficult shift to make.

Another way to put it is that the self is a structure or a process of assembled familiarities. Insert the unfamiliar and we change the experience structure as a whole. This is what underlies the experience of culture shock. Suddenly the items at the grocery are not familiar, the language is not familiar, and there is little to reaffirm one's reality constructs. Quite the opposite, almost everything contradicts what we have known. This is also the reason, beyond the physical danger, that earthquakes are profoundly disturbing. We depend on and expect the ground beneath our feet to be solid, reliable, and stable. Its movement shakes the foundation of our psychological world as much as it does the foundations of our houses. Hallucinogens and other "mind altering" drugs alter our neural connections, changing our understanding of the meaning of things, and therefore our sense of identity. Other stimuli, whether visual (a glorious sunrise, for example), auditory (music, for example), or somatic (the experience of pain, for example), or even olfactory, can similarly alter how we experience ourselves. When we ask people attempting to resolve a conflict to consider alternative views or new narratives, to be open to opinions or perspectives that differ materially from what they have known or believed, we are asking them to see the other in a new light and therefore, to shift or alter their own identity construct, at more or less central or peripheral levels. There is no clear typology of which aspects of our reality and identity constructs are more difficult to change and why. The arrangement will vary according to individual and circumstance. But we can be certain that when we see a heated conflict, some important parts of the individuals' neural identity constructs are being activated, parts that they are disinclined to alter.

The degree to which and the ways in which a conflict will be experienced as an identity threat will vary. Sometimes, a negative element of a party's self-image, a negative self-story, is triggered. For example, in interpersonal conflict, a statement by one party may trigger an experience of low self-esteem or patterns of guilt or shame in the other party. These patterns of self-experience, deeply or strongly encoded, can be difficult to change as they comprise a habituated part of self-identity, of self-definition. This is the challenge of psychotherapy. The transition from one set of beliefs to another is a delicate process for people in a conflict or decision-making situation, especially to the degree that those beliefs are fundamental. It is these kinds of transitions that conflict resolution workers seek to cultivate, facilitate, and manage.

As an outside observer, we may wonder why the Israeli Jews and the Palestinians, for example, seem so unwilling (as a generalization) to create a new narrative, to change their minds. We may believe or assume that changing the narrative is entirely at their discretion and wonder why they so willingly engage in continuing the violence that is so evidently harmful to both communities. But it can help to remember that we ourselves hold stories in our own lives that make up our understanding of the world that we would have equal difficulty changing, even absent the stakes and the history that exist in the Israel/Palestine conflict, whether those stories be, for example, our perceptions of the homeless, our family members, our alma mater, those on our side or the other side of the political aisle, or an opposing sports team. It is not simply a case of willfully changing parts of our understanding of the world that make up parts of our self-identity. Habits of the mind, embodied in neural structures, are as difficult or more difficult to change than are habits of the body. The physical therapist has more direct access to the body than does the psychological therapist or the conflict worker.

Relationship

To say the obvious, in conflict resolution work we are dealing with relationships. Conflict happens in relationship. In a conflict relationship, the dynamics of dependence, independence, interdependence, trust, cooperation, competition, power, influence, and safety come to the fore. Conflict threatens the structure of relationship or tests its stability.

As it turns out, in relationship, we face ourselves as much as we meet the other as our neural structures of meaning are activated by the other.[43] This is one of the challenges we face as conflict workers, helping people take responsibility for themselves and their part in the conflict. In the heat of conflict, we can be resistant to self-reflection as we attack and defend in the face of perceived threat.

The potential for injury in relationship is great.[44] We speak of our feelings being hurt. We can cry with the pain. The emotions and feelings experienced in conflict, of sadness, fear, anger, shame, guilt, relief, etc. are felt in the body. Tucker (2007, p. 258–259) notes, "Recent research using magnetic resonance imaging of brain activity has shown that the networks responsible for physical pain appear to form a basis for the adult's response to the psychological pain caused by social rejection . . . Rejection hurts." In agreement, Cozolino (2014, p. 106) emphasizes that:

> The cingulate becomes activated when we, or those we love, experience physical pain as well as when we experience social exclusion. The common underlying neurobiology of physical and social pain may help us to understand why the quality of our relationships has such a profound effect on our physical health.

One of the premises and corollaries of the embodied understanding of consciousness is that, just as mind is not separate from body, we are not entities separate from the world. We are a part of our environment, are in constant interaction with our environment, and are changed by our environment. As Mark Johnson (2007, p. xii) puts it, the mind is "embodied meaning that emerges as structures of organism-environment interactions or transactions." Our identity is made up, in large part, of the people in our lives, each of them on a continuum from most to least intimate and important. Our behavior in the world is largely behavior in relationship. Hood (2012) reports on a study in which bowlers at a bowling alley smiled only 4 percent of the time after a good score when facing away from those they were bowling with and 42 percent of the time when they turned to face them. Our behavior is communicational and communal, from facial expression to body poster and movement to the dynamics of vocalization.

Realizing the deep interdependence and inter-relatedness of organism with environment contributes to how we perceive and understand the interactions between and among the parties as they affect each other's physical selves. As I've been emphasizing, the brain changes in response to experience, including, and perhaps most importantly, relational experience. As Cozolino (2014, pp. xv) puts it, "relationships are a fundamental and necessary condition for the evolution of the contemporary human brain" and "when we interact, we are impacting each other's internal biological state and influencing the long-term construction of each other's brains" (Cozolino, 2014, p. 6). This is the profound nature of what we are working with when we are working with people in conflict.

Trust, Betrayal, and Trauma

It's a commonplace to say that trust is the glue of relationship. The primal importance of trust to our fundamental survival concerns runs so deep that we are mostly not aware of it as an omnipresent factor. Trust has to do with the degree to which we can rely upon the interfaces we have with external reality, both physical and relational. I trust that if I lean against a wall, it will support me. I trust the ground beneath my feet. I need to be able to trust my perceptual experience of the physical world in order to navigate within that world safely and successfully. So it is also with my social relationships. We ask to what degree we can rely upon and be safe in the presence of the other. Trust is established on the basis of experience. We learn (encode) how something is, whether a physical object, a person, or a relational dynamic, and we expect it to remain consistent. When there is variability, we learn about the pattern from repeated exposure. We can deal with the variability when it includes some constancy. We want the patterns to be predictable.

Repetition reinforces the neural structures. The longer and more frequent our relationship with a physical or relational phenomenon, the more we have the experience of "knowing" it and the more we trust it to remain as it has been. As I discussed earlier, expectancies are established. When expectations are violated in a betrayal, the violation of trust creates a disruption at the neural level. Expectancies are not confirmed but are contradicted. Our understanding of the world proves to be wrong. What we thought we knew to be true turns out to be mistaken. The unexpected has happened and it is like walking into a wall we hadn't seen. We must reconstruct our understanding of the world. The ground has shifted. Our world is shaken. We are undermined. There is a kind of breaking in betrayal. We speak of our trust being "broken." We speak of our understanding or confidence being "shattered." Neural networks crash like software or hardware gone wrong. Parts of our worldview "collapse," and to that degree, our identity structure is shaken or weakened. If I were to sit on a chair and, rather than it supporting me as I expected, my body passed through the chair landing me shockingly and painfully on the floor, I could say that the chair betrayed me. What I had believed to be true of it was suddenly no longer true and I would find myself questioning everything I know about the physics of the world, and perhaps much else.

This is why betrayal in trust relationships can be so disturbing and difficult to recover from. The discovery of marriage infidelity or lying breaks critical parts of our understanding of the external world that are important components of our identity structure, shakes those neural networks as an earthquake shakes physical structures. Theft and other crimes of malicious or intentional injury break what we call the social contract, the set of relational assumptions and agreements upon which we base our relational expectations. Belief in a fundamentally just and safe world (along with other primary shielding assumptions such as, for example, that we are the center of things, that we won't die, at least not today, or that we're right, at least more right than wrong) provides primary protective security. When that belief is confuted, we speak of being violated. It is a part of the body that is shaken or injured, in the form of neural structures that were experienced as sound but then are rent like a spider's web. We experience a kind of internal chaos or confusion until our neural structures settle into a new normal. Parental violence similarly betrays and harms the child at a deep physical level beyond any more superficial injury. Neural matrices of safety are broken.[45]

Trust is a bit like humpty dumpty. Once broken, it's not simple or easy to rebuild it. To recover from betrayal, a single positive experience will not likely be sufficient to reestablish secure trust-meaning neural matrices. We hear victims of betrayal speak about the offender having to prove his or her trustworthiness, and proof is achieved through repeated affirming experiences that will forge new or renewed neural circuits. The process of recovery sometimes involves what we call apology and forgiveness, which require, reflect, and convey shifts in the reality constructs of the participants, a rewiring of their neural meaning matrices.

If past experience has involved repeated trauma or betrayal or violence, expectancies will have been thus formed and more positive behavioral experience will not be received easily or with full confidence. The "rewiring" that is the necessary embodiment of recovery from past trauma is as difficult as the betrayal of trusted relationship is painful. Hostile past experience establishes very durable neural records that can be difficult to overcome, replace, or amend. This helps to explain why some conflicts are so persistent and difficult to shift. The relationship dynamics become fixed in memory to a degree that inhibits or is resistant to change.[46] Recovery requires the creation of new narratives of security or re-empowerment, or other sustaining narratives, the creation of new neural matrices of meaning or the restoration of previous matrices.

Priming, Mirroring, and Affect Contagion

The phenomena of behavioral priming, neural mirroring, and affect contagion are examples of external stimuli activating elements of the perceiver's internal neural structure.

There is a good deal of literature on priming in mediation, most of which focuses on priming techniques mediators can use that may encourage more constructive communication and promote movement towards resolution.[47] But parties will be primed by each other as well, often in not so helpful ways as the verbal or physical behavior of one will activate neural circuits in the other that make communication more difficult and particular responses more or less likely.

In priming, a perceptual stimulus, consciously or unconsciously received, activates neural pathways that make it more likely that subsequent behavior, immediately following the prime or following shortly thereafter, will take one form rather than another. The prime facilitates subsequent neural processing in the direction of the prime (Tucker, 2007, p. 106; Haidt, 2013, p. 67, Bergen, 2012).

As but one of many examples, an experimental demonstration of the priming phenomenon is described by Bergen (2012) in which subjects asked to turn a knob as soon as they can determine that a sentence flashed on the screen before them makes sense will do so faster if the action described by the sentence is in the same direction as the knob-turning. The read description primes the subject's knob-turning by preparing the neural pathways having to do with direction of movement. Conversely, if the sentence references directional terms opposite the direction in which the knob turns, the knob-turning will be slower because associations with opposite directionality will have been activated. In another experimental example, after completing tasks in a research experiment, subjects who had been subliminally primed with words having to do with the elderly (tired, wrinkled, old) left the laboratory and walked down a hall to leave the building more slowly than those who were not so primed. In another study, subjects rated abstract ideographs more favorably when the ideographs were observed while the subject pulled a lever towards themselves (welcoming prime) than when pushing the lever away (rejecting prime) (Bergen, 2012). There are numerous other experimental demonstrations of the effect.

An explanation for the priming phenomenon is that the neural connections involved in the primed behavior are stimulated by the prime so that subsequent activation meets less resistance on those neural pathways. The neural pathways involving the primed behavior are prepared by being activated by the prime, making it more likely that subsequent perceptual and cognitive experience will tend along those neural pathways. It is as if the primed behavior is already partially initiated by the prime. This explains also why the influence of a prime is short-lived. The priming effect only influences perception and cognition in close temporal proximity to the prime (though the results of the prime, the primed behavior, may endure for a longer period), after which the prime becomes lost among subsequent perceptual stimuli that will prime for other behaviors.[48] Looked at in this way, we are always being primed by the conditions to which we are exposed, moment-to-moment. Intentional priming is only the manipulation of a neural characteristic that is always active.

There has been much talk of mirror neurons since neuroscientists at the University of Parma accidentally discovered several years ago that the same motor neurons in the brains of macaque monkeys that would be involved in a physical action were activated by the observation of that action performed by another. This phenomenon is a specific case of the general function of neural activation and reflects, also, the integration of brain functions, cognitive and motor. When I observe someone smile or ski or lift a box or sing, the stimuli of the perceptual experience activate those neural structures within me that would be involved were I to perform those behaviors.[49] My "knowing" of these behaviors is imbedded in the neural matrices that would allow me to perform the behaviors. In the conflict resolution context, tension in one party, for example, perceived by the other party is likely to activate the neural structures, including motor neurons, involved in the experience of tension. The degree to which this mirroring effect will be activated will depend on present circumstances and the history of experience of the observer. But the potential for this kind of mutual influence is always present. Cozolino (2014, p. 56) notes that:

> The networks that receive and send social communication are interwoven with others that regulate our own emotions, moods, energy level, psychological health, and ability to fight off illnesses. Anxiety is contagious . . . and, transmitted via mirror, imitation, and resonance systems, it alerts our muscles to respond; it activates our fear and alarm circuitry through the amygdala down through the HPAA axis and spreads throughout the body.

He goes on to say that this kind of infectious tension results in a reduction in our ability to learn new information and to problem-solve.

In these ways, expressed emotions by one party will have an effect on the other parties who perceive the expression.[50] The effect is neither predictable nor necessarily one-to-one. Discouragement or optimism expressed by one or several parties may spread to others but may perhaps activate a variety of responses, depending on the life experience of the perceivers. It is known that seeing fear in the face of the other will trigger our own brain in one of several ways, either to be on the alert to a potential threat, to lookout for danger, or to help the other who appears to be in trouble. In response to someone who looks fearful, we may feel dominant and safe or fearful and unsafe (Cozolino, 2014). The mutual influence of parties on each other will always be a matter of degree and dependent on many variables, external and internal, present and past, specific to the individuals involved.[51]

Knowing and Certainty, Learning and Change

As I noted at the beginning of this discussion, and to say what perhaps seems too obvious to mention, conflict and conflict resolution have to do, in part and at a foundational level, with what we believe we know and how certain we are, or feel a need to be, about that knowing. In relationship, we meet each other with our knowings about the world and our structures of identity. In conflict, our knowings are at odds.[52] As I have been emphasizing, knowing and certainty are neural phenomena, though we don't directly experience the physical underpinnings.

The process of resolving conflict is one of learning and change. To learn, we must be willing to not know, or at least to loosen our attachment to what we think we know,[53] and to become new.[54] Yet such a large part of our cognitive experience tends towards an attachment to what we already know.[55] We use the term "ingrained." We are "anchored" or "wedded" to our knowings. We resist the feeling of not knowing, as if it is a kind of being set adrift. We tend to cling to (as with a life raft) our beliefs, especially in conditions of perceived threat. Even as I write these words, I experience aspects of this phenomenon as I need a certain threshold level of certainty in my knowing in order to write them, regardless of the correctness of my knowing. The balance between knowing and not knowing is delicate.[56] We all experience the need and desire to know, to be certain, to be right, as we do also the discomfort of doubt and uncertainty.

We witness dialogues becoming polarized when the issues being discussed are contentious. It is instructive, if not somewhat discouraging, to witness a disagreement in which the opinions on each side are presented as objective facts over which the battle then rages. Each side claims to see and speak the truth and accuses the other side of all manner of ignorance and moral laziness or worse. "My truthiness is more true than your truthiness," goes the cartoon. These days, the comments sections at the end of articles posted on the Internet and Twitter exchanges offer easy access to such spectacles of self-righteous anger and vituperative indignation in the face of disagreement. In these circumstances, it is difficult for those involved to share their perspectives as possible interpretations of reality or as personal observations to be placed side by side with the other's equally legitimate personal observations and then to consider their differences with interest and respectful inquiry.

Tucker (2007, p. 3) reports Claude Shannon's definition of information as that which reduces uncertainty and he continues (p. 140), "Learning, the process of accommodating information, only occurs when you are surprised – when there is uncertainty and it is reduced by information." I add, and Tucker agrees (personal communication), that the surprise necessary for learning can also occur when there is certainty which is reduced by the surprise of new information, creating uncertainty that can provide the healthy, constructive and, to some degree, uncomfortable context for new learning.[57] That said, if information is that which reduces uncertainty, we have to be willing to be uncertain in order to have our uncertainty reduced. When we are too rigidly certain of what we already know, we will be immune to new information.[58] Again, we know these dynamics observationally. We can better understand the behaviors on the basis of the underlying neural dynamics.

Whenever we speak of knowing, the question of objectivity arises. What are we able to know? How accurate can be our understanding of reality? The premise of embodied consciousness leads to conclusions about the nature of truth and knowledge. Access to mind-independent reality is both limited and personal. So the answer to the objectivity question is "No," by definition, by the nature of the organism.[59] The closest we can come to what we call "objectivity" is through reality-testing our subjective experiences with others and through consensus-building in which we bring together our different and sometimes differing perspectives to build a joint and common understanding of the world. Truth, for our purposes in human relationship and communication, is consensus-based. There are methods (mathematics, science) that likely, though not certainly, get us closer to accurate understanding of external reality but the fundamental principle holds that "it depends on how you look at it" and each of us is limited to our necessarily egocentric perspective.

The need to see ourselves as being right in our understanding of external reality flows naturally and necessarily from the embodied basis of identity and knowing. Most fundamentally, the need to be right is not the result of a defect in character but arises from the organism's motivation to achieve accurate environmental assessment. We can't easily or, more importantly, healthily live in a perpetual condition of complete uncertainty, or of denying what we know, or of believing that what we know is wrong. For one thing, basic physical survival requires that we are able to rely upon the accuracy of our assessments of our environment. But additionally, psychological health depends on and is reflected in a consonance between what we believe we know and our own validation of that knowing, as long as there is a sufficiently close correspondence between what we believe we know and the external, mind-independent reality. To some significant degree, we must be committed to our mental constructs. When willingness to be open to new perspectives becomes general denial of or pervasive doubt about our self-experience, identity integrity and relationship capacity become impaired. There is a basis for our need to justify our beliefs and behavior, whether at the individual or the group levels. Again, it is a question of balance in the healthy state. Working in conflict, we must understand that the balance can be precarious, the scales can be tipped by external conditions, and the stakes can be high for the parties.[60]

Any statement becomes questionable in its assertion, including this one. Any assertion presents the challenge to challenge. A proposed certainty begs to be tested. So, in conversation, we are always on the verge of disagreement.[61] As you read these words, you will find yourself prompted by the assertion of the statement to question the statement.[62] Certainty always stands on the thin ice of uncertainty, much as "maybe" is the same as "maybe not." Social science research and our experience demonstrate that, in circumstances of threat, we will tend to protect our certainties even when the data undermine the certainty.[63] As one example, experimental research suggests that adherence to negative stereotyping increases in conditions of conflict, threat, or uncertainty. Stereotyping provides a kind of certainty, an illusion of security in believing we know what is true by rigidly defining the unfamiliar other within a known category.

Because we are working to facilitate change of one sort or another when we are working with people in conflict (change of mind, change of heart, change of understanding, perspectives, beliefs, perceptions, relationship, positions, objectives, etc.), it is helpful to be aware of, and sensitive to, how difficult change can be.[64] Change is not impossible. We have many examples in our own lives, and in stories of the lives of others. Rabid anti-Semites or racist extremists have been known to realize (to see the real, to know the actual) the error of their previous beliefs, to "see the light." But change is not simple or easy in many circumstances and for good reasons, as I have been discussing. The momentum of belief resists opposition. The stronger, the more forceful, the more aggressive the opposition to our beliefs, the greater our resistance can be. Change must be cultivated gently. Success will be furthered by demonstrations of care, kindness, indeed, love for the other whose views we hope to change.

Tucker and Luu (2012, p. 6) discuss the blocking effect by which a conditioned stimulus, such as a tone, that is paired with an unconditioned stimulus, such as food, to elicit a response, such as a lever press, even when presented without the food, will be blocked if the response is first trained to a different stimulus, such as a light, in which case presenting the light and the tone together will not result in the conditioning of the tone, even after many pairings. This could be a partial explanation of our difficulty in changing our present perception of another based on current cues that do not easily override the cues (the conditioned stimuli) from our past experience of the other. Based on this analog, there will be resistance to allowing new cues to replace the old conditioned cues. This research might also indicate why it can be so difficult to recover from past traumatic events, the triggers being so strong and difficult to replace. At the same time, the learning of new cues is facilitated by the presence of surprise, when actual stimuli differ from what is expected, particularly an aversive surprise. "Learning thus emerges from the need to change" (Tucker and Luu, 2012, p. 6). If circumstances are familiar and consistent with past experience, old cues are more difficult to replace with new cues, perhaps due to the blocking effect.

Notes

1 "When discussions are hostile, the odds of change are slight" (Haidt, 2013, p. 79).
2 "Comprehension is the vicarious experience of the described events through the integration and sequencing of traces from actual experience cued by the linguistic input" (Rolf Zwaan as quoted in Bergen, 2012, p. 72).
3 "a substantial body of evidence from the cognitive sciences supports the hypothesis that meaning is shaped by the nature of our bodies" (Johnson, 2007, p. 9).
4 "One threat of exposing ourselves to one another in language is that we may be called on to change. What may be made clear is that the ideas of others are in some sense better than our own ideas ... The willingness to change one's mind is often thought to be a condition for genuine argumentation" (Crosswhite, 2013, p. 141); "In order for argumentation to take place, one must be willing, in principle, to be convinced of the other person's point of view" (Crosswhite, 2013, p. 77). Note that within the discipline of rhetoric, argumentation refers to responsible, nonviolent dialogue the goal of which is learning and growth.
5 For a review of some of the research on interactional influence on the brains of interlocutors in the communication exchange, see Hasson et al (2012).
6 "The interpretation of communicated information involves activating a context of previously held beliefs and trying to integrate the new with old information. This

process may bring to the fore incoherencies between old and newly communicated information. Some initial coherence checking thus occurs in the process of comprehension. When it uncovers some incoherence, an epistemically vigilant addressee must choose between two alternatives. The simplest is to reject communicated information, thus avoiding any risk of being misled. This may, however, deprive the addressee of valuable information and of the opportunity to correct or update earlier beliefs. The second, more elaborate, alternative consists in associating coherence checking and trust calibration and allowing for a finer-grained process of belief revision. In particular, if a highly trusted individual tells us something that is incoherent with our previous beliefs, some revision is unavoidable: We must revise either our confidence in the source or our previous beliefs. We are likely to choose the revision that reestablishes coherence at the lesser cost, and this will often consist in accepting the information communicated and revising our beliefs" (Mercier and Serber, 2011, p. 60).

7 "When I communicate with you I am trying to change your mind. I am trying to act on your mental state. I'm not just putting out a kind of signal for you to decode. And I do that by providing you with evidence of a mental state in which I want to put you and evidence of my intention to do so. The role of what is often known in cognitive science as "theory of mind," that is the uniquely human ability to attribute complex mental states to others, is as much a basis of human communication as is language itself" (from talk by social and cognitive scientist Dan Sperber at https://www.edge.org/conversation/dan_sperber-an-epidemiology-of-representations).

8 "The person we may most need to reason with might be an enemy of our present point of view, our present attainments, but also a profound friend of our next self, the one we are hoping to become, without yet knowing it very clearly" (Crosswhite, 2013, p. 78).

9 Clive Hamilton, in discussing psychologist Leon Festinger's research into cult behavior, noted, "He wrote that we spend our lives paying attention to information that is consonant with our beliefs and avoiding that which is not. We surround ourselves with people who think as we do and avoid those who make us feel uncomfortable" (Hamilton, 2010, p. 96).

10 "In its communicative function, language is a set of tools with which we attempt to guide another mind to create within itself a mental representation that approximates one we have" (Scott Delancy as quoted in Feldman, 2006, p. 259).

11 "Argumentation (by which is meant principled communication in the tradition of rhetorical practice) is an attempt to purify reason of violence" (Crosswhite, 2013, p. 107).

12 "the meaning of an utterance can best be expressed as a linked set of (embodied) schemas" (Feldman, 2006, p. 285).

13 The difficulties are further exacerbated with written words that do not even carry with them the meaning aids of tone, pitch, and pacing.

14 "Each word can activate alternative meaning subnetworks . . . These subnetworks are themselves linked to other circuits representing the semantics of words and frames that are active in the current context. The standard neural best-fit matching mechanism activates additional related concepts as part of choosing the most appropriate meaning. The meaning of a word in context is captured by the joint activity of *all* of the relevant circuitry: contextual, immediate, and associated" (Feldman, 2006, p. 287).

15 "the images you and I see in our minds are not facsimiles of the particular object but rather images of the interactions between each of us and an object which engaged our organisms, constructed in neural pattern form according to the organism's design . . . And since you and I are similar enough biologically to construct a similar enough image of the same thing, we can accept without protest the conventional idea that we have formed *the* picture of some particular thing. But we did not" (Damasio, 1999, p. 321).

16 "Such evocation requires, among other things, that the listener or the reader share enough experience with the author" (Feldman, 2006, p. 259).

17 "Recent findings suggest that not just a person's face but their whole body posture can trigger non-conscious perception of the person's emotions in an observer. It therefore makes sense to assume that, like facial expressions, body postures belong to a category of biological stimuli to which we are evolutionarily prepared to respond" (Tamietto and de Gelder, 2010).

18 "As a series of phenomenal experiences, consciousness is necessarily private – it is tied to an individual's body and brain and to the history of that individual's environmental interactions. That history is unique" (Edelman, 2005, p. 141).

19 "Human language and thought are crucially shaped by the properties of our bodies and the structure of our physical and social environment" (Feldman, 2006, p. 5).

20 David McRaney, in his book *You Are Not So Smart*, speaks of this attachment to our beliefs when he says, "Once something is added to your collection of beliefs, you protect it from harm. You do this instinctively and unconsciously when confronted with attitude-inconsistent information. Just as confirmation bias shields you when you actively seek information, the backfire effect defends you when the information seeks you, when it blindsides you. Coming or going, you stick to your beliefs instead of questioning them. When someone tries to correct you, tries to dilute your misconceptions, it backfires and strengthens those misconceptions instead. Over time, the backfire effect makes you less skeptical of those things that allow you to continue seeing your beliefs and attitudes as true and proper" (as quoted at https://www.brainpickings. org/2014/05/13/backfire-effect-mcraney).

21 "the brain . . . has means to coordinate the segregated perceptual events that occur when . . . a stimulus strikes the retina. The net result of such coordination is perceptual categorization – the carving up of the world of inputs into objects significant for a given animal species' recognition. The brain carries out pattern recognition" (Edelman, 2006, p. 20).

22 "When the other is significant for us, as a source of either affection or danger, countless . . . evaluative processes become activated. Those of us who can better predict the intentions of others have an obvious advantage in terms of safety, competition, and mating. Neural networks dedicated to the evaluation of others have a long evolutionary history" (Cozolino, 2014, p. 5).

23 "To the extent that they incorporate the residuals of experience that are encoded within our representational networks . . . the interpretive structures of consciousness must be historical, the developmental products of personal life histories" (Tucker, 2007, p. 132).

24 "Our experience of others is created at the interface of our memories of people in our past and our experiences of people in our lives today. Thus we never experience a person as totally new but rather as some blend of our expectations, implicit schema, and who he or she really is" (Cozolino, 2014, p. 138).

25 "When memory dominates the corticolimbic pathway, then processing is *limbifugal* (outward). When sensation dominates the pathway, then processing is *limbipetal* (inward)" (Tucker, 2007, p. 176) and "The density of neural pathways is as great going from the limbic core toward the neocortical shell as it is from the shell to the core. Memory reaches out to sensation as much as sensation gives the evidence of perception" (Tucker, 2007, p. 176).

26 For a thorough review of reactive devaluation, see Lee Ross's chapter 2 in Arrow et al (1995).

27 Full discussion available at https://www.edge.org/conversation/hugo_mercier-theargumentative-theory

28 Again, see Haidt's discussion in the source listed in Note 27.

29 See his discussion of the theory at https://www.edge.org/conversation/hugo_mercierthe-argumentative-theory

30 Categorization is, for one thing, an efficiency strategy. We can know one tree, and we can know many tress. But we can't know each one of all trees. Each new tree we meet,

we can recognize as part of the "category bucket" of trees without having to know it for itself.

31 "In our daily life we continuously perceive – mostly unconsciously – the objects and events around us by classifying those objects and events into categories, and by matching them to previous experience – that is, by matching them to established cognits in our cortex" (Fuster, 2013, p. 44).

32 "Perception is the categorizing of the world that surrounds us . . . In our daily life we continuously perceive – mostly unconsciously – the objects and events around us by classifying those objects and events into categories, and by matching the to previous experience – that is, by matching them to established cognits in our cortex" (Fuster, 2013, p. 44).

33 This is the reason we may experience some discomfort with what is sometimes and revealingly called disfigurement, striking birth marks, severe scarring from burns, or birth anomalies.

34 Some consider religion to be the ultimate such filling in, in our circumstance of greatest possible absence of information. Conspiracy theories, in their less paranoid forms, emerge from the conjunction of unsatisfactory and/or incomplete evidence and an ideological goal not supported by the available evidence. In this regard, religion could be called a grand conspiracy theory. Of course, those with religious beliefs would disagree. And those without would say of that disagreement, of course, that's the nature of conspiracy theories. And round they would go.

35 "The brain is embodied and the body is embedded . . . If we include the brain as your favorite organ, you *are* your body" (Edelman, 2006, p. 24).

36 "We all have the same brain systems, and the number of neurons in each brain system is more or less the same in each of us as well. However, the particular way those neurons are connected is distinct, and that uniqueness, in short, is what makes us who we are" (LeDoux, 2003, p. 303).

37 "One's working self is thus a subset of the universe of possible self-concepts that can occur at any one time – it is the subset that is available to the thinking conscious person at a particular moment, and is determined in part by memory and expectation, and in part by the immediate situation. These features of the working self explain how one can have both stable and mutable motives, and how motives can be conflicting or dissonant. The working self is a central part of one's mental apparatus. It influences perception, attention, thinking, memory retrieval, and storage, and guides action" (LeDoux, 2003, pp. 255–256).

38 There is a difference between our experience of self and the neural function that produces the experience. Our experience of thinking is different than what thinking is, just as our experience of seeing is different than the physical processes that produce sight. "The opacity of introspection is a fundamental limitation. We must understand that the mind is not subjectively transparent. We have to construct our knowledge of the mind carefully and systematically through scientific analysis of the evidence" (Tucker, 2007, p. 18).

39 "The cost of new learning may be abandoning your old self" (Tucker, 2007, p. 100); "Once you have learned, your old self is not to be seen again" (Tucker, 2007, p. 121).

40 "From our neural perspective, primary metaphors can be seen as a normal consequence of associative learning" (Feldman, 2006, p. 201).

41 "Logos is in part the references things bear to each other. The being of things lies not in their being detached from all relation to one another, but rather in the internal references that link them to each other" (Crosswhite, 2013, p. 175).

42 "Change your brain, your body, or your environments in nontrivial ways, and you will change how you experience your world, what things are meaningful to you, and even who you are" (Johnson, 2007, p. 2).

43 "We exert such influence (on each other) in every encounter because we never experience each other outside of a communicative event" (Crosswhite, 2013, p. 17).

44 "However, the way in which violence sometimes hovers around a dialogue helps to remind us that a struggle is taking place, that the exposure of our weakness is something we do not just naturally accept. We feel it as a violence, and we often fight back. And in this process we become suspicious of 'persuasion'" (Crosswhite, 2013, p. 141).

45 "The neurodevelopmental effect may be one of rapid differentiation of the connections within the child's developing neural networks. In an environment dominated by threats, the continual engagement of the redundancy bias would lead not only to a focusing of attention reactively, but to the restriction of brain growth to neural networks that are immediately relevant to coping with threat. Because brain development is continuous, the adaptive scope of cognition and neurodevelopment provides continuing constraints on the possibilities for future development" (Tucker and Luu, 2012, p. 133).

46 "A *hedonic cathexis* (Freud's term for a positively charged attraction) can be a powerful force in the mind, but it pales in comparison to a hostile cathexis . . . hostility binds memory with unusual strength and tenacity. A hostile encounter spawns motivational reverberations that are powerful enough to distract you from focusing on anything else" (Tucker, 2007, p. 209).

47 A Google search conducted August 26, 2015 of "priming in mediation" listed 213,000 results.

48 See, for example, Carter et al (2011) (available at http://labconscious.huji.ac.il/wp-content/uploads/2011/03/Carter-etal-Long-term-effects-of-American-flag.pdf), as reported in Hoffman and Wolman (n.d.).

49 "we imagine sounds using the brain regions that allow us to hear real sounds" (Bergen, 2012, p. 35).

50 "In the unaware observer, undetected emotional stimuli can also induce spontaneous facial reactions that reflect the affective valence of the stimuli, as recorded using electromyography (EMG). This spontaneous tendency to synchronize our facial expressions with the emotional meaning of other individuals' expressions is likely to play a part in social interactions" (Tamietto and de Gelder, 2010, p. 704).

51 "the visceral, emotional responses to observing another's emotion are not necessarily productive of real empathy. These are primarily responses of emotional contagion, primitive feelings that mirror perception with little integration of more complex facets of experience. Cows show emotional contagion, but we would not consider them capable of deep empathy" (Tucker, 2007, p. 267).

52 "If we know that our world is necessarily the world we bring forth with others, every time we are in conflict with another human being *with whom we want to remain in coexistence*, we cannot affirm what for us is certain (absolute truth) because that would negate the other person. If we want to coexist with the other person, we must see that *his certainty – however undesirable it may seem to us – is as legitimate and valid as our own* . . . A conflict is always a mutual negation. It can never be solved in the domain where it takes place if the disputants are 'certain.' A conflict can go away only if we move to another domain where coexistence takes place. The knowledge of this knowledge constitutes the social imperative for a human-centered ethics" (Maturana and Varela, 1987, pp. 245–246).

53 "The Platonic *logos* is a leading, not a seeing or grasping or knowing. It is more a reverent way of inquiry than a method for reaching final conclusions or arriving at a knowledge of the final being. The latter can simply not be a realizable goal for a Socrates whose essential intellectual virtues include ignorance" (Crosswhite, 2013, p. 34).

54 "When we choose stability and the continuity of personal identity, we can assimilate only events that the current representational model expects. When we choose change, we accommodate. Identity is sacrificed, and we are informed . . . Learning is not just the linear accretion of data. It also requires an accommodation of fundamental changes to the structure of the mind itself" (Tucker, 2007, p. 135).

55 "learning within the sensory and cognitive domain is often a type of match learning. It takes place only if there is a good enough match of top-down expectations with bottom-up data to risk altering previously stored knowledge within the system, or it can trigger learning of a new representation if a good enough match is not available" (Grossberg, 1999, p. 36).

56 "The new rhetoric may be the only philosophy that praises those who ruminate, hesitate, are reluctant, doubtful, but ultimately able to act prudently" (Mieczyslaw Maneli, as quoted in Crosswhite, 2013, p. 54).

57 "The modern animal learning evidence shows that the primary signal for new learning is often disruptive: the disruptive event signals that current expectations are wrong and that change is required" (Tucker and Luu, 2012, p. 13).

58 "This reciprocity of information and uncertainty causes what we might call the 'information paradox.' Information has meaning only in the context of need and incomplete knowledge . . . In abstract terms, we can see how data become information when they have a relation to a context and complete a pattern" (Tucker, 2007, p. 4).

59 "Interpretations of the world are by their very nature motive-memories, infused with egocentric needs and presumptions. Pretending objectivity without understanding the fundamental subjective basis of the mind is to invite bias to operate freely and fully cloaked in the preconscious domain of motive blindness" (Tucker, 2007, p. 247).

60 "A distributed information system is inherently holistic: Once it has learned a concept, the system cannot learn a new idea without disrupting the existing one . . . New learning may always require sacrificing old assumptions. Information is change. Becoming informed turns out to be an act of self-transformation, and the first step is a kind of self-destruction. Learning, when the information is personally significant, requires abandoning the old self" (Tucker, 2007, p. 20).

61 "Because they lead to the transformation of the old self, the changes required for accommodating new information cannot be accepted without a struggle" (Tucker 2007, p. 134).

62 "the assertion is not a mere assertion at all; it is a *claim* . . . Such claims not only answer questions, but they also provoke questions, because explicit claims are essentially questionable" (Crosswhite, 2013, p. 212).

63 "Once firmly established, a neural network that links a thought to a feeling of correctness is not easily undone. An idea known to be wrong continues to feel correct" (Burton, 2008, p. 98).

64 "Current evidence suggests that there is *no erasing* in the adult brain . . . long term memory of facts, skills, or situations is captured by structural changes in the connections between neurons. There is no process for selectively reversing these changes. That is why it is so hard to alter your behavior patterns or to change the beliefs of others. The only known neural mechanisms for changing behavior involve inhibiting a pathway or bypassing it with a more active alternative" (Feldman, 2006, p. 38).

5

WHAT CAN WE DO
WITH THIS INFORMATION?

Applications to Practice

Now we come to the question "What now?" What can we do with this information in professional practice and in our daily lives? To say again, the conflict resolution field is in its early stages. Its theories and practices have been developed by sensitive and astute students of human social behavior who have used introspection and observation, along with study of related disciplines, to better understand the relational dynamics of communication and conflict. From that work, we have developed approaches that are conducive to improved communication and a greater capacity to resolve differences collaboratively. What we have come up with works some of the time and to some degree. We know that the application of conflict resolution practices, especially with the assistance of a third party, improves the chances that those involved in a conflict will be able to find their way through the thickets to a resolution that is more satisfying than the alternatives. But it would be a mistake to complacently assume that we have arrived at a mature practice of established methods, or that improved conflict skills have been satisfactorily distributed throughout society. As I mentioned earlier, while we can point to many successes and accomplishments in reducing destructive or unproductive responses to differences, we see also failures, unsatisfactory outcomes, and insufficient reach into some of the more vexing arenas of disagreement in the world. Clearly, there is more to be done to reduce negative outcomes of inevitable conflict and to help ourselves access the information latent in conflict to improve relationships and make good decisions.

It is likely that successful intervention strategies that conflict professionals, or any of us in our daily lives, currently use address, by definition if they are successful, the underlying neural experience of the parties, in one way or another. Otherwise, they wouldn't be successful. For example, our efforts to model and facilitate active listening, to create safe contexts, to encourage perspective taking, to implement joint fact-finding processes, to support the consideration of alternative narratives, all target, even if unintentionally, the neural basis of cognition. That said, will attention to the underlying neural dynamics of human behavior lead to shifts in practice interventions that might produce better results? Will understanding the neural roots of consciousness and behavior enable us to facilitate better communication and more collaborative relationships in our personal lives and with clients who find themselves at odds? These questions are the focus of this chapter.

When we speak of conflict resolution work or mediation, we are necessarily referring to a wide range of types of conflict and of conflict settings involving anywhere from two people to a large group, multiple groups, or to ethnic or national entities. There are practice specifics that apply distinctively to the various contexts and issues. Process design for a family dispute will be very different than that for a multi-party public dispute or an inter-ethnic or international dispute. Constraints we face in working with a workplace dispute will differ from those we might face in a divorce case. Working with youth in schools will be significantly different than working with adults in a commercial dispute. In considering the role of neural function, we can make generalized observations about how people behave in conflict and about conflict resolution practices, and those observations will apply widely. But looking at each conflict circumstance will reveal specific opportunities, limitations, and adjustments based on the particular characteristics of those settings.

In seeking ways to improve practice based on a neural understanding of human behavior, we will face limitations imposed by the circumstances of the conflict and the resolution setting, limitations of time and other resources, limitations inherent in the structures of the organizations and systems within which we work, limitations imposed by party expectations for the process and their willingness to understand conflict and their own behaviors, and limitations of our own abilities. There is no final solution to the conflict resolution problem. We are not like brain surgeons. We have no meticulous tools. We don't have direct access to the brain that remains a kind of black box into which we can't see.

The dynamics of consciousness and cognition are complex and subtle beyond complete understanding, at least at present. At best, the neural perspective will contribute to our understanding of conflict and to some measure of practice improvement. We are left still with the artistic work of engaging with other human beings with imprecision and humility in the face of our limitations. People bring their disputes to a conflict resolution setting within the context of their complex lives and their extended biographies. On the one hand, we work with them as whole human beings because they bring all of whom they are to the conflict resolution process. Yet, on the other hand, we have access to and can deal with only parts of the complex set of stories they carry within them.

It is in this sense that conflict workers are sometimes faced with the question of the distinction or apparent occasional overlap between therapy and conflict resolution. We know that the objectives and methods of the two types of processes are different. But in both cases, human beings with all their subtle complexities of history, temperament, and capacity are involved.

One aspect of therapeutic processes involves making implicit memories conscious so that their effects can be understood and modified. In conflict resolution, the contents of implicit memory can be quite active in the conflict relationship, but our ability and the parties' willingness to access and consider those memories may be limited. For example, people with a history of physical or emotional abuse are often highly attentive to facial expressions, looking for small changes in eye gaze or facial movements that might suggest potential danger. This can lead to misperceptions and misunderstandings and cause relationship stress. Generally, there is a wide divergence of facial expression recognition capacity among people of different psychological tendencies. Those who are anxious and sensitive to rejection place greater focus on negative expressions; those who are avoidantly attached are less attentive to facial expressions; those with attention deficit disorder have difficulty reading angry and sad expressions; those with depression are better at detecting sad faces (Cozolino, 2014). As third parties, we may not be able to identify and account for these variations even as they may affect the resolution process. We temper our expectations and recognize the limitations of practice while we work at various points along a continuum from settlement to transformation.

In the sections below, I look at some common elements of a mediation or conflict-resolving process from the neural embodiment perspective to consider how our intervention strategies and tactics might more intentionally take into account the neural experience of the parties. I offer the discussion not at all as definitively prescriptive but to encourage thinking about how we currently work and how our work might be adjusted to be more effective based on a neural understanding. Most of what I discuss will not present a dramatic departure from current practice but rather will suggest a change of emphasis, timing, structure, duration, or focus, or will offer explanatory support and validation for current practice approaches. I have arranged the list of topics in four categories. The first category looks at how the neural perspective sheds light on a number of theoretical issues (neutrality, mediator influence, impasse, issues, positions and interests, recovery from betrayal or injury, settlement, educating parties and the public, and reflective practice). The second addresses implications for some of the phases of a conflict resolution process (first contact with the parties, first phase of a joint session, party story-telling, joint reality construction, options generation, agreement-building, between sessions and post-mediation). The third deals with some practice issues (location and setting, trust-building, active listening, activations and reactivity, emotions, expectancies management, priming, values conflicts, and somatic interventions). Finally, the chapter discusses five process design issues (caucusing, online mediation, site visits, an educational phase, and linking progress at the negotiation table with represented constituencies).

Theoretical Issues

Neutrality

Over the years, there has been much debate and discussion in the conflict resolution field about the term "neutral" and the concept of neutrality as they apply to the role of a third party, with some arguing for the usefulness of the term and others claiming that neutrality is a false and misleading premise.[1] As is the case with many debates, there is sense on both sides of the discussion and the perspectives are not mutually exclusive. There is a sense in which we, as third parties, can be neutral in the way the term is often intended. Our goal is to not favor either side but to work on behalf of all involved. By another understanding of the term, we will not and cannot be neutral. As a noun, the word is a useful term of trade to refer to one outside a conflict and without a stake in the outcome who is engaged to assist those who have a stake in the outcome in their attempt to resolve the conflict collaboratively. Used in this way, the term does not describe a psychological state but, rather, designates a role.

As a neutral, we also are subject to the constant and unavoidable experience of trying to figure out the meaning of the external reality to which we are exposed. We are not immune to the meaning-making function of our neural embodiment. We must assign meaning to incoming stimuli as we listen to parties relate their accounts of reality, and the meaning we make will be determined by the specifics of our lived experience. Our own neural circuits will be activated by the incoming information of party appearance, behavior, words, and relational dynamics. The parties will make their impressions on us. We will, unavoidably, make judgments, have opinions, make assumptions, and be susceptible to our own biases and stereotyping as our perception of the parties activates aspects of our past experience and as we try to make sense of what we perceive. We embody our own set of value systems and preferences. We have our own identity that will engage with and respond to party behavior in our own idiosyncratic ways. For these reasons, we cannot *be neutral*, but we can act *as a neutral*. We are not an empty vessel or a blank slate, but we can manage our internal experience in order to be effectively neutral.

We confront our non-neutral neural experience when, for example, we become susceptible to the apparently convincing nature of a party's recounting of events when conducting interviews for a workplace or public deliberation conflict assessment. Much as we work to be impartial, we may experience the convincing impressions made by the stories we hear from our first informant and then experience internal dissonance as we hear contradictory or very different stories from successive interviewees to whom we are more or equally sympathetic. Less consciously, the implicit biases we embody may impinge on our perceptions of the parties, as will the other perceptual biases that plague human relational experience.

The practice of becoming an effective neutral has not so much to do with not having "non-neutral" responses to our experience of the parties and their stories but with recognizing our responses and not acting on their basis. We can exercise our ability to delay our response to the incoming stimuli of party behavior. With practice, we get better at not "believing" the stories we hear from parties or the stories we can tend to tell ourselves about the parties. We can create a type of understanding that allows for the coexistence of mutually contradictory accounts, what might be called a "maybe capacity," a looser attachment to hypothesis formation that allows us to be receptive to, and to convey our openness to, each party without fully subscribing to their account or to our own internal responses to their account. We recognize that each party has his or her understanding of reality, an edifice of identity constructed over time in the neural matrices of their body. We make it a practice to shift away from right and wrong framings to the equal legitimacy of party experience, even when their stories are contradictory, an approach that is sometimes termed "multi-partial." We recognize that we have responses to our perceptual experience of the parties and their stories and we mindfully cultivate a distance or separation from those responses, in effect assigning a different meaning understanding to our responses. We learn to appreciate our own desire to know and be certain, and to moderate that natural tendency with regular reminders to maintain the humility of uncertainty.

This is one of the paradoxes of third-party work. On the one hand, we evaluate and interpret as we seek to understand the conflict. On the other hand, we resist that tendency and do our best to refrain from forming opinions or drawing conclusions about the parties and their stories, or from taking too seriously any opinions or impressions that are activated within us. We cultivate an even-handed stance in relation to our own experience as well as to our experience of the parties. Understanding and accepting our own neurally based response experience helps us manage our engagement with and reactions to the parties and helps us maintain a "neutral" stance, effective if not actual.

Case Example: Every mediator has had the experience of feeling noticeably more favorable to one party than to the other or others. This is hopefully only noticeable to us and not to the parties. It's likely, in fact, that in every case our resonance with the parties will vary among them. Usually, the variance will be minor and unobtrusive.

But consider a case in which one of the parties has a particularly grating personality, perhaps narcissistically arrogant, apparently unwilling to take much responsibility for his (in this case, a male) participation in the relationship. Each time the other party expresses a perspective or a desire or interest, our protagonist seems to dismiss or ignore the content and carries off onto another self-centered tangent. Do what we will, we seem unable to find a way to help our increasingly frustrating party engage constructively.

We try helpful questioning and attentive inquiry. We validate and affirm. We attempt some educational interventions. We demonstrate modeling and mirroring. We engage in some role-playing. We pull out some directive tools. Worse still, the party reminds us a bit of our difficult father or another challenging personality from our past. How do we maintain our multi-partiality when our sympathies are not at all evenly distributed? We might begin to notice erosive claims on our confidence generated by our lack of success that begin to stimulate old narratives of incompetence.

Reminding ourselves of the neural reality of our experience can help us make sense of the feelings that arise. Acknowledging our biases can allow us to "get some distance" from our experience activated at the neural level, making it easier to maintain our equilibrium and continue supporting both parties and a fair process. Denying our biases risks having them influence our behavior.

Mediator Influence

However we understand the concept of mediator neutrality, there is no doubt that we will influence the parties in many ways and unavoidably, whether we define ourself as a facilitative or a directive mediator. First of all, what purpose would there be to mediation if we had no influence? And second, it is impossible to be in any relationship without mutual influence. Our goal is to have a positive influence in the parties' problem-solving and also, when necessary, an influence that helps the parties come to the collaborative negotiation table in the first place. Even the most facilitative, least directive mediator will influence the parties. Our skill lies in part in understanding and taking responsibility for our influence.

In neural terms, parties will be more or less open to our influence and their willingness will vary according to many factors, one of which is our behavior. One of the attributes of a good mediator is an ability to sense (perceive) what parties need in order to participate at any particular point in the process or in order to participate in the first place. The accuracy of our perceptions will vary, but when we are right, we will influence their state of being, their understanding of the process and their relationship to the process, their willingness to engage in the process and with the other party or parties, and their understanding of the conflict. With the right words and the right tone, we influence their internal experience, their neural activity. We can be a bit like a great salesperson or like a conman (or conwoman) as we influence party decision-making, our focus not so much about the settlement outcome but on how the parties negotiate and on keeping them in the process. Without the third party, the parties have been unsuccessful. They are at an impasse or have been unable to communicate effectively. The difference we make must change the parties at some level.

The obvious tool of mediator influence, wherever we may fall on the directive/facilitative continuum, is the language we use to talk about the issues involved.

As I discussed earlier, words are nonsense syllables to which meaning has been assigned. Meaning is not absolute, universal, or inherent in the words we use or the parts of the world to which our words point. Meaning is personal, idiosyncratic, variable, and imposed, though, fortunately, it is most often sufficiently common within a language group to allow for communication and understanding. Engaging with parties, there will be times when we need to pay particular attention to the words we use with them about the issues and possible agreements in order to be sure that we are speaking in terms that carry the parties' meanings. In a workplace case, what nuances of meaning do the parties associate with words like "boss," "supervising," "time off," or even apparently benign terms like "meetings" or "planning"? In a divorce case, how are the parties using such terms as "parenting" or "bedtime" or "diet"? Not only do we work to confirm commonality or differences among the parties in the meaning they assign to the terms they are using, but we must also be careful that our use of terms carries meanings that match, as closely as possible, the meanings they associate with the terms.

If our mediation style is to offer suggestions or propose possible solutions, we must ask ourselves whether the framing of the suggestion imposes or presupposes a picture that is at odds with the parties' perspectives or blends well with their views. And will the suggestion be equally satisfactory (or unsatisfactory) to both parties or dovetail more closely with the neural constructs of one party's worldview than the other's, creating a perception of bias in favor of one of the parties?

Impasse

The occurrence of impasse is to be expected when working through a conflict resolution process since a condition of impasse is, in one way of thinking about it, what brought the parties to the table in the first place. The essential question in a collaborative conflict resolution process is whether the parties can move past the impasse state that will otherwise either endure or require resolution in a rights- or power-based setting.

During a resolution process, there can be many causes of impasse and a variety of strategies for attempting to overcome an impasse. If an impasse is reached, there is, to say the obvious, something causing the impasse, something blocking the way forward on the road to resolution. Impasse needn't be cause for despair but rather for renewed commitment to the process of inquiry, exploration, and discovery. What is the block?

For our purposes here, it is interesting to consider impasse in neural terms. Do the parties have different meaning associations with the issues? In other words, are they talking about two different things, holding two different neural meaning-pictures that don't coincide, while thinking that they are talking about the same thing over which they believe they are in disagreement? Have they not been successful in either understanding the other's worldview or in being understood? Is their ability to creatively problem-solve and consider options hampered by experience of threat, lack of safety, or concerns about the implications of possible outcomes? Have they not been able to adequately articulate their needs, either because of reluctance or insufficient conscious awareness, and are they therefore not able to consider options for next steps? Are proposed or possible solutions at odds with some fundamental aspect of their worldview that prevents them from being able to accept a proposed new reality? Each of these possible barriers has obvious neural structure bases. We can better understand the nature of impasse within the conceptual framework of neurally encoded reality and identity structures. Thinking in these terms can offer the conflict resolution practitioner some insights into what interventions might budge the impasse.

It's interesting to consider the term "break" that we use to describe what we attempt to do with an impasse. There is a rigidity to an impasse. The parties are locked in unyielding attachments to their points of view, as if two irresistible forces meet two immovable objects. We also talk about being stuck in an impasse, as if the gears are frozen, are not meshing. The parties are at loggerheads, at a stand off. In neural terms, the structures of meaning within each individual are not able to accommodate each other. They don't fit together and there is an unwillingness by one or both parties to make the shifts in meaning structure necessary for a workable fit. In adversarial settings, mutual opposition continues until one side prevails over the other. In collaborative, interest-based resolution processes, we try to help parties through the impasse by somehow finding ways to get their meaning structures to fit sufficiently well together that they can forge a joint reality, an agreement. Again, there are many reasons for lack of fit, perhaps different definitions of terms, misunderstandings, different understandings, or incompatible or apparently incompatible needs, states in which a proposed solution doesn't correspond equally well to the meaning matrices of both parties. Perhaps we would do well to abandon the breaking metaphor and think more in terms of helping the parties find ways to shift neural structures, soften attachments to adopted perceptions, or seek new experience that will expand understanding sufficiently to allow new perspectives to be adopted.

Working as a third party, we can feel confounded and frustrated by an impasse state and not know where to look for a way to loosen the frozen process. The parties are stuck and we can feel stuck as well. What to do? Thinking about impasse in neural terms can help us understand a possible basis for the impasse facing us and to feel less intimidated by its occurrence. Rather than be daunted by impasse, we can honor it and see it not as an impediment but rather as an indicator that calls for more understanding. With this approach, we don't focus on the impasse. Rather we allow continued learning to soften the impasse until it dissolves.

Issues

One of the first and obvious steps in a problem-solving, agreement-building process is to identify the issues at stake. What are the problems the parties are trying to resolve? Identifying issues can seem misleadingly simple. Ask the parties what they believe the issues are, write them down, and move forward to address them, one by one, identifying interests and other relevant factors along the way. However, though parties may agree that a particular issue is involved and may all use the same terms to refer to the issue, the meaning or significance of that issue may vary among the parties. As third parties, we can make the mistake of thinking that the parties are talking about the same thing, when, in fact, they are experiencing two different meaning-stories to which the same words are applied. If we move on too quickly from the identification of issues without devoting sufficient time to understanding the meaning of each issue for each party, we risk creating confusion and may inadvertently produce more positional bargaining. Parents and their teenage daughter in conflict about what time she will come home from a Friday night party may think they are arguing about the same issue, but it may represent for the parents, in their neural matrices of meaning, an entirely different subject than it does for their daughter. For the parents, meaning matrices of authority, parental responsibility, control, safety of their daughter, perceptions of risk, and relief from worry are perhaps activated. For their daughter meaning matrices of trust, independence, reputation with her peers, and the evolution of relationship in moving towards adulthood may be involved. Some of these elements can be framed as interests, for example, the parents have an interest in perceiving themselves and being perceived as responsible parents, have an interest in their daughter's safety, and have an interest in being relieved of worry, regardless of and more important than the positional question of what time she will come home. But do the parents have an interest in control or does the issue involve meaning associations having to do with control that are triggered by the issue? Is the evolution of relationship and movement towards adulthood an interest of the daughter or a meaning association? As another example, in the conflict between the Israeli government and the Palestinian Authority over West Bank settlements, aside from the forcefully stated positions and the underlying interests having to do with security, autonomy, and statehood, the issue has deep meaning significance related to history and the land that is distinct for each party.

Issues, positions, interests, and meaning associations are intimately interwoven. Though it can seem that issues, once articulated, are the most obviously and easily defined and clear of the four, their meaning may be more obscure or opaque than we recognize. And we can mistakenly assume that uncovering the parties' interests will reveal what the issues mean to the parties. But meaning can be a layer deeper than interests. In such cases, we may wander into confusing territory by moving too quickly from issues to interests, goals, and solutions without first better understanding what it is that the parties are talking about in the first place when they identify an issue. What does the issue mean in their world?

Case Example: Jane and Tom came to mediation as an already divorced couple several years after their divorce and a year after Tom had remarried.
Among the issues they wanted to address were the frequency and content
of texts sent by Tom's new wife Mary to Jane and Tom's children when they
were with Jane. Jane reported that over the year of Mary's new presence as
step-mom to the children, Mary had been texting the children "incessantly"
(in Jane's terms) when they were staying with Jane, and further that some of
the content of the texts were critical and not respectful of Jane. Both Jane and
Mary had clear positions. Jane: "Keep the texts restricted to the hours of six
to eight p.m. and with no mention of Jane in any way." Mary: "What's the
big deal. I should be able to communicate with the children when I want,
and besides, it's not that often and I never talk about Jane." It is quite standard mediation practice in such a case to ask the parties what is important to
them and what they would like any proposed solution to address (in other
words, their interests). In this case, Jane said, "I don't want my time with the
kids invaded by Mary. In other words, I want them to have space to be with
me, without her being so present. And I also don't want Mary to undermine
my role, and I don't want the kids to have to deal with the stress of hearing
less than supportive messages about me." Mary said, "I want to be able to
continue to build my relationship with the kids. They're most of the time
with Jane and only with Tom and me every other weekend, so I want to be
able to maintain our relationship during that time. And I don't want Jane to
be dictating or controlling my relationship with the kids." And then there
was Tom. He said, "I want there to be peace between Mary and Jane. And
I don't want to be in the middle of this. I don't want to be on one side or
the other. I lose either way. I just want something that they're both happy
with. Also, I don't want the kids to feel that they have to choose mom over
step-mom or have to experience or deal with stress between Jane and Mary."
Proceeding to considering options that might satisfy the expressed interests,
we kept coming up against impasse. Nothing seemed to work. From the
frustration of impasse, the conversation fortuitously moved to a deeper level.
Mary was worried that Tom still loved Jane and didn't know what that meant
for their own relationship. She also felt insecure in her relationship with the
children and competitive with Jane as the mother figure. Jane was worried
that Mary would become too important a figure in her children's lives and
that her chatty texting style would take the children away from her in some
way. She also was angry with Tom for having moved 60 miles away, even
though it was for a job, the income of which benefited both of them, and
that left her with more of the parenting responsibility taking care of the children. Tom felt guilty for having left the marriage, felt not fully resolved in his
relationship with and feelings towards Jane and struggled with wanting her

(continued)

> *(continued)*
>
> approval. These meaning associations were deeper and distinct from inter-
> ests to be satisfied by any given solution and revealed that they weren't, in
> fact, talking about the same factual issue. I witnessed the liberating results of
> their honesty (with themselves and with each other) as they relatively quickly
> formulated a plan that, in retrospect, came so easily once they'd figured out
> what they were really talking about. Not only had they uncovered what the
> issue meant for each of them but, as it turned out, the different meaning
> associations became the issue. Without bringing the meaning associations
> into the room, it would have been difficult, if not impossible, to find a satis-
> factory solution to the presenting problem.

Positions and Interests

The embodied nature of cognition sheds light on what is actually involved in the
bedrock negotiation terms-of-trade "positions" and "interests" and how people
engage with and respond to these two cognitive experiences. We tend, by nature,
to be a positional species. If this weren't so, we would not witness the prevalent
phenomenon of positional responses to conflict and we would not have to work
so hard to help negotiating parties move from their focus on positions to attention to their interests. If we were an interest-based species by nature, we'd see less
unresolved, destructive, or violent conflict.

There are reasons for our positional nature rooted in, among other things,
the physiological demands of navigating the environment in order to survive.
As we are exposed to the perceptual stimuli of our environment, we must make
decisions moment to moment, and to make those decisions, we must determine
what we believe to be true and act on that basis. Our preference for positions is
a reflection of our reality assessment, reality construction, and identity formation
needs. A position is a solution that matches and supports the party's assessment of
reality. Positions answer questions posed by perceptual experience, with answers
that we believe will satisfy our actual or perceived survival needs, whether those
needs be physical, psychological, or social.

As I've discussed, there is comfort in knowing, in being certain, and in feeling in control. Positions provide the illusion of knowing, certainty, and control.
Further, positions satisfy our problem-solving, pattern-seeking nature. They provide answers to the questions a conflict presents. Finally, positions are a kind
of bulwark to our identity constructs. Interest-based negotiating can appear to
weaken or challenge our identity as it calls into question what we believe we
know and what we believe should happen. However, positional bargaining
appears to affirm, by the assertion of the position, our beliefs about what is right,
true, good, and real. There is security in having a position. A position answers a
question with a certainty. What should happen? This is how it shall be!

Faced with an issue, our first response tends to be to adopt a position, to propose or assert a solution, just as we tend immediately, and often vociferously, to take sides, agree or disagree, or voice an opinion about any subject that is raised, and just as we do our best to explain any new perceptual stimuli within the borders of our present understanding of the world. Positions are the parties' "I know."

The shift from positions to interests is one from asserted commitment to a particular outcome, to a condition of outcome uncertainty, and therefore from comfort to discomfort. We feel more vulnerable when asked to put aside our positions and to focus on our interests. With the assertion of a position, the outcome is named. With a focus on interests, the outcome is unknown. A shift from positions to interests requires a level of trust and a willingness to not know, to enter into a problem-solving, learning mode. With a position, we feel safer behind the protection of its strong assertion. The over-confidence of a position allows us to feel right and righteous. In contrast, letting go of our positional stance and moving to interest-based problem-solving confronts us with the possibility that we may have been wrong in our assessment of the situation or that our original idea of what should happen will not be validated.

As I suggested earlier, in the context of conflict or in conditions of perceived or actual threat, our visceral tendency is to cling more tenaciously to our positions, to our beliefs about what is real, right, true, and good, to our egocentric worldview, and to whatever control we can muster. With an outcome in accordance with our position, neural networks of belief and knowing don't have to be restructured, rather they are confirmed. When confronted with a positional stance by the other, a party will tend to feel attacked and threatened. The assertion of a position feels secure to the holder of the position and threatening to the recipient faced with the positional demand. Shifting to interest-based dialogue can feel more uncomfortable to the individual expressing his or her interest and less threatening to the recipient.

Because we hold to positions for these neurally based reasons, as practitioners, we should not be cavalier in our request that parties shift from their positions to focus on revealing their interests. They may not be ready to abandon the protection of a firmly stated position. It may be necessary first to attend to questions of safety, security, and trust before asking parties to put aside their positions. Confidence-building or trust-building measures can be a first step prior to relinquishing anchoring positions. Even as parties may reveal interests while engaging in their storytelling about the issues involved, they may need to maintain the protective security of positional framing for longer than we, as mediators, might expect, assume, or desire.

Helping parties move from positions to interests, the mediator might consider what a party might need in order to feel sufficiently comfortable to put aside his or her positional stance. Might there be another framing that can provide the security of a strongly held position? Even when parties realize, on a rational level, that it is in their interest to set aside their positions, at a visceral level, doing so may feel to them too vulnerable or may seem to them to reduce their bargaining power. Sometimes an interest can be expressed as a strongly held position in order to maintain a party's sense of strength, self-respect, and control. For example, in a national border dispute negotiation, the position, "We will control this body of water!" might be replaced with the strongly stated interest, "We will be guaranteed a sufficient and uninterrupted water supply and guarantees of passage in any settlement agreement!" However the transition from positions to interests is accomplished, sensitivity to the neural basis for the experiential quality of positional and interest-based stances will help us better understand party behavior and provide a framework for helping them navigate the transition.

Recovery from Betrayal or Injury

It is often the case that there has been betrayal and/or some level of injury in a conflict, whether the injury be economic, physical, psychological, or social. In these cases, to resolve the conflict, the consequences of betrayal and injury must often be addressed, one way or another. The results of betrayal are etched in the physical reality of neural embodiment. As I discussed earlier, betrayal "shatters" neural structures of meaning, structures of meaning about the external world, the other, and also of the self. What we thought we understood of the world is brought into question or is destroyed, and therefore, to some degree, the understanding of the self is brought into question and must be reconstructed. The mind copes in one way or another by establishing new neural structures, but may also remain somewhat in a condition of chaos of unknowing, seeking to make meaning of what has happened and to create a structure of meaning for the new world into which the betrayal has thrown us. Recovery requires the creation of new structures of meaning that answer questions, that reconstruct the world and the self within the new context.

Though mediation or conflict resolution processes are not therapy, they may be part of a therapeutic process in which parties are able to re-define or re-establish relationship after an episode of betrayal. In a divorce case, in which one party has had an affair that has contributed to the break-up of the marriage, the party betrayed struggles with trying to understand who their partner is. The betrayal has confuted what they had previously understood, has changed their internal picture of the person they thought they had known. The new information of the betrayal has disrupted or destroyed previous networks of knowing and has to be incorporated into their new understanding of the world. The betrayal can also call into question their confidence in the reliability of their perceptions. This can be very unsettling.

In a recovery process, apology often plays a part. What is apology, actually? What is happening in an apology exchange? For one thing, an apology is, in part, a validation of the other's reality, a confirmation of the reality, an acknowledgement that something did indeed happen that warrants the apology. "You are not crazy.

I did do something that hurt you." An apology is also an acknowledgement and confirmation of common values and standards. The apology creates a shared reality of knowing and meaning. In these ways, apologies provide a kind of soothing and can be part of the healing process. The internal injury, at the neural level, is healed in the sense that rent neural connections can be re-established or new and stable neural connections can be established.

Settlement

Questions about to what degree and in what ways a mediator engages with the goal of reaching a settlement and with possible settlement options have always been the subject of much discussion within the conflict resolution community. Does the mediator make suggestions for possible settlement agreements, and if so, in what way? Does the mediator attempt to push the parties towards a particular settlement agreement or towards settlement of any sort? How attached is the mediator to achieving settlement? Do we measure success only in terms of achieving a settlement? Is the goal of the process settlement of the issues, resolution of the conflict, or transformation of the individuals and their relationship, however these terms are defined? Short of making specific settlement suggestions or overtly directing the parties, what influence does the mediator have on the direction and perceived goals of agreement seeking, and how? How conscious is the neutral about his or her assumptions concerning settlement and how explicitly might those assumptions be addressed with the parties?

Clearly, parties are looking for solutions to their conflict. They very often enter into a conflict resolution process with strongly held ideas about what a satisfactory settlement must include and begin their negotiation maneuvering to achieve those settlement goals. Very often, they attempt to convince the mediator of the rightness of their justifications. Even parties willing to shift away from positional bargaining will critically evaluate possible settlement offers and options. One way or another, the third party will be pulled into the settlement tussle. Mediators themselves are not immune to the appeal of reaching settlement agreements. There is an undeniable satisfaction in closing the loop. Resolution produces relief in the third party as well as in the primary parties, and for the third party, almost independent of the content of the resolution.

It is not uncommon that a party will look to the mediator for some assurance that a set of settlement agreements is reasonable or fair, seeking validation of the new filaments of neural meaning matrices being formed. This presents the mediator with the challenge of helping the party know whether or not to strengthen those meaning matrices while not inserting his or her own beliefs, biases, and perceptions. One of the ways we do this is with questions that help the party tie the proposed settlement agreements to more established elements in the party's world about which the party feels more certain: interests, beneficial consequences, or perhaps to some independent facts, measures, or standards.

One of the commonly stated third-party goals regarding settlement is that agreements be durable. To be durable, the parties must be sufficiently satisfied with the outcome of negotiations to continue to be satisfied post-negotiation. One way of testing settlement satisfaction and agreement durability is by asking the parties how the new post-resolution reality fits into the larger contextual frameworks of their lives. Are there places where the fit isn't quite seamless, where the agreement grates with other elements of their world or self experience? Is there anything else that needs to be discussed in order to improve the fit? Can we test for "buyer's remorse" before it has a chance to occur? We may be somewhat reticent to ask questions that reality-test a settlement agreement once achieved, fearing that to do so might threaten the stability or continued acceptance of the agreement so recently and arduously reached. But we know that our third-party responsibility is to do what we can to insure that agreements will be implemented. Asking parties in an interpersonal conflict to check how newly articulated agreements fit with the rest of their world is analogous to having parties in a public policy negotiation check back with their constituencies and/or superiors for ratification to confirm that there are no problematic implications of the agreements within the real world context within which the agreements will be implemented.

The final step of accepting an agreement once formulated can be particularly sensitive as the parties consider the implications, internal and external, of the shift in their world that the agreement represents. This is the time when third parties sometimes see a reactive stepping back or away from an agreement that seemed in the bag, so to speak. One or another of the parties may suddenly see the agreement in a different light. Its meaning changes. Progress achieved in one session is challenged or brought into question at the beginning of the next session. The experience can be of two steps forward and one step back or sometimes one step forward and two steps back as the parties struggle to make of the negotiation elements meaning that works. Seeing the phenomenon in neural terms can help the third party make sense of and be patient with this pattern.

Case Example: One of my cases involved a very complex business restructuring that involved a host of issues including buying back shares from some of the early investors in order to create space for bringing in new capital, changing the management structure and individual roles for the two founding partners, and separating the wholesale and retail portions of the business. Within the narrative, there were power struggles for control, differing fiscal analyses and interpretation of financial data, and sharp differences of opinion about strategic direction and the decisions needed. More than any other case I've been involved in, agreements that were reached repeatedly blew up, one meeting's progress in tatters at the next meeting, phone calls late in the evening to pull out of agreements apparently reached that afternoon, right up to the end when one of the parties refused to sign what we thought was the final document. Each collapse required renegotiation. It seemed that every time we thought we were actually done, with an agreement in place, something else would come up that threatened to torpedo the whole settlement. The parties were desperate to avoid what they saw as the likely alternative to a negotiated agreement, litigation with investors and between themselves that would threaten the life of the business and their financial well-being. Yet each of them seemed unable to pull back from the brink. The closer we got to the grail of a final agreement, the higher were the stakes and the more potentially disastrous each change of mind seemed. One explanation for the repeated withdrawal from agreements is that the proposed settlement at each stage did not fit, in one way or another, into the more global reality construct of one or the other of the parties. Realizing this helped moderate my experience of frustration with their apparent inconsistency and unreliability. Though figuring out what prompted each new retreat was often difficult, thinking in neural terms helped me formulate questions that got at how they experienced the situation and where the friction points were. Contingent agreements were attached. Language was refined. Holes were plugged. The ship survived the storms and they were able to continue forth with the wind of a successful settlement agreement in their sails.

The moments after a set of agreements has been accepted and documents signed are interesting and significant. They often call for a response from the mediator that supports the parties' experience at this final point in the process. Whatever the mediator may say and do, if well done, will address the experience of the parties in those moments when a solution has been found and the parties are faced with the end of the conflict and, hopefully, are ready to go on with the rest of their lives. Sometimes there is relief and a kind of lightness in the accomplishment. Perhaps the parties will experience some remorse for what happened during the conflict. Parties may feel a degree of disorientation in the face of the new reality they have agreed to. In other instances, the negotiations will have been particularly difficult and the settlement not entirely happy. In some cases, ongoing relationships will continue after the settlement has been reached. In others, the parties will not see each other again. Whatever the quality of the settlement experience, it will present a transitional moment that must be navigated. Handshakes, hugs, affirming words, expressions of respect, appreciation, congratulations, or acknowledgement can be part of completing the process and helping the parties make the transition to their new reality.

Educating the Parties and the Public

Perhaps the area of greatest opportunity, but also perhaps the greatest challenge, for the conflict resolution practitioner is in helping the general public better understand how people tend to function in conflict so that they are better able to achieve the resolution of differences that they come to us for help with?

As things stand now, for the most part, conflict resolution interventions are fit into the nooks and crannies of our social structures, whether within the legal system, public policy decision-making processes, workplace protocols, or the arrangements of our private lives. To a large extent, alternative conflict resolution practices have been superimposed upon previously established methods and institutions for resolving disputes. To the degree that collaborative conflict resolution approaches have altered the design and formats of social engagement, they have been more supplementary than revolutionary. We can see this in the introduction of mediation in workplace and employment dispute management, in the courthouse, in our attempts to incorporate collaborative decision-making approaches in the public policy realm, or in peace-making interventions in the contexts of international or interethnic conflicts. Our culture hasn't fully taken on and prioritized collaborative conflict resolution as a core principle animating the methodologies of our social structures. Rather, it might be said that we are at a stage of dealing with symptoms more than getting at the root of the problem with a more comprehensive social change effort.

To the degree this is the case, we will be limited in our ability as a field to effect dramatic change in how people deal with differences. We will continue to find ourselves working with specific disputes but not more broadly altering how people understand and engage in the processes of communication, perception, and relationship in the face of differences.

It is typical to hear from those working in the conflict field how life changing their own conflict resolution learning process has been for them. Conflict will always be uncomfortable given that conflict presents threats to our self-identity. But there is also no doubt that we can become more secure in the face of conflict, that we can become more conflict-friendly and conflict-competent, as we sometimes put it. This has certainly been true in my own life. I was very much more afraid of and confused by conflict before I entered the conflict resolution field, first as a student and then as a practitioner, than I am now. I was conflict-averse and conflict-incompetent. More than I realized, I saw conflict as both a threat and a failure. I was ignorant about the dynamics of conflict and communication. I was unable to step back from conflict in order to manage it with intention. I had few tools, didn't use them very effectively, and was unaware of what I didn't know. I would guess that most practitioners and students of conflict resolution can speak of an experience analogous to mine when my daughter commented on my improved parenting. We discover through the study of conflict that we can learn how to accept, understand, and better deal with the differences and disagreements that are an unavoidable and inherent part of our relational lives. The benefits of conflict study that practitioners experience are not yet widely distributed throughout society, in spite of the many public trainings offered and school-based programs implemented.

I would say that the conflict resolution field has a responsibility beyond providing access to good-practice professional conflict resolution services, a responsibility to educate, to disseminate to the general public the knowledge and understandings we develop and use in our own education. Fisher et al's (2011) ground-breaking book *Getting to Yes* is a good example of delivering conflict resolution understandings across the divide between the professional and academic worlds and the general public. We have more to do in this regard. Imagine how public discourse and private relationships would change if a larger percentage of the population understood what we have come to learn in our work with conflict and communication. We'll never succeed in putting ourselves out of work but we may make our work easier by expanding the level of self-understanding we can cultivate in society.

It is difficult to change a culture's structures, whether they be economic, political, legal, or educational. There is an inertia to them. And they exist within larger webs of social organization so that change in one area requires change in others. That said, over the past 40 to 50 years, the conflict resolution field has definitely contributed to some changes in how people handle differences and resolve disputes, as we see in the public policy sector, in the family area, in the workplace, and in our courthouses. That said, I think it is fair to say that we have much more to do. Of course, we are faced with a not insignificant challenge in trying to gather, prioritize, and distill the body of relevant knowledge and to deliver it to a wider audience at times and in ways that work.

Aside from the opportunity and challenge to more widely disseminate the theoretical understandings and practical tools of conflict management to the wider public, education is an important part of a practitioner's toolbox when working with individual parties. We know that people tend to have a negative view of conflict and feel uncomfortable in the face of conflict. This is so for a number of reasons, including those I have been discussing. But the feeling of discomfort is heightened also by the fact that parties often feel incompetent in the face of conflict. The confusion and fear typically associated with the presence of conflict are amplified when we feel we don't know how to handle conflict. Beyond the other reasons I've talked about, we will be even more likely to respond defensively, to flee, to avoid, or to attack when we don't feel we have the skills to respond in more constructive ways. Incompetence often leads to avoidance and defensiveness. With more understanding comes more mastery. With more mastery comes more confidence. With more confidence comes more mastery. The cycle is positively reinforcing. The acquisition of more knowledge about conflict, its causes, and how better to work with it, can be the catalyst initiating the cycle. One of the goals of therapeutic processes is that the individual achieves more awareness of his or her self-experience and its antecedents, in order then to be more able to understand and manage behavior and achieve change. Similarly, in conflict resolution, greater understanding of the roots of internal conflict responses can support salutary changes in behavior. Being unaware of the neural underpinnings of conflict experience, for example, we can be misled to believe our responses are unavoidable products of external circumstances, a kind of fundamental attribution error. Recognition of the neural underpinnings of our experience can help us step back from and gain some perspective on our responses, allowing us, for example, to reduce attachment to beliefs and certainties that are unhelpful and to make choices conducive to constructive resolution of disagreements. Indeed, to note what is obvious, it's the very usefulness of conflict understanding that is the reason we teach what we do in conflict resolution training programs in the first place. With more understanding of conflict and communication, we're better able to work effectively with parties. The more we are able to share this kind of information with parties in conflict and with the general public, the more easily and likely we'll be able to achieve our goals of helping people be successful in their conflict resolution efforts.

Direct education about theoretical concepts has always been one of the strategic options available to mediators as they seek to help parties resolve a conflict.[2] For example, when I present material on in-group/out-group behavior or the dynamics of personality style differences to groups I work with in organizational settings, the information is most often transformative. The information gives them a new way of understanding their behavior, the sources of the conflicts they've been dealing with, and new ways of thinking about how to prevent or manage those conflicts. For another example, helping a divorcing couple, or a couple trying to work through conflicts in their ongoing relationship, understand how structural realities (e.g. both working full-time with three children under the age of six, and just barely making enough money to pay the bills) or relational patterns (e.g. not talking about contentious issues with respect, trust, and demonstration of care for each other) can be the cause of conflict over specific issues can dramatically alter how they understand and deal with their issues. With a recognition that the source of their conflicts might lie elsewhere than the particular issues they find themselves fighting about, they can then partner in addressing the problems at their root. For another example, awareness of the reactive devaluation phenomenon can help negotiators mitigate or moderate its influence. Knowledge is power. Theory-based information provides support for parties' executive-function behavior management, helping them increase the delay between conflict stimulus and response and modify behavior, even when some of the causes (basic personality style differences, for example) are not always accessible or susceptible to change. With understanding, parties' sense of competence increases, and following, confidence, capacity, and comfort also increase.

How might our mediations change if we were to include a more substantial educational phase? This approach is often a part of multi-party public collaborative negotiation processes in which the parties engage in joint fact-gathering and mutual education on the issues and, sometimes also, on interest-based negotiation theory and practice, prior to actually getting into the nitty-gritty of the negotiation itself. Workplace communication, negotiation, and conflict resolution trainings serve a similar function, attempting to create a culture of understanding and capacity that reduces conflict and improves the handling of conflicts that do arise. Might outcomes of mediations in other settings be achieved more efficiently if we were to add an educational component at the outset, perhaps devoting an entire initial meeting to conflict education including, in distilled form, some of what we provide in practitioner education and training and some of the ideas discussed in this book? It's possible that the cost of a session devoted entirely to this kind of education and information exchange would be more than recouped in the more efficient and productive negotiations that would likely result. Such a change in practice would require the buy-in of the parties who, at least at this point in the evolution of our practice, do not expect to devote time to an educational phase prior to working on their conflict.

Parties with whom we work will most likely not be accustomed to thinking about their experience and behavior in neural terms, but with this conceptual framework, they might be more willing, for example, to engage in the practice of meaning confirmation (active listening) when they understand the neural basis of potential misunderstanding. They may be more able to reduce aggressive communication with an appreciation of the visceral intimacy of the spoken word. They might find it easier to be tolerant of differences when they can place their experience within an understanding of the neural basis of identity. They may be more able to soften their attachment to positional certainty, more easily accept that their perceptions are not necessarily the whole story, and tolerate uncertainty in the problem-solving setting with an understanding of the neural encoding function and the neural stability/plasticity balance. Understanding neural activation might help parties be more compassionate towards each other and themselves, help them see that reactivity is not a symptom of character flaw, and help them be more sensitive in their communication, recognizing how and why triggering happens. The question then becomes how we can present and convey the essential information about neural embodiment in formats that are accessible and that parties can absorb within the limitations of our work with them. Educational materials for the general public will support our work with prospective parties and ways to simplify and condense the information for presentation within the confines of the mediation setting can further the goals of a conflict resolution process.

Reflective Practice

There is a long tradition of thought across a range of practices on the need to be a reflective practitioner and how to achieve reflective practice.[3] The imperative to be a reflective practitioner almost goes without saying, whether one is learning to play an instrument or to be a neurosurgeon. How can we engage well and improve in any kind of practice without being reflective? This is as true of work with physical objects and handcraft as it is of work with people, but especially critical in work with people since the cost of mistakes will have significant impact on others. The importance of reflective practice is commensurate with the level of responsibility we have to those we work with.

Working with others in conflict, we are dealing with issues of understanding, perception, and knowledge, and we are involved in relational experience. When we become involved as a third party, we are not separate from the conflict relationship though we are not one of the parties to the conflict. We join in the conflict in our role. As earlier discussed, we are not entirely an independent, objective, or unaffected entity. We will categorize, stereotype, project, make attributions and assumptions, favor and prefer, mishear and misunderstand, apply our own story templates to the parties' situations, and so on. Donning the hat of the neutral or multi-partial third party does not free us from the characteristics of our own neural embodiment. Reflective practice is the means by which we can moderate and manage the vagaries of our own cognitive experience.

As I've been emphasizing, when we meet new parties, our perceptual experience of them will activate meaning matrices from our past experience. When we hear their stories, associations from our own past will be activated. The danger present in un-reflective practice is that we will not recognize the distinction between who they are and who they are for us, and the difference between what their stories mean to them and what their stories mean to us. Reflective practice allows us to acknowledge the difference and to be more proficient in paying attention to who they are, what they mean to each other, and what their stories mean to them. We can keep ourselves somewhat "out of the way" so to speak, and be more able to be with the parties in their world.

Transference and countertransference are phenomenon well documented and studied in doctor/patient and therapist/client relationships. Transference and countertransference are not necessarily or always pathological events. They occur in many (most? all?) relationships, to one degree or another. They are neural events analogous to priming and akin to stereotyping and categorizing. Transference is the transfer of a past perceptual/emotional experience that we had with one person (especially a parent) redirected onto another person in the present. Countertransference is the term used when the transference experience is from doctor to patient, therapist to client, or, for our purposes here, from mediator to party. Unexamined and, worse, unrecognized, countertransference will interfere with helpful relationship. Awareness of a countertransference experience will allow the mediator to regulate and manage his or her emotions and perceptual experience.

Given that we are, indeed, neural beings, that our consciousness and cognition are emergent properties of our neural embodiment, recognition of the tendencies and characteristics of neural function will add dimension and depth to our reflective practice. Greater self-understanding makes us better practitioners because it is our "self" that is involved in our practice.[4]

Stages of a Process

First Contact with Parties

Parties are very likely to consider or to enter into a collaborative conflict resolution process with some level and mix of skepticism, confusion, suspicion, distrust, uncertainty, anger, and fear. They may feel insecure or overconfident, or both, insecure about the process and overconfident about the correctness of their positions. They will be concerned about whether they are right or wrong (and consequently, perhaps, good or bad) and whether they will lose in the process (lose control,[5] resources, respect, or face). The process may be a new and unfamiliar experience, and they may wonder what it entails. They will feel uncertain about what will be asked of them. They may not trust the other side, the process, or the third party. In the face of these uncertainties, they will likely want to hold more firmly to their own beliefs about the world and the issues involved in their conflict. They will likely be, as we say colloquially, defensive. They will expect an attack on their position(s), which is to say, an attack on their understanding of the world, and therefore an attack on themselves, on their self-definition. Parties will be protective of their internal status quo, particularly at the beginning of a process that will ask them to change, to one degree or another.

Of the many things we can be afraid of losing in a conflict, we are afraid, most fundamentally, of losing our understanding or grasp of what is right and what is true about the world. Money and other resources over which people may be in conflict are important but external. More important is what those external elements mean to us, the internal representations that exist as neural structures of understanding or belief that give us our bearings in the flux of perceptual experience. As I've been emphasizing, we're not just dealing with issues and information when parties first approach us. We are dealing with the structure of their identity, embodied in their neural reality. This is one of the reasons why people get so hot (quite literally sometimes) about the disputes they find themselves in. The stakes are often higher than the issues seem to warrant. We feel it so important to be right because being right is an identity issue, an issue about knowing. Conflict is an epistemological phenomenon.

Given all this, upon first contact with a neutral, parties typically are eager to assert their understanding of the situation, how right they are and how wrong the other side. Their efforts serve two purposes. First, their aim is to convince us of the rightness of their position and experience, which is to say, to create neural pathways of understanding in us that correspond to their neural matrices of meaning, either because they fear we might favor the other side's account or because they want to make of us an ally in their opposition to the other party. Second, they want to affirm and reinforce their own neural meaning structures in the face of the challenges to their reality constructs they expect to experience in the anticipated negotiation.

As third parties, we are faced with the question of how to acknowledge the parties' internal experience while not reinforcing the neural networks of their established beliefs about the issues at stake. How much should we encourage parties to talk about their side of the story upon first contact or in caucus prior to meeting in joint session (if prior caucusing is the mediator's practice)? There is no standard answer to this question that will universally apply to every situation. It will depend, in part, on how the mediator works with the exchange should he or she choose to engage in a relatively extensive interchange with each party prior to the first joint session. A mediator, meeting separately with the parties at this initial stage, may be able, through such tactics, among others, as priming, acknowledging, framing and reframing, trust-building, and normalizing the possibility of there being other ways to look at the situation, to help the parties soften their attachment to their stories and to create confidence in the possibility of co-creating a collaborative solution to the problems at hand with the other party or parties. The exchange can serve to build party trust in the mediator, develop rapport and an experience of support that will facilitate subsequent willingness to hear the other side and consider shifts in perception during face-to-face sessions. That said, without conscious intention and careful management of the conversation to further the resolution process, there exists the danger of contributing to a hardening or reinforcing of positions with too much re-telling of the neural network stories.

Arguments can be made for the utility of both approaches, whether to devote very little time or substantial time to party story-telling prior to the initial joint meeting. Whatever choice we make as mediator, anchoring our engagement with the parties in an understanding of the neural basis of their experience will help to guide our interaction with them by providing a framework within which to think about the dynamics and possible results of story-telling at this point in the process.

First Phase of Joint Session with the Parties

I'll discuss caucusing (whether pre-joint session or mid-process) in a later section but, for the moment, let's assume that the parties meet first in joint session with the third party after only a relatively brief pre-session phone contact or no prior contact with the mediator.

Standard mediator training typically includes a process template that begins with an opening stage during which the mediator talks through some combination of mediation explanation, process road map, third-party role, principles, objectives, communication expectations and agreements, and solicits any questions the parties may have. The mediator has the option of covering these details at the beginning of the first joint session or prior to or in a combination of the two. Whatever the mediator's preference and style, we know that delivery of this information can and should contribute to the creation of a safe and structured context that promotes the building of trust, reduces stress, and lays the foundation for anticipated problem-solving. But one of the questions a mediator will ask himself or herself is how much time to devote to introductory information and in how much detail. We don't want to flood the parties with too many words and ideas when their attentional capacity is taken up by other concerns. Some parties will arrive in a sufficiently calm state for which beginning with a relatively extended introduction can serve to achieve goals of settling into the mediation room and building relationship and trust with the mediator. But when parties arrive in a state of disturbed agitation, they may not be able to take in much external information. There is no one recipe for these third-party decisions. Some calm and quiet talk about mediation and our role may give even highly upset parties time to settle a bit, some breathing room as we gently welcome them even if they are not able to take in much of the content of what we are saying. However, too long or complicated an introduction may serve only to increase the parties' agitation as they experience our talk as an irritant grating against their internal upset. Instead, keeping our opening remarks very brief may be more helpful. Thinking in terms of neural experience and neural activation can provide some guidance for our third-party decision-making during this phase. What level of detail, what pace of speech, how long our sentences, what tone, what terminology to match parties' backgrounds and styles will help the parties feel more comfortable, safe, and able to participate? Of the characteristics I discussed in Chapter 3, activation and reactivity, expectancies, and the balance between the dorsal (self-to-world) and ventral (world-to-self) systems are most at issue here. Additionally, it can be helpful for the practitioner to keep in mind the fundamental intimacy of communication, the impact of words entering the identity structures of the parties, and the tendency to defend against incoming information in conditions of threat, insecurity, or uncertainty.

Case Example: Two parties in a workplace conflict arrive at my office for their first session clearly upset. One of the parties has trouble making eye contact with me. From the few words said and the behavior between them, it is clear the conflict is flaring. I know that this is their first experience with mediation. What do I do? I expect that they have questions about the mediation process, how safe it will be for them within the workplace context, what is expected of them, about the external pressures to settle their conflict, what will be done with any settlement agreement, what will happen if they are unable to settle, etc. I also want to create a foundation or common framework for how we will work together. But because of their evident upset in the moment, I decide to dispense, for the time being, with any introductory commentary. I take a purposefully visible deep breath and exhale slowly as I look at each of them with compassion, a gentle smile, and a slow nodding of my head. Trusting that their process questions and more peripheral concerns

(continued)

> *(continued)*
>
> can be addressed later, after a quiet pause of a few seconds, I begin, "I'm getting that you're both feeling pretty stressed and upset. If I'm right, shall we start by paying attention to how you're doing right now?" And off we go. In this case, the approach worked, leading us into the substance of their problems as well as their process concerns. I was able to insert explanations of mediation and my role and answers to their questions as we went along. Another approach may have worked just as well. There's usually more than one way to feed a cat. But my sense is that if I'd delved into an extensive opening statement instead of meeting them where they were in their present upset, I'd have risked losing them, at least for a time.

Research suggests that creating contexts that incentivize and normalize cooperative behavior results in higher levels of default cooperative pro-social behavior over time and in other contexts.[6] There is a kind of priming effect that entrains people towards more cooperative behavior. In professional practice, we are aware that our words and behavior with the parties in these early stages can be conducive to a change of mood in the parties, a movement towards greater willingness and ability, hopefully, to be open to collaborative, mutual problem-solving relations. Remembering that the parties' experience is neural and therefore physical, provides an almost tangible experience of what's happening with the parties as we provide reassurance and confidence-building, soothing their troubled and distracted neural networks.

Party Story-Telling

An individual's actions in the world arise out of and make sense within the context of their self-identity story. As Hood (2012, p. 134) puts it, "(The) authorship of actions requires the illusion of a unified sense of self." We need an identity story in order to act in the world. Our actions are motivated by, are justified by, and reflect the stories we have of the world and ourselves. Our stories of the world and ourselves give meaning, reason, and rationale for our actions. We are each the protagonist in our life story and, as mentioned earlier, one important corollary of our self-story telling is that we want to feel good about ourselves in our story. We don't want to be wrong or bad. Even if not entirely heroic, we don't want to be the villain. And yet, in conflict narratives, it is often the case that each party is defining the other, and feels defined by the other, in exactly those terms, the villain or the mistaken. In this regard, we see the dynamics of in-group/out-group behavior in which a group's positive self-identification is often bolstered by defining the out-group in negative terms.

Seen in this way, part of our job in helping parties restore relationship or resolve conflict is helping them redefine the problem and possible solutions in terms that allow each of them to be understood in more positive terms. For this reason, we speak of face-saving, respect, acknowledgement, and recognition. Changing negative narratives can help positive movement happen.

Case Example: One of the more moving divorce mediations I conducted was one in which the wife of the couple was wheelchair bound. She had been injured in a car accident about a year prior and was paralyzed from the waist down. The husband was asking for the divorce and this was, of course, very difficult for both of them given that her mobility and ability to care for herself were significantly compromised. The marriage had been breaking down prior to the accident. They had tried to keep it together as they dealt with the aftermath of the accident. For whatever the reasons, they'd come to this point of divorce. There were many issues to be dealt with, of course, but most significant was the meaning of the divorce for their self-perceptions. The husband felt a great deal of guilt for leaving the marriage when his wife was facing her disability. The wife was struggling with the impact of her paraplegia and the additional commentary of divorce on her self-image. It was these two personal story elements that clouded and overshadowed all the logistical and economic issues involved in the divorce. It was difficult, initially, for them to talk about the emotions involved. But to their credit, they were able to summon the courage to confront the pain and fears that were so heavy and present for both of them. In spite of the problems they had had in their marriage, it was evident that they cared for each other, though the care was a bit buried beneath feelings of guilt and anger. To move forward, they needed to make sense of what was happening in each of their life stories and to find some sort of positive self-definition within the painful reality. The alternative was the husband defined as the guilty party abandoning his disabled wife and the wife defined as the angry and bitter abandoned victim. Neither of them wanted these narratives for themselves or for the other. Neither of them believed these stories to be the accurate representation of who they were. Together, they were able to build an understanding that they felt was more accurate and healthy of the meaning of their marriage, the divorce, the events leading to it, and their role and responsibility in the unfolding story. Once they'd achieved that, the other more mundane issues, with all their complications, were more easily sorted out.

Just as parties understand their conflict within the self- and world-stories by which they make sense of external reality and their location within that reality, so also any actions to address a conflict and any agreements proposed to resolve a conflict must make sense, in one way or another, within the parties' self- and world-stories.

The task of helping parties who are uncertain about or resistant to coming to the negotiating table or entering into a mediation involves helping them find ways of making sense of the choice to participate within their understanding of things. For a party ready to bolt from a negotiation, their BATNA (best alternative to a negotiated agreement),[7] rightly or wrongly, seems to make more sense than continuing to negotiate. In order to remain in the negotiation, they must revise their meaning-making, the story they tell themselves about the situation. Any proposed settlement in a conflict resolution process must somehow find a fit within the parties' stories and will require some adjustment to those stories. The reverberations of a settlement agreement through the intricate webs of the parties' identity structures will be more or less extensive and profound depending on the significance of the issues and the specifics of their resolution.

As we work with the parties, we are not only working with issues, options, and information and data. We are also working with the internal neural contexts within which these elements find their meaning. The more we can understand, and help the parties understand, the meaning that the conflict elements and possible resolution elements have for them, the more able we and they will be to discover and create what is necessary to find and accept solutions.

If parties are to negotiate a resolution, they must be able to be present in the negotiation. But it is difficult to be present, to participate in a negotiation process, when our stories, and therefore ourselves, are under attack. In oppositional conflict, the two sides have been, in effect, attempting to deny and discount the other's reality experience. In order for parties to be present, opportunity must be made for their stories to be fully present in the mediation room. Not one story or the other, not one story in opposition to the other story, not one story right and the other wrong, but each party's story understood and accepted as legitimate and free from attack in the mediation room. It's not a question of whether the parties' narratives of reality are accurate, right, or true, but that they exist, even though they are mutually contradictory, at least sufficiently so to have created the conflict in the first place. We must first make space for them to be safely coexistent. Each of the parties' stories must be recognized, their neural structures acknowledged and validated, even though not agreed with.

This is where we must start, allowing the reality of each party's experience to exist. As long as the pattern of attempted "mutual destruction" continues, each party will defend his or her neural understanding because the denial by the other is a denial of the self, and the self must survive. Change will not happen when under attack. The battle will continue. The beginning of a resolution process must be in accepting and understanding the other's reality. When we engage in conflict to replace their worldview with ours, then it is natural that they will defend and counterattack. However, when we see conflict as the meeting of differences, then we can place the different perspectives side by side and see the process of working through those differences as one of inquiry to develop more understanding. The preliminary agreement or first step in a resolution process will be that both worldviews exist, free of attempts to destroy one or the other understanding. Only when there is safety for their presence can each individual begin to consider revisions to the structures of meaning that comprise their identity. By acknowledging and accepting their experience (their stories), we confirm and allow their existence. We create the conditions within which they can be as they are. In doing this, we establish some security for each party. We shift the narrative from a battle between two opposing worldviews to the co-existence of two different worldviews. By affirming each, we remove their need to defend and aggressively assert. We soothe what has been disturbed and threatened and even, perhaps, injured by the conflict. As I noted earlier, all this does not differ from standard mediation practice, but recognizing that the parties exist in their neural structures provides a clearer and more solid basis for practice and can provide a framework within which the mediator can think about how much needs to be done to achieve this early goal of mutual story-telling.

The time necessary for this phase of the process will be determined by the situation and the needs of those involved given what has happened to date in the conflict. As parties tell their stories, clarifications and explanations will likely be necessary, questions asked and answered, and reactions and responses managed. However much time is necessary, this phase should not be short-changed because it provides the foundation and the context for moving forward. Without the information revealed in their stories, the parties won't have the necessary material with which to work. The story-telling can make visible and known what is otherwise private and hidden. It may be necessary in some cases to work individually and separately with the parties to help them build trust in the third party, in the process, and in themselves within the mediation setting. Whatever the case, one way or another, our goal is to move the parties from the experience of oppositional story-telling to coexistent story-telling. Accomplishing this step opens the path to next steps in the problem-resolving process. The need to recognize, acknowledge, validate, and affirm continues throughout the mediation as parties attempt to identify what is true for them, to communicate, and to consider shifts in positions.

Accomplishing the goal of getting both or all parties' stories "on the table" and visible can be easier said than done. They may resist being completely forthcoming because to do so feels too vulnerable or because they believe it will weaken their position. They may also tend to formulate their stories in opposition to the other's story, reverting to the attack mode of self-assertion and attempts to de-legitimize the other's story. These tendencies will run contrary to the goal of making space for both stories to co-exist. This is one reason we encourage parties to speak in what is often called "I-language," to counter the tendency to frame the account of their own story in terms that discount or oppose the other's story and blame or negatively characterize the other.

We talk about trying to reach common ground and also about how much common ground parties actually share (shared interests, for example, or shared experience). Given that people come to a conflict and to a resolution process with different pictures of the world based on their different life experiences, time must be devoted to understanding what those different pictures are, in order to identify where they differ, to what degree, and where there may be areas of agreement. In making visible the stories of each party, we can begin to see what the conflict is actually about and what is getting in the way of resolving it. Without disinterring the assumptions, beliefs, and understandings imbedded in their stories, we are liable to miss some of the sources of the conflict, impediments to resolution, as well as areas of agreement or commonality.

Recalling past events can reinforce the remembered events, returning the party to the emotional experience of the conflict. This is particularly a risk in circumstances that have included some level of trauma. At the same time, avoiding attention to the history of the conflict will not make the past disappear. The neural structures of those past experiences will remain if they are not somehow retold in a context that allows for a shift in present understanding. In other words, the past has to be retold somehow in order for the established neural pathways to be restructured or amended to give the past a new meaning in the present, sufficient to allow for settlement or resolution. The meaning of the past is not fixed. Its meaning changes according to the changing light of the unfolding present. The parties can be helped to blend the retelling of what has happened with revision of those stories based on new information, understanding, objectives, and motives.

The term "venting" sometimes refers to a type of re-telling of the past. In this sense, venting is a returning to the scene of the accident, so to speak, of actually returning to the emotional experience of a past event. To the degree that such story-telling involves emotional flooding for the teller and accusations about or attacks on the other party, the process will likely not be helpful, or will present barriers to constructive change. There can be a thin line between sharing stories for the sake of greater mutual understanding and further hardening conflict narratives in the process of re-telling. As much as possible, the telling of conflict stories is best *about* rather than *within* emotional or feeling experience. That said, there may be times when a party is overcome by the emotions associated with the conflict story, in which case a different intervention will likely be necessary, whether in joint or separate session.

Case Example: I once worked with two business partners who were also cousins in a close-knit large extended family. They came to mediation to try to dig themselves out of a severe relational and co-management breakdown that had been deepening over the past year or so. They were under significant stress with the prospect of the possible demise of their business. The prospect of failure had significant personal as well as financial implications. Extended family members had invested in the business. Family relationships as well as financial well-being were at risk. Their once close relationship was on the verge of collapse. Instead of focusing on present problem-solving, the parties seemed compelled to tell their narrative of events over the past three years to prove intentional mismanagement and even possible fraud by the other. The more they recounted their stories, the more heated they became until their interchange moved suddenly from tense but relatively calm (uncomfortably controlled) discussion to heated yelling and angry name-calling. One moment, they were sitting across from each other and the next moment they were both on their feet straining across the conference room table red-faced and swearing at each other about what had really happened and what the other had done. Both were completely emotionally flooded. The more they yelled their accounts at each other, the more cemented their stories became. It was as if with each vituperative sentence, another layer of certainty was laid down, another ply to add strength to their righteous conviction. To pull them back from the brink, I stood up with them, calming them with a gentle hand on each of their arms and coaxed them to sit down with a vocal firmness sufficient to exceed their volume. I briefly acknowledged and normalized their strong feelings in order to help them save face after their undignified outbursts, and then brought them back to the goals they had expressed at the beginning of the mediation session, reiterating their motivation to recover a relationship that had been close, trusting, and productive. Acknowledging again their strong feelings and the stress that they were experiencing, I suggested that they turn away from each other and take some moments to attend to their breathing. After some moments of stillness and settling, I suggested that they remain turned away from each other while I asked them prompting questions to uncover some positives from the past and their aspirations for the future. I wanted them to remain not facing each other in order to minimize triggering activations and to help them get in touch with themselves. They agreed and subsequently the mediation proceeded productively, leading to further sessions in which they resolved the fraud suspicions (unfounded, as it turned out), addressed the mismanagement accusations (unintentional but actual mismanagement that was acknowledged by both who admitted being in over their heads with the demands of their growing business), and arduously established some stepping stones for a way forward. In the early stages of their mediation, the repetitive re-telling of the past only served to deepen the ruts of their conflict. It was only later, when they had paved a new and smoother path, that they could revisit and revise their stories of the past.

Joint Reality Construction

Once the mediator and parties have been successful in getting the respective stories safely expressed, heard, and understood, the next phase is the gradual collaborative building of a new reality, which will be, it is hoped, a more shared reality. The parties can now speak with some knowledge of the other's experience and can, in crafting a new reality, begin to include the other's perspectives, understandings, and needs. The prior phase of story-telling has allowed them to expand their understanding of the situation beyond their own experience to include the experience of the other, giving them a more common language and set of data points with which to begin problem-solving. At this stage, it is hoped that their identities feel less threatened as their stories have been heard, accepted, and confirmed during the earlier stage, establishing security in which the attack and defend cycle is a less necessary part of the conflict relationship, though the conflict itself remains.

With an understanding of the neural basis of our reality constructs, the importance of what is called joint fact-finding (the building of shared understanding on the basis of accepted data from mutually agreed-upon sources) in multi-party, public, collaborative resolution processes takes on a more concrete meaning. We can also better understand the challenge of reorienting an adversarial right/ wrong battle to a process of joint inquiry and problem-solving. In order to learn together, the parties must be willing, to some degree, to not know together and this requires an adjustment to the level of certainty with which they likely entered the resolution process, certainty about their understanding of the conflict, about relevant data and the interpretation of the data, their beliefs about what would constitute a right outcome, perhaps certainty about their BATNAs, and even their understanding of who the other party is (the meaning associations they have of the other party within their worldview). In another way of saying it, they must be willing to still the voices of confirmation bias.

The list of interventions that can be used to help parties maintain their equilibrium during the transition to joint problem-solving and mutual learning will depend on the circumstances of the case. In multi-party public collaborative dispute resolution processes, presentations by neutral and independent experts are often part of the joint learning process. The timing of such interventions is key. If the parties are not ready to receive information that might contradict or expand their understanding of the issues, introduction of the new data from an outside source may be counterproductive, tending to lead a party to harden his or her position. As David McRaney puts it in his book *You Are Not So Smart* (2012):

> Once something is added to your collection of beliefs, you protect it from harm. You do this instinctively and unconsciously when confronted with attitude-inconsistent information. Just as confirmation bias shields you when you actively seek information, the backfire effect defends you when the information seeks you, when it blindsides you. Coming or going, you

stick to your beliefs instead of questioning them. When someone tries to correct you, tries to dilute your misconceptions, it backfires and strengthens those misconceptions instead. Over time, the backfire effect makes you less skeptical of those things that allow you to continue seeing your beliefs and attitudes as true and proper.[8]

In other settings, a particular exercise that demonstrates the bigger picture or alternate points of view or an illustrative movie that moves the parties past their limited views or expands their emotional experience might help open new ways of seeing the situation they face with their erstwhile adversaries.

The goal is not, of course, to get the parties to agree about everything, to see the world in the same way. But if they are to reach agreements that resolve the conflict sufficiently to allow them to proceed with their lives free of the impasse or road block that the unresolved conflict has created in their lives, they will necessarily have to make some adjustments in how they see parts of the world involved in the conflict issues and those adjustments will have to move in the direction of some shared understanding. This is, after all, what we mean by agreement, sometimes defined as "the state of being in accord" and "unanimity of opinion; harmony in feeling."[9]

> Case Example: There is a controversy swirling on the Big Island of Hawaii over the placement of yet another astronomical telescope, along with the dozen older telescopes already there, on the mountain known as Maunakea. On one side, are those who see the new telescope, able to peer more deeply into the cosmos than any telescope yet built, as a critically important contribution to our grand species enterprise of knowledge advancement, and among those even some who see it also as consonant with the spirit of the mountain and with the values of those who have used the mountain for various purposes over the generations. On the other side are those who see the placement of the 30-meter telescope as another desecration of the sacred mountain and a further encroachment by foreigners on an indigenous cultural space, an encroachment that must be resisted and reversed.
>
> In this example, we once again see those involved experiencing the conflict in an either/or frame in which the outcome must be a win for one side or the other. Resolution in these terms may settle the dispute but will leave the conflict to abide and fester and the community divided and unhappy. As is sometimes observed, a win/lose result is often, especially in these types of circumstances, ultimately a lose/lose outcome.
>
> The conflict over Maunakea is one of worldviews and, as we have been discussing, worldviews are embodied in the encoded neural matrices of meaning within the proponents and opponents. The disagreement is a neural
>
> *(continued)*

(continued)

event. Each of those involved carries a picture of the mountain within them, "wired" in their neural networks, and those pictures differ and clash. The mountain exists mind-independently as a screen onto which the advocates project their deeply held meanings. To find an enduring and generally satisfactory solution requires a new mountain within the parties. The mountain will abide; the people have to change themselves. The change will not be total; the parties can't be expected to radically transform their view of the mountain. But if a generally accepted solution is to be found, their mountain meaning must be expanded or supplemented. The parties will have made a new mountain that includes somehow both their mountains.[10]

Options Generation

As I've discussed, the ability to make new neural associations (creativity) is reduced in conditions of low trust or perceived threat. Under threat or in the fear condition, we are less free to consider new ways of knowing the world. Given that conditions of low trust and perceived threat are common in conflict situations, we can make the mistake as mediators of asking parties to engage in the generation of options (brainstorming) when they are not yet in a cognitive state most conducive to making novel neural linkages. Recognizing the interconnected dynamics of trust, safety, and creativity, we might spend more time developing the relational context between the parties before asking them to move to the generation of solution scenarios. There is a danger in focusing too early on solutions when division between the parties remains their primary experience. Certainly, our ultimate goal is to get to solutions, when possible, but to get there, we must attend to what the parties need in the present moment. Prematurely moving to a solution focus may set the parties up for an experience of failure in which they conclude that, indeed and as they believed, the case is hopeless. Impasse then will not be the result of incompatible objectives but a problem of timing.

As mediators, we may tend to want to get solutions too quickly for various reasons: because we want to be efficient with the parties' time; because we want to experience the success of forward movement; because we want to be perceived, and to perceive ourselves, as effective; or because we are uncomfortable with what might appear to be lack of progress. In conflict resolution work, sometimes we need to go slow to go fast. Parties may benefit from more time spent in building trust, in getting comfortable with the process, in forging communication and relationship channels between them before delving into possible solutions. Preliminary trust-building at the beginning of a mediation process, even if relatively brief, provides the context for beginning to discuss the issues. More trust is necessary for parties to be willing to reveal and explore their interests. The movement to options generation requires a further shift from adversarial relationship to a degree of cooperative partnership, a shift from opposition to a more or less willing co-creative engagement.

Agreement-Building

As I've mentioned, our attachment to previous beliefs and ideas can be difficult to loosen. Even when an idea we previously held has been proven to be incorrect and we acknowledge a changed understanding, the feeling of its correctness can remain. The familiar neural pathways don't disappear immediately or completely. We don't turn from one understanding to another on a dime, and this is particularly so with some beliefs more than others. As I've been discussing, shifts of perspectives or beliefs, shifts in how we see and understand the world happen at the physical level. To repeat my earlier observation, when we ask someone to change his or her mind, we are speaking not only figuratively but literally. The body must change as our pictures of the world and ourselves change.

As I've also discussed, some changes are simpler and more easily accomplished than others. The depth of significance of any particular understanding or belief varies along a continuum from superficial to profound. I sometimes imagine the issues of a conflict as threads that are either quite simple to pull from the web of neural connections or are very much more intricately interwoven in the fabric of identity as it exists in the parties' neural structures. The more complexly interwoven, the more careful and attentive we must be in our attempts to help a party accomplish the shifts required for resolution. What other threads are attached or implicated? What knots must be gently teased apart? Or, using another metaphor, what new pictures must be painted and what images will be sufficiently compelling and convincing to replace or revise the old images set in neural structures more or less colorfully?

So, among the first questions to ask as parties consider the elements of a possible agreement are whether any shifts are required in order to accept the new stories that the proposed agreements represent, how difficult are these to make for each of the parties, and what might they need in order to make those shifts. Of course, often there are external constraints and realities to consider, for example, budget limitations, elections or other political factors, BATNA calculations, etc. But for our purposes here, it's the significance of the parties' internal meaning matrices and what may be needed in order to change or amend those networks in support of the post-resolution world that are of concern. We may sometimes overlook the fact that all shifts of perspective are not equal and therefore neglect to ask the questions, "How difficult is it to accept this agreement, and why, and what might you need in order to make the shift?" Noticing a party's resistance to a proposal, option, or scenario, we can respond by slowing down and taking time to check in with the party's understanding and experience, devoting more time to learning how the party sees the proposed reality, what meanings the new potential reality might carry with it for each party, and what relationship those meanings might have to other elements of the party's worldview. Based on the embodied consciousness perspective, we might pay more attention to the transition from one narrative or position or understanding to another, the "passing of the neural baton" so to speak. The old story doesn't disappear with the adoption of a new story. In many cases, there needs to be a bridge from one story to the other. The phrase "caught in the past" is revealing in this regard.

As parties make conciliatory gestures or consider proposals for possible settlement agreements, they may need help to maintain their dignity (perceiving themselves as being respected by the other), their sense of being in control (perceiving that their assessment of what is real or true is not completely wrong), or their self-respect (perceiving themselves as not being out of touch with reality). The moments of transition during which a party lets go of one point of view and accepts a new point of view can be delicate. Parties may need some extra help and encouragement during this phase. We may ask what might be offered in exchange for the apparent relinquishment of control or the abandonment of a previously held belief or perception. In negotiations involving an ethnic conflict, for example, it might be helpful to highlight and reinforce elements of ethnic identity through cultural or historical presentations as the parties contemplate agreements that require a shift in their strongly held beliefs. Given how profoundly disturbing it can be to be faced with disagreement about our beliefs or to shift our perception of reality, the transition from how the parties saw the world to agreements that embody a new understanding must be gently guided.

There's something also about honoring the experience of the past as parties consider revising their perceptions of the conflict, the issues, and the other party. Replacing a previous perception with a new understanding needn't discount the former if we understand that our experience is a mix of past and present circumstances. The past needn't be judged on the basis of the present. Previous perceptions and understandings may have made sense given the conditions of the past. New understandings are found with the benefit of current experience that was not available to the parties in their past circumstances. Seeing things this way, the parties needn't discount their past experience even as they revise their understandings on the basis of new perceptual experience (new information and new experience with the other party). With this framing, change can perhaps be more easily accepted.

Case Example: Understanding that any given topic exists in a larger web of neural interconnections will help us be sensitive to the fact that a proposed settlement that addresses the specific issues the parties brought to mediation might have implications for other elements in the lives of the parties that might not, at first, be obvious. I once mediated a painful dispute that had been brewing for months between two co-workers and that had erupted in the workplace a number of times. When the conflict became so disruptive that it was interfering with their work performance, management asked that they consider mediation, to which they agreed. After a lot of deep work on the history of their relationship, the complaints they each had and changes that they wanted, and mutual learning about each other's experience, they were able to resolve past events and build agreements to create a better context for their ongoing work together. To all appearances, their work was done and I drafted their settlement agreement. At our final meeting to iron our a few small issues, it became evident that they were worried about how their co-workers would feel in the aftermath of their conflict and the mediation. They were unsure how their co-workers would respond to their emergence from the mediation process. Further discussion revealed additional issues of trust/distrust, face and reputation, supervisory style, how they would communicate with their co-workers, and what meaning they would make of the past and their present newly reformed relationship. As a result, among other additions to their agreement, they decided to jointly craft, with my assistance, a message to their co-workers that framed the whole event in a way that felt satisfactory to both of them, actively taking control of meaning-making in the workplace.

This was done without any reference to the neural basis of their experience but it illustrates how any particular issue will be linked to other issues in ways that may not be immediately apparent. Some of those interconnected issues will be in close enough proximity, neurally speaking, that to ignore them might undermine the durability or thoroughness of an agreement. In this case, if we hadn't taken the time to explore what related issues might be involved, their working agreements might have foundered within the larger network of their co-workers. At the time, I was anxious that asking further questions would disturb the newly achieved harmony, and indeed it did to begin with, threatening to rekindle the conflict and move the relationship two steps back after our successful step forward. But in the end, the risk paid off and the additional work produced a more complete agreement.

Between Sessions and Post-Mediation

Recognizing that positive shifts of perspective and understanding that are achieved during a conflict resolution process can be subject to reversion to previously held positions upon a party's return to his or her pre-mediation environment suggests that effective conflict work sometimes requires "upriver" work with parties' home circumstances. If our responsibility includes helping the parties build durable agreements, our work may extend outside the mediation room. Parties may need help in devising incentives or strategies to convert negotiation advances to long-term incorporation in the implementation settings, what might be seen as analogous to converting short-term memory to long-term storage.

Understanding this in neural terms, we can see that the history that created the neural wiring of the conflict experience is not necessarily easily or quickly replaced by the new perceptual and cognitive experiences that have led to agreements within mediation. The fact that a divorcing couple arrives at agreements in mediation about how the exchange of children from one parent to the other will be handled doesn't insure they will be able to successfully implement the exchange in the contexts of their actual lives that have produced the relational problems that brought them to mediation. Perhaps some practice within the mediation room is necessary, or at least more discussion. In more difficult cases, the parties might agree to have a trusted friend or family member present for the first few children exchanges, or it might be necessary to create some other kind of buffer between the parties in a particularly high-conflict relationship.

Case Example: In one of my cases, a divorcing couple made the unusual request that I be present at their home while they divided personal and household items. They had agreed in mediation on a method for dividing their belongings but had been unsuccessful on their own despite their commitment in mediation to refrain from the aggressive and sometimes violent behavior that had characterized a good deal of their relationship, and despite a lot of discussion and strategizing during a mediation session about how they would go about successfully implementing their plan. The neural pathways of their antipathies and distrust were deep-set. Try as they did, without assistance, they were unable to "re-program" their perceptual experience of each other. As they attempted to divide their personal belongings on their own, long-established and dysfunctional matrices of meaning were reactivated to the exclusion of their more recent new agreements and commitments. They required my presence to reinforce the newly established but comparatively tenuous meaning matrices of their recent agreements.

In multi-party public negotiations in which the people at the table represent constituencies and organizations not present, it is common practice to make sure that progress at the table is accompanied by sufficient communication between meetings with the represented groups to insure that, as agreements are crafted and considered at the negotiating table, the constituencies represented are kept current. In a negotiation that is progressing successfully, representatives at the table are changed by the relationship-building experiences among them and by new information that has contributed to changing perspectives and emerging agreements.

Decision-makers away from the table or members of represented constituencies will not have had a similar experience. Work may need to be done within a constituency to take members through a process that helps them develop understanding conducive to supporting and ratifying the agreements reached by their representatives at the negotiating table, agreements that might initially seem to them to contravene held values, to represent an unacceptable allocation of resources, or to not sufficiently achieve envisioned goals. To reiterate, agreement-building is a neural event. People require some sort of experiential process to promote the shift from one set of meanings to another.

Stipulations to include monitoring, review, and evaluation of agreement implementation are sometimes a part of a comprehensive settlement agreement and are often common components of multi-party, public collaborative negotiation processes for a variety of reasons specific to public policy decision-making and the management of public resources. One of the reasons this is so in the public policy arena is that personnel responsible for implementing agreements may change over the period covered by the agreements. People will leave their jobs, retire, be promoted or transferred, or elections may result in new people being involved. Those responsible for the ongoing implementation of agreements may not have been involved in the agreement-building process. In neural terms, they won't have been exposed to the perceptual experiences that produced the understandings upon which the agreements were founded. This may or may not be a problem. In some instances, there will be no resistance to implementation because the newly involved individuals responsible will take the agreements for granted as a given part of their new work environment. In other instances, those newly responsible for continuing implementation may either not understand the bases for the agreements or may disagree with the agreements. To the degree that continued implementation is a concern, parties to a negotiation may include in their agreement methods to address such future circumstances. These may be in the form of documentation sufficient to shift neural maps of understanding or directives or job description requirements sufficient to override objections (unless, of course, the new individuals are in positions of power that allow them to abandon or revisit former agreements with which they disagree).

Practice Issues

Location and Setting

That we are interactive with our environment, not separate from it, underscores what we already know of the significance of setting for a conflict resolution process. The setting will influence, activate, and prime the parties in one way or another. The features of a meeting space that we know to have impact on the parties are viscerally experienced. Seating spacing between the parties, how each is oriented towards doors and windows and to the mediator, air circulation and temperature, presence of food and water (a mentor of mine always had a bowl of nuts or other nibbles on her mediation table), size of the room, ambience (paint color, lighting, etc.), and office location all contribute to the experience of the parties and their ability to engage in the resolution process.

Case Example: I recall a case in which members of two local California Native Tribes were invited to several meetings of a negotiation made up of corporate interests and local, state, and federal government representatives (elected officials and agency staff). The location was familiar and comfortable to all the latter individuals but was, to a degree, foreign territory for the Tribal members. We were not meeting on their home turf. The cultural norms and expectations within the room involving dress and behavior belonged to the non-Tribal participants. Perception of the room and what was activated within each of the individuals that gave meaning to the setting was different for everyone. This is always true, of course. We are always in different rooms, each of us being different, but in this case the difference was material, affecting the quality and content of communication. The power dynamics that existed between the Tribal representatives and the others at the negotiating table on the basis of history and culture were accentuated and reinforced. Over the course of our meetings, I wondered how the engagement might have differed if the meetings had taken place in a Tribal location?

In another case, I had met several times with a divorced couple in my smaller mediation room that included four comfortable chairs around a small round coffee table. The parties had been divorced for several years and had decided to use mediation to improve their co-parenting communications that had been characterized by much distrust, anger, and fighting. In mediation, they had been able to establish a new framework for their co-parenting relationship that resulted in their communications being more cooperative and collaborative. At one point, they agreed that it would be helpful if the ex-wife met with the ex-husband's new wife to work through some areas of disagreement and friction between the two of them. For this purpose, I proposed that we meet in a larger conference room with a full-sized conference table. From what the parties told me of the tense relationship between the two women, my smaller meeting room felt too constrained a space, forcing a level of intimacy that I believed the parties would have had trouble tolerating. The larger meeting room provided space for more separation sense of safety and the full-sized conference table provided a needed buffer of protection.

There is research demonstrating that subjects given a warm drink to hold (for example, a warm cup of coffee) will subsequently experience warmer feelings of regard towards other study participants than will those who briefly hold an iced drink. So also will a comfortably warm meeting room increase feelings of safety and relaxation and will counter feelings of aloneness, tenseness, and stress.[11] Such studies illustrate the physical basis of psychological experience, the embodied basis of emotional experience and affect.

Trust-Building

A primary task, when parties come to work with us, is to build trust that will begin to lay the groundwork upon which they will be willing to make the changes necessary for resolution. That trust between or among parties is low or even absent does not preclude the use of a collaborative process to resolve a dispute. In fact, one purpose of an effective conflict resolution process is to build trust where it is low or nonexistent. Conflict resolution processes are designed to build trust in a variety of ways. We build parties' trust in ourselves as third parties through our behavior (our physical appearance and movements, including our vocal behavior, tone, modulation, pace, volume) and the content of our communication, as well as the aspects of place that I've mentioned, location, room layout and décor, etc. We help parties build trust in each other by helping them speak honestly about what is important for them and hear what is important for the other.

It is interesting to think about trust in neural terms. In relationship, perhaps nothing is as primary and primal as our experience on the trust/distrust continuum. We are concerned with our safety, physical and psychosocial. Psychosocial safety requires that our understandings will be confirmed and validated, or at least encouraged, recognized, and acknowledged as legitimate, and that we will be welcomed, affirmed, and included.

As a generalization, in circumstances of insecurity, uncertainty, and threat, we prefer not to be surprised or contradicted. In one way of looking at it, trust has to do with predictability. Can I depend on you to behave in the way you say you will? Part of the dance we see in the early stages of a conflict resolution process has to do with the parties figuring out whether and how much they can trust the other or others. Once sufficient trust is established, we can more easily tolerate disagreement and contradiction.

This is not to say that when basic trust criteria are met in relationship we are entirely tolerant of surprise or contradiction. But when a relationship shifts to the status of significant conflict, the rules change, so to speak. As I've discussed, it is inherent in conflict and disagreement that our understandings, and therefore our identity, are challenged, and the threat of physical violence remains a potent subtext. Within the context of a trusting and safe relationship, disagreements are managed and different points of view can co-exist without threat to self. But in an antagonistic or adversarial conflict relationship, the stakes change and parties are more likely to experience the need to protect themselves and defend against what feels like threatening assaults on their views about the world, their beliefs and opinions, their reality constructs. The organism bristles with defensive strategies in the face of perceived threat and unpredictable antagonism.

In addition to the question of interpersonal trust, parties in conflict may experience fluctuations of intrapersonal trust, how much they trust themselves, either chronically or in the particular conflict situation. Low self-trust may inhibit a party's ability to participate in fruitful negotiations or willingness to consider alternative perspectives or specific settlement terms. In that event, it may be necessary to look for ways to reassure or reinforce the party's self-confidence. In some circumstances, this might involve encouraging a party to obtain outside review of the terms of a proposed settlement. In other circumstances, introducing independent expert opinion into the process will support a party uncertain about his or her meaning constructs. Sometimes the development of contingent agreements that address what-if scenarios can help a party take a settlement step in the face of internal uncertainty.

Case Example: Mediating a divorce case, I was presented with two individuals whose levels of intrapersonal trust differed greatly. The husband, in his early 40s, was confident and gregarious. He had made a not insignificant fortune with his own self-made business. He was expert in and comfortable with fiscal calculations and money management. He provided for all the material needs in the relationship. His wife, 29 years old, was a quiet introvert who spent most of her time with the horses on their horse ranch. She had never had to contribute to the household income. Over the course of my first two sessions with the couple, the husband did most of the talking, including often speaking for his wife, while she said very little and never more than a few words at a time, in spite of my efforts to create space for her to speak and to encourage her to express her perspectives and experience. Aside from the various power imbalances between them (income, comfort with money management and control of finances, household decision-making, age and experience, force of personality, etc.), the wife had almost no trust that she could know what she wanted and could assert herself. In the absence of sufficient self-trust, the negotiations could not arrive at a fair or ethical conclusion. Meanwhile, the husband was quite comfortable with the dynamics of their decision-making. He was accustomed to being in control and was not motivated to change the dynamics. Though he was resistant to the idea, I helped them agree that she would meet with a counselor, a financial advisor, and a lawyer in order to bolster her self-confidence and increase her grasp of the financial and legal aspects of the divorce process in order to provide a more solid basis from which to negotiate their divorce settlement. To his credit, the husband was willing in the end, though grudgingly, to shift his internal blueprint of the relationship. Over the course of the mediation, with the support of the external experts, the wife was able to practice and develop more self-trust that changed not only her participation in the facilitated negotiation but also changed the dynamics of the relationship and altered the husband's experience of himself and his soon-to-be former wife. It was remarkable to watch the two change their (neurally based) identity constructs.

Research indicates that, "we develop trust based on attunement and reciprocal interactions and are untrusting of those who appear unresponsive or misattuned to our state of mind" (Cozolino, 2014, p. 194). Unresponsiveness and an absence of being attuned to each other are characteristic of conflict relationships. In conflict, by definition, we are not attuned. We see things differently. When we are divided by conflict, we are very likely unresponsive to each other, fixed in our own certainties and fears, and often unwilling to extend reassuring conciliatory gestures. Anything we can do in a conflict resolution process to increase interactional responsiveness and develop more attunement will build trust and help to create an environment more conducive to productive problem-solving and agreement-building. For example, processes of active listening, acknowledgement, and recognition promote and reflect responsiveness, one party to the other. Sometimes shared humor (introduced with due caution and sensitivity to possible unintended consequences) can help to break the ice and produce an experience of mutual attunement. Shared experiences of eating together or site visits are known to produce relationship-building advances conducive to subsequent joint problem-solving.

To say it again, remembering that the parties' experience is neurally based can help to ground our practice, anchoring it to the reality of physical embodiment, helping to explain party experience and behavior, and providing justification for practice interventions.

Beyond Active Listening: Mutual Understanding and Acceptance of the Other

It's one thing to have parties express their stories, but unless each party is able to hear, understand, and accept the legitimacy of the other's story and each party has the experience that he or she is understood, our job isn't done. Both parts of the communication process are necessary, the speaking part by which each party's understanding and experience of the situation are expressed, and the listening part by which each party understands the other party's story, and conveys that understanding to the speaker. Mediators will commonly provide a behavioral model for the parties by engaging in active listening practices.[12] This is common practice in conflict resolution work. Understanding the neural basis of experience helps to illuminate the importance and the difficulty of this part of the parties' communication exchange.

It is easy to forget that we don't actually experience the internal world of the other and we tend to assume that their experience is like ours, indeed, is the same as ours. On this basis, we can believe that we understand the other, that we "get" what they are saying about their experience. So often we superimpose our experience onto their reports, and think we understand them when really we are only understanding our own experience. When we are in disagreement, we evaluate the sense of their words against our own meaning matrices and find them lacking, forgetting that their words make sense within the meaning matrices of their understanding.[13] To counter this tendency, we must listen closely to understand the meaning of their words in the context of their world rather than the meaning of their words in our world.

Even with well-intentioned active listening practices, misunderstanding and inaccurate assumptions can continue. Even when we repeat what the other has said, in their own words, to confirm and convey understanding, we may not realize that the words we are exchanging carry different meanings for each of us. Restatement, in these instances, will be insufficient without mutual inquiry into what the salient words mean to each of us. Words hide as well as convey meaning. It is the meaning behind the words that we must get at in a conflict resolution process.

Until the understanding portion of the exchange is achieved, it will be difficult, for obvious reasons, to make progress in the problem-solving. Without understanding the other's experience, the parties will be working in the dark, or will be working with only their own understanding of the issues and the situation, which may not match the other party's experience, and will very likely be based on projections about the other's experience. There must be a sharing of neural maps, so to speak. In Bush and Folger's (1994) terms, these are the twin aspects of acknowledgement and recognition. From the neural perspective, when we are heard as we mean to be heard, when we feel understood, our neural networks are acknowledged and validated and we are reassured. We certainly prefer that the other agree with us for that would confirm our reality constructs. But short of agreement, just being heard and understood provides relief in the experience of being known. If either party doesn't feel heard and understood, it will be as if his or her story doesn't exist in the mediation room, and therefore as if he or she is not known or present, as if her or his existence is denied.

As we know from experience, it can be difficult for parties in conflict to listen to the other's story without discounting it or defending against it. After all, the conflict is based on disagreement to begin with. The story told by the other delivers a set of meanings, assumptions, and expectations that likely don't correspond to and often directly contradict the neural structures activated in the listener. Additionally, the incoming stimuli in the moment often activate meaning matrices established in the past that stoke the conflict fire. The listener will then experience inner disturbance in response to the incoming stimuli of the speaker's words, making it difficult to actually hear the meaning of the speaker's words. Instead, the listener may hear only what is activated within, without being able to understand the meaning the words have for the speaker. In these instances, there is little delay between stimulus and response, whether the response is internal or behavioral.

Case Example: Conflict within the large accounting department of a national nonprofit organization had festered and grown since the arrival of a new chief finance officer (CFO) 18 months prior to my being called to work with the group. There were many issues involved in the conflict and a story too long to tell here. But one of the issues had to do with staff feeling disrespected by the new CFO and the new CFO feeling stonewalled by some of the staff, particularly a key staff person who had acted as the informal CFO prior to the new CFO's arrival. The accounting group had suffered through three previous and relatively short-term CFOs who turned out to be less than competent leaders. Between the departure of the last of these and the arrival of the new CFO, the group had had to manage on its own for almost a year and a half, doing its best to keep the fiscal house in order while the organization was experiencing significant expansion of services and overall growth. For all their best efforts, the two audits conducted before the new CFO's arrival produced numerous errors and omissions. The Board of Directors and funders were very agitated and the new CFO was committed to righting the ship and producing a stellar audit, for which he had only six months to prepare. With his strong leadership, the audit came through completely clean. But the success was experienced differently by the CFO and the staff. Each time the CFO sang its praises to the Board, funders, and in the office, staff heard a lack of respect for their previous work that had led to two poor audits. They heard no recognition for the fact that they had kept the organization afloat through very difficult circumstances. Their resentment was expressed in morale-eroding gossip and in resistance to helping the CFO accomplish his goals. The CFO didn't understand why he was having so much trouble winning the approval of his staff given the fact that he kept proclaiming how well they had done in producing a clean audit. The more he talked about the great audit accomplishment, the more they heard disparagement of what had gone before. By the time I arrived, his frustration was turning to anger. Trust was low all around and communication was stuck. In a second all-staff meeting, we were able to uncover the different meanings that staff and the CFO heard each time he proclaimed the audit success. This was the key that unlocked the door to a set of other issues that they were then able to work through and resolve.

Furthermore, listening to understand will be made more difficult if the speaker's words are said with an explicit intention to replace or undermine the listener's understanding or story, as is the norm in the conflict dynamic. We will tend to be less willing to let the other's words enter into us if we feel they are attempting to change us. We will be less willing to be influenced by their words. If, however, the mediator has convinced and reassured the parties that the intention is not to replace understandings but to help each express their experience in an exchange that is not intended necessarily to convince the other, then the listener will find it easier to take in the other's story and to place the speaker's picture next to his or her own.[14]

I spoke earlier of the distinction between internal motivational priorities (the self-to-world dorsal system) and responsiveness to external contextual information (the world-to-self ventral system). This conceptual framework, based on our neural anatomy, can provide a language with which to understand imbalanced behavior along the continua of speaking and not speaking and listening and not listening. The two modes, the dorsal self-to-world and ventral world-to-self, correspond to the speaking (self-to-world) and listening (world-to-self) behaviors we try to help parties achieve in mediation. We want parties to be able to speak what is true for them but not to the exclusion of taking in (literally) what the other is saying. We want parties to be receptive to the other's communication but not to the exclusion of attention to their own needs and what is true for themselves. Understanding that there is a physical basis for the predominance of one pattern over the other provides an explanation to the practitioner for behavior that might otherwise seem arbitrary, baffling, and frustrating. The conceptual framework can provide explanatory justification for the devotion of more time to helping a party shift behavior from one extreme or the other. As discussed earlier, bias towards greater reliance on the dorsal system involving internal motives for self-regulation is associated with greater elation whereas bias towards greater reliance on the ventral system involving somatic perception of the external world for self-regulation is associated with greater anxiety (Tucker and Luu, 2012, p. 105). If we see a party exhibiting more manic behavior, we may want to help him or her pay greater attention to external stimuli, in other words greater attention to the other party and what the other party is saying. Similarly, if we see that a party is exhibiting greater anxiety, we may want to help her or him pay more attention to their internal needs and motivations.

The process of expressing (and, therefore, revealing) one's story can produce learning for the speaker as well as for the listener. In the heat and chaos of conflict, in which they may be subject to fear-based neural flooding, or simply in the conflict tug-of-war to be right, the parties might not be fully aware of what is important to them, and might be unable to see the larger picture that likely exists beyond their own parochial understanding. Parties can easily be short-sighted about their true interests and how to most likely find the path to satisfy them. There can be a kind of blindness when we are overcome by the emotions stirred up by conflict and are preoccupied with survival in the face of what we experience as an assault on our existence or, at least, on our worldview. Conflict is like a battle and finding resolution requires that everyone come out from behind the defensive walls of their castles of certainty and rightness to venture into the open fields of neutral territory to sit and learn together. To come out from behind those walls, people must, of course, feel safe, at least safe enough to venture forth into the shared problem-solving space.

> Case Example: I'm reminded of the question, commonly heard by conflict resolution professionals and negotiation coaches, a young woman asked me as she was considering mediation with her ex-husband to deal with a contentious custody and parenting disagreement. "Won't it be a sign of weakness if I suggest or ask that we meet in mediation?" Conflicts are seen as a battle. Putting down our swords and shields is not easily done. This young woman was filled with distrust. The distrust was a reflection of concern for her safety. As we know, we can be afraid of various possible losses in conflict and concerned with protecting various parts of our internal and external worlds. In this case, she was concerned about losing parenting time, losing control over her young son's development, and losing income in a reduction of child support payments. But she was also concerned about losing the battle of beliefs about what was right for their child.

In the process of speaking our own story and listening to understand the other's story, we can experience breakthroughs. "Oh, I didn't understand that!" or "Oh, now I get what it's been like for you" or "I've been afraid that . . ." or "As I say that, I realize . . ." etc. With attention to our own inner experience in conflict situations, we can know the resistance commonly felt to accepting or allowing the restructuring of neural matrices of meaning reflected in these types of expressions. In conflict, we are disinclined to change and disinclined to see the other's point of view. But with willingness, there can be a shift from seeing the other party as threateningly different and a member of an out-group (even if an out-group of only one member or of a vaguely defined out-group of bad people) to seeing the other more generously as "much like me" in many ways and now a partner in problem solving.

Activations, Reactivity, Projections, and Attributions

Neural networks are unavoidably activated by the perceptual stimuli of our surroundings. In a conflict relationship, just seeing the other can activate feelings of anxiety, fear, anger, or distrust, as well as one's self-stories about the conflict.[15]

Patterns of behavior that are part of the conflict's history, that are familiar and therefore, on some level, reassuring, will be triggered.

In conditions of perceived threat, the emotional components of activated neural circuits will tend to predominate. For us to moderate and manage the emotional elements of our activated associations, threat must be reduced sufficiently to allow prefrontal executive function regulation of our responses. A state of fear will inhibit thoughtful consideration of the issues and possible solutions. Whatever we can do to reduce in the parties their perceptions of the other as enemy or adversary will help produce conditions more conducive to joint problem-solving. Thus Roger Fisher's well-known dictum to be hard on the problem, not on the people. This shift reduces demonization and encourages a sense of partnership, and therefore safety, in the problem-solving.

Helping parties understand and be explicitly conscious of the activation phenomenon can allow them to apply neocortical executive function management to their limbic system emotions when they become angry, fearful, or aggressive. With awareness, a party can understand that he or she is being activated and can accept but not be ruled by their feelings, and the other party can recognize that the other is in the grip of feelings and not need, necessarily, to react, though they might, in which case, their understanding of the reactive state can help to keep it in perspective so that the parties are not overwhelmed by or driven by their feelings. Vulnerability to emotional contagion can be reduced through awareness, understanding, and the development of better boundaries.[16] In these ways, a viscous escalation cycle of activation and response can be avoided or interrupted.

Our projections are activations of the neural traces of our own past experience by the stimuli of present circumstances. This is not to say that we cannot have accurate understandings or close to accurate observations of others. All our experience of the other is perceptual, of course, and our understanding of the other, whether accurate or inaccurate, is determined by the activation of established neural structures or the creation of new neural connections. But the distinction of projections is that, like transference and inaccurate stereotypes, they are the imposition of an inaccurate interpretation on the other, the application of one's own meaning associations onto the other. Paranoia is a more extreme and pathological example of environmental cues activating neural matrices of understanding that don't accurately match the external stimuli.

In all social interactions, we seek to understand or assign meaning to the behavior of the other. In friendly or loving relationships, our explanations of the other's behavior are positive or benign. But in conflict relationships, we tend to interpret the other's behavior negatively, attributing to them malicious intent, dishonesty, deceitfulness, ignorance, obstructionism, and so on. It's a commonplace to say that our picture or image of the other changes according to the dynamics of the relationship, but this is part of what we work with in a resolution process, the attributions and meaning stories the parties have toward and about each other.

Nervous system arousal and response cued by those around us underscores the importance of mediator behavior (actions, facial expressions, statements, voice modulation, etc.) that can encourage trust or not, calmness or not, and feelings of safety or not. However, our ability to determine how we will influence the other by our words and actions is partial. You may have had the experience, for example, of behaving in a manner to reassure someone only to find that they were put off by your behavior. What our behavioral and vocal messages will activate in the other will vary according to circumstances and the individuals involved. This is one of the challenges of communication. As a third party, we may not know what is activated in the parties by the presence of the other, even as whatever is activated influences the party's behavior in the resolution process.

Case Example: I mediated a case involving two members of a Native Tribe in Oregon. One of the parties was a member of the Tribal Council (the central governance body) and the other a younger member of the Tribe. It was clearly apparent that issues of respect for an elder were activated in the communication dynamics. What was not apparent were the political dynamics between the families to which the two parties belonged. Each party's perception and experience of the other was colored by the activation of meaning matrices established over a long history of conflict and animosity between the two families, none of which had to do with the employment-related dispute that brought these two individuals to mediation. The projections and attributions derived from that history interfered with the parties' ability to resolve the current issues and to actually perceive who the other was in the present, free of that history. At one point in the mediation, a brief reference to the history was made. That proved to be the key that unlocked the impasse they were stuck in. By bringing the historical narrative to the surface, the parties were able to recognize and manage the neural activations that had been obstructing progress (though they didn't frame it in those terms) and distinguish between the family histories and their current conflict issues.

Emotions

We make a distinction between what we call "emotional" and "rational" responses only because our complex brain allows for what we call thinking, characterized by logic and reason. Because only mammals were seen to have neocortical regions of the brain and because thinking and reasoning were considered to be, if not exclusive to, at least more advanced in mammals, the conclusion was drawn that the cognitive processes of thinking and reasoning were exclusively mediated by the neocortex and emotions were relegated solely to the limbic system. This was the belief paradigm in the earlier part of the 20th century until it was discovered that damage to parts of the limbic system led to severe reduction in cognitive function. Gradually, the previous distinction assigning emotion to the limbic system and cognition to the neocortex broke down. As it turns out, the whole brain is involved in cognition and emotional response, the neocortical and limbic systems mutually engaged in the cognitive processing of perceptual experience (LeDoux, 2003).

There is also a tradition that claims that emotion and reason are in opposition and that to maintain control and to be able to make sound decisions, emotions should be minimized and rationality maximized (Churchland, 2002, p. 219ff.). Though this viewpoint has been largely abandoned, it continues to have its allure because of the nature of our internal experiences of emotion and thinking. Damasio (1999, pp. 41–42) expresses the understanding that the:

> Selective reduction of emotion is at least as prejudicial for rationality as excessive emotion. It certainly does not seem true that reason stands to gain from operating without the leverage of emotion. On the contrary, emotion probably assists reasoning, especially when it comes to personal and social matters involving risk and conflict.

He goes on to say (p. 42) that it's not that emotions are a substitute for reason or that we should decide solely on the basis of emotions:

> It is obvious that emotional upheavals can lead us to irrational decisions. The neurological evidence simply suggests that selective absence of emotion is a problem. Well-targeted and well-deployed emotion seems to be a support system without which the edifice of reason can not operate properly.

Patients whose ability to experience emotions has been destroyed by a brain tumor or injury have a very difficult time making decisions, even though their other cognitive capacities and their intelligence have not been impaired (Lehrer, 2009; Churchland, 2002). This kind of evidence reinforces the idea that decision processes have to take into account emotional needs and responses. If we don't know what we feel, we can't know what we want. If a party continues to feel some level of fear, doubt, or anger about a proposed agreement, this is likely an indication that more can be done to produce a more optimal resolution.

For good reason (pun not intended), mediation is seen as a rational process of problem-solving and the discipline has struggled with the question of what place emotions play in the process. We can't exclude emotions from the mediation room. Emotions will be involved unavoidably. While they can impede problem-solving if not addressed and managed, they can also provide useful information critical for crafting satisfactory and durable agreements. That said, there is no doubt that emotions can be difficult to deal with.

Our primary response to the world around us is at the visceral and feeling levels. It is only after the infant has reached a certain point of development that the capacity for rational thought is added to its response repertoire, and then only as an additional dimension of cognition, not separate from or independent of the visceral, emotional response to experience of the world. The neural circuits associated with what we call emotion are the first to respond to a given stimulus within the first few milliseconds of perception. It is on this basis first, prior to cognitive awareness of our perception, that we assess what the stimulus signals in terms of its meaning for our well-being. As Lack and Bogacz (2012, pp. 41–42) put it:

> The human brain will instinctively assess stimuli through emotions first, within the first few milliseconds of exposure to a stimulus (especially one creating feelings of fear), before the brain is able to have a cognitive appreciation of this emotion or stimulus . . . It is only after conscious awareness of a stimulus (after approximately half a second from original exposure to the stimulus) that a person is conscious of a stimulus, and can begin to self-regulate and try to overcome scripted patterns of behavior.

In conditions of threat, limbic responses will predominate and our ability to over-ride emotional responses through self-awareness and self-regulation will be reduced.

Particularly in conflict resolving efforts, we can tend to resist or avoid, either as parties or as a third party, the expression of emotions, believing that they will interfere with problem-solving and communication and fearing we will lose control. We know from personal experience and from observation that conflict involves some mix of fear, anger or rage, frustration, sadness, and despair. We often call these emotions "negative," probably because they don't feel good and because they can lead to undesirable and destructive behaviors and outcomes. But if they exist, if they arise in response to or in the context of a conflict relationship, they are better dealt with when accepted as legitimate than when denied or repressed as wrong, bad, or harmful. By changing the frame, we can diffuse their power to interfere with resolution. At the neural level, emotional circuits are always firing in the integrated brain. On the one hand, we want to moderate and manage their activity, to not let them overwhelm relational and communicational capacity. But on the other hand, ignoring or denying emotional responses will not make them go away and will likely interfere with or prevent sound decision-making and durable agreements.

Just as it is so that there is always an emotional component to any cognitive experience, so also is it true that neocortical regulation of emotions is always possible, given the right circumstances. By "opening the channels," so to speak, neural connections between the limbic system (and perhaps especially the amygdala) and the frontal cortex can be exploited. Interest-based negotiations and collaborative problem-solving approaches ask of parties that they apply neocortical oversight to the issues and relationships involved precisely in circumstances that tend to trigger heightened limbic system responses (fight/flight/freeze). Our challenge in collaborative conflict resolution processes is to achieve a balance between the identification, acknowledgement, and expression of emotional responses and the application of neocortical reason to the issues. There is often information embedded in emotional experience that, when accessed, can help the parties determine preferred decision-making. Our goal is to structure the conflict resolution process to allow emotions to be voiced without them being expressed as an attack on the other, without the other experiencing their expression as an attack, and without a party being overwhelmed by their experience of emotion.

There are two ways in which the expression of emotion can be experienced as an attack, one related to content and the other to form. In conflict situations, the expression of emotion is often framed as an attack against the other rather than an expression of personal experience. This is the content portion in which the expression of emotion is stated in terms that convey a message to the other, "You are bad, wrong, guilty, nasty, malicious, dishonest . . ." etc. It is also often the case that strong emotions expressed in the context of a conflict are made as statements and assertions of fact. In both instances, the other party will likely, if not necessarily, become defensive and may counter-attack with his or her own feelings, initiating an unproductive escalating cycle of emotional experience and expression that may have been preventing resolution of the issues at hand to begin with. Common conflict resolution practice speaks of the importance of "I statements," of not characterizing the other when expressing our own feelings and perceptions. Thinking about this in neural terms explains why the two approaches produce different results. In the case of personal attack, the listener has to defend against or exclude the incoming messages that do not fit well with established neural structures of self-definition. In the case of clear expression of personal experience that is owned, the listener is able to take in new information about the other. Of course, other dynamics can come into play when, for example, the listener doesn't believe what the speaker is saying about his or her emotions, in other words, when the incoming message conflicts with previously established neural meaning structures about the other, but that is another issue.

The term "venting" is often used in mediation to refer to a form of expression of emotion. The metaphor suggests a salutary release of pressure. But it also suggests a kind of uncontrolled and dangerous explosion that overwhelms both the speaker and the listener. The problems of the latter can outweigh the benefits of the former. Venting is not the most useful method of emotional expression when it activates feeling states from which the party cannot escape. Instead, the expression of emotion will be more useful when it is part of a revelatory process of inquiry and discovery in which the parties explore what is true for them about the issues at hand. We don't want the expression of emotion to reinforce neural pathways associated with the conflict impasse. Rather, we want to encourage neocortical recognition and expression of emotion avoiding limbic dominance that results in an experience of overwhelm, what is sometimes referred to as flooding, both terms useful euphemisms for what is happening at the neural level.

One approach to producing conditions favorable to the productive expression of emotions is normalizing the fact that parties have strong feelings about the issues at hand. With permission for their expression, they can then become part of the learning that is a necessary part of a conflict resolution process. Learning how we feel and how the other feels provides information that can help in the development of mutual understanding, one of the key objectives of a conflict res- olution process. It is often our fear of emotions that causes problems, and our fear of that fear. Only when emotions are named and acknowledged can they then be subject to self-regulation and used in the process of finding a way forward. Until they are named and acknowledged, they will tend to influence negotiations in non-constructive and unconscious ways. Denial or repression of emotions may be possible in the short term but may obstruct the achievement of satisfactory agreements or negatively impact the durability of agreements.

Expectancies Management

To remind, we meet each new moment on the basis of our experience to that point. That experience is encoded in neural matrices that are more or less suscep- tible to change in response to new experience according to the stability/plasticity balance.

We know that people have a tendency to reject information that contradicts their expectancies (confirmation bias). New information must be of a quality or kind that overcomes this resistance, or must be delivered by a trusted and influ- ential source, so that dismissal or denial is no longer as likely.[17] Even in those circumstances in which new information is delivered from a trusted source, there can be a disturbing impact on the party faced with having to accept the new information, especially when it confronts the party with the prospect of having to change deeply held beliefs. A party may experience a kind of hitting bottom in which the reorientation or reorganization necessary produces a loss of confi- dence or a kind of disequilibrium. As mediator, we can be sensitive to the fact that a party may need some form of reassurance, comfort, and support as he or she deals with the disorienting experience of taking in new information that not only doesn't conform with but may actually contradict the party's expectancies. Those moments of "Oh, I didn't know that" or "Really, is that true?" or "You mean what actually happened was . . .?" present boundaries that are not always easy to cross. The process of resolving a conflict involves these kinds of transi- tions; conflict resolution is about change.

Becoming aware of and acknowledging our expectancies, and the degree to which they may color our understanding of the present, requires a level of self-reflection and disclosure that can be difficult to cultivate and achieve, particularly within the context of a conflict relationship. Parties will embody a set of expectancies about the other party, about the conflict between them, or about the likelihood or possibility of achieving a satisfactory settlement, or any settlement at all, based on past experience with the other party or past life experience generally. Revealing those expectancies requires a level of self-disclosure that is not the norm in conflict relationship. We more typically keep hidden, from the other and sometimes even from ourselves, the assumptions we carry about the other party and the conflict situation while we act in accordance with those premises. See, for example, the extensive work being done on the phenomenon of implicit bias. Implicit bias is a reflection of the collection of neurally embedded expectancies created by our formative experiences, personal and socio-cultural. We are exposed to stereotypical cultural messages of the other that are then encoded in our neural meaning structures of knowledge. When our implicit biases are revealed to us,[18] we are often surprised when they don't match our self-description. "This is not who I am!" we might respond. And to a degree, our claim is accurate. This is not who we are, in one sense; the biases are not necessarily what we believe. But we have absorbed cultural messages, embedded in neural structures, that contribute to the full scope of our knowing and to our behavior. To remind, what we know is who we are. What we know is more than what we are aware of.

Attempting to uncover expectancies that may be influencing party engagement in the resolution process is working at a meta-level with the conflict, or what might be called a sublevel or meta-sublevel, trying to get beneath the conflict behaviors to some of the motivating elements of internal world-definition as they apply to the present conflict. This can be helpful to the degree that certain expectancies are influencing how the parties are engaging with each other in the conflict resolution process. If one party has certain expectancies about the other party or is pessimistic and unhopeful about the process based on past experience, it can be difficult to make progress without addressing those expectancies. Part of our work is uncovering those hidden barriers to resolution progress. This is not to say that direct attention to identifying and articulating expectancies is the only way to deal with them. Shifts can be achieved just through new experience with the other or positive experience within the conflict resolution process. But there can be instances when identifying and making explicit underlying assumptions can be helpful in breaking an impasse or opening a path for forward movement. Becoming consciously aware of expectancies that might be interfering with movement forward can allow parties to consider what might help them shift unhelpful expectancies to create conditions more conducive to a change in relationship and outcome.

There can be challenges or dangers, however, in attempting to uncover hidden expectancies that are negatively influencing the resolution process. For example, the expectancies may include some bias against or negative judgment or evaluation of the other that will be difficult for the target party to hear and deal with or that might take the conflict to a deeper level, complicating our efforts to resolve the dispute at hand. It is not so much a problem if the expectancy is something along the lines of, "I just don't believe we can solve this problem" or "I don't believe these things ever work out" or "We'll never get over the hurt" or "There aren't enough resources to fix this problem. It's zero sum and I'm going to lose." It can be more difficult for the other to hear something like, "I know he's dishonest and so I can't trust him" or "She's . . . and I've never liked their kind" or "All he's thinking about is the money, I'm sure of that." When these latter types of assumptions are unspoken, they will impede or undermine negotiating and problem-solving. But getting them out on the table risks further inflaming the conflict, or igniting new conflict. Somehow, we have to create the context in which the distinction is made between the parties' expectancies and current reality so that parties can share difficult information as puzzle pieces to work with in resolving the conflict problem.

We seek to encourage parties in these directions with some of our common prompting questions, without reference to neural system expectancy, when we ask, for example, about their experience interacting with the other party or parties historically, or when we try to uncover areas of mistrust and what the parties expect from the other, or how each party believes the other party perceives them, or how confident they feel that a good resolution can be achieved, and what they believe might be in the way of achieving resolution. Many questions that we commonly ask parties seek to get at expectancies that may be influencing the resolution process. A theoretical understanding of expectancy and the impact of expectancies on current perception may lead us to paying more attention to helping parties become aware of and articulate what they bring to their interaction with each other. And providing the parties with the theory of neural expectancy and activation may make it easier for them to risk the vulnerability that accompanies awareness and honest expression of expectancy biases, and may help parties be less reactive to the articulation of the other's expectancies.

Priming

As discussed earlier, priming is always happening. We are primed one way or another by all our perceptual experiences, conscious and unconscious. Each new set of perceptual experiences erases or reduces the priming effects of the immediately preceding perceptual experience.

A Google search of priming in mediation will produce a long list of articles. We know that our words, our behavior, and the setting of our mediation office will prime the parties. However, there are limits to how much control or management of priming is possible. To the degree that priming is used as a tool in mediation, it is not an exact science. Beyond some general assumptions about words and behaviors that are likely to be conducive to collaborative work, we can't be sure what words will have what priming effect for a given individual.

The room, the location, the time of day, or the season will be primes for the parties, but in ways we can't predict or know. Our physical behavior, when working with parties in conflict, will influence them. Perhaps I will sit forward to express focused attention or perhaps I will sit back to express relaxation or to provide a party with the experience of space, comforting and safe. We know that our posture (how open or closed), our facial expression (smiling or tense), and our breathing (relaxed and deep or rapid and shallow) will affect the parties. But not only will the degree of effect vary, but the direction of effect is uncertain, dependent upon how our behavior is experienced by the other. Because the priming effects of our behaviors as third party are not always obvious, when we are unsure about our influence, sometimes the best approach is to ask. Asking can build trust and model good communication.

Dealing with Values Conflicts

That values conflicts are especially difficult to resolve is common knowledge. An understanding of the neural basis of consciousness can help us understand why this is so. Value-based conflicts are more deeply embedded in the neural architecture of identity than, for example, resource conflicts that will be encoded at more superficial levels of identity.

Values conflicts are about who we are whereas resource conflicts are about external matters. Certainly, the outcome of a resource conflict can have significant survival or well-being implications, and resource issues can be tied to values concerns, as is the case, for example, in the Israel/Palestine conflict. In that case, conflict over land is a conflict over identity, as well. The division of money or property can involve fairness values and rights issues. Though resources are external to the self, their meaning can be a significant part of self-definition and self-viability. But at the neural level, values and moral/ethical imperatives are more deeply woven into the construction of self and world-view than are resource perceptions. This is why it is easier to compromise, to yield, or to make tradeoffs in resource conflicts than it is in values conflicts. Shifting from a values-based position requires a greater or deeper alteration of the neural latticework of self. Additionally, as Kouzakova et al (2014) note, to abandon or revise a values-based position also risks rejection or exclusion by one's in-group that is a part of one's extended neural self-identity construct. Part of our job as practitioners is to help the parties determine to what degree the conflict as it is understood threatens identity as it involves values-based elements. If the parties are not aware of or have not identified the values-based elements, they will be driven by them without understanding the source of the conflict impasse or difficulty.

Kouzakova et al (2014) distinguish between threat and challenge motivational states in response to conflict, the former characterized by the belief that one has insufficient resources to deal with the demands of the situation and the latter by the belief that one has sufficient resources to deal with the demands of the situation. Research demonstrates that the threat state results in low cardiac output and high vascular resistance whereas the challenge state is accompanied by high cardiac output and low vascular resistance. People in a values conflict will show a stronger cardiovascular threat profile compared to people in a resource conflict. Kouzakova et al go on to discuss two types of goals, safety and security on one hand and attainment and growth on the other, the former characterized by a prevention focus in which people guard against loss and the latter by a promotion focus in which people aim to reach desired goals and are more willing to risk in order to achieve those goals. Kouzakova et al report that research has shown that those with a prevention focus are less open to change, and, relatedly, more risk averse. Their research indicates that those involved in a values-based conflict will revert to a prevention orientation, making reaching a resolution to the conflict more difficult.

Given this, it is important to determine whether there are values dimensions to a conflict that seems at first to be about resources or other external issues (for example, contract interpretation, scheduling coordination, activity preferences, strategic planning, etc.). A values conflict will involve a stronger threat state and prevention-focused conflict response strategies whereas a resource conflict will tend towards a stronger challenge state and promotion-focused conflict response strategies. Of course, it is possible that, if both parties are experiencing a challenge state of goal pursuit, the conflict could shift to behaviors perceived as threats.

Harinck and Van Kleef (2012, cited in Kouzakova, et al, 2014) demonstrated that when people face an angry counterpart, they tend to give a more defensive reaction in a values conflict than in a resource conflict. When the other party in a values conflict expresses anger, people remain more firm in their position, become angrier themselves, and are less willing to yield than when anger is expressed in a resource conflict.

Conflicts that involve values are another instance in which explicit party education may help parties better deal with their cognitive and behavioral responses.

Somatic Interventions

With the premise that there is no separation between mind and body, with mind inherently of the body, the experience of conflict will be a corporal as well as a psychological phenomenon, or, to put it another way, the psychological is corporal, only experienced differently. The linking is evident, for example, in the presence of elevated heart rate, perspiration, and the physical responses of flight, fight, or freeze in conflict circumstances. This suggests that there are opportunities to help people cope with and find their way through the thicket of conflict via somatic as well as intellectual/verbal interventions. Somatic interventions by themselves will not be sufficient to resolve conflicts. Parties must apply their thinking skills and must communicate with each other to solve their problems. But since conflict experience will involve the body unavoidably, somatic interventions can provide significant supplementary support to the conflict resolution process.

There is a growing literature on the adverse effects of stress on our ability to engage well in relationship.[19] Studies of stress response demonstrate a negative impact on cognitive capacity as well as on physical health. In a state of poorly managed stress, and more extremely in conditions of neural flooding, we are less able to process information, to understand what someone is saying, and to engage in creative problem-solving. In response to the threats experienced in conflict, our bodies will tend to tighten. Techniques that increase relaxation will improve parties' ability to self-regulate and to engage with the other during the more stressful portions of a resolution process. Loosening body tightness will loosen the mind's tightness. As Tucker (2007, p. 77) puts it:

> Interestingly, it often seems that a reflective mental process requires a certain degree of relaxation; the anxiety of worrying about things engages not only a focused mode of attention but the motor system and muscle tension as spontaneous side effects as well. Apparently because of the mechanistic link of anxiety with the motor system of the anterior brain, relaxing muscle tension serves to decrease anxiety and allow a broader, more aesthetic mode of awareness.

Body awareness can help parties identify fear or other responses, and this awareness can provide information helpful to their resolution process. Interventions will depend on circumstances and mediator style. A mediator might suggest, "How about we all stand up and move around a bit, shake out some of the tension?" or "Shall we take a stretch break?" Just taking a break, perhaps a bathroom break, to allow calming when a party experiences neural flooding is a somatic intervention. In multi-party public policy/environmental negotiations, the physical activity of site visits and walk-abouts are known to create windows of negotiating opportunity. It's known that intentional breathing can reduce some of the somatic symptoms of stress response and improve cognitive function in stressful circumstances.[20] Suggesting that the parties take time to breathe and pay attention to their breathing can help them create delay in their activated responses to the conflict stimuli, allowing them to be better able to reflect, consider, and listen.

Generally, what are referred to as mindfulness practices will help parties be more effective in a resolution, agreement-building, decision-making process. An increasing amount of attention has been given to this subject in the conflict resolution literature over the past several years.[21] However, the introduction of mindfulness understandings and practices into conflict management and negotiation training has been minimal, perhaps due to constraints that restrict inclusion of information from the relevant multi-disciplinary source material available, and also, perhaps, because of uncertainties about the limits of professional identity and qualifications. Practitioners may feel uncomfortable introducing interventions that have not been a part of standard practice, or may feel incompetent to incorporate and manage body-based or mindfulness interventions. And parties may be resistant to intentional and explicit somatically based interventions that run counter to their expectations for the process. Though it might be helpful to identify areas of tension in the body and to work with the parties to relieve those tensions, both the parties and the third party may be hesitant to explore such approaches. That said, the reality of somatic involvement in the conflict experience and the impact of stress on cognitive and relational capacities suggests this is an area ripe for further investigation by the practitioner community and an opportunity to broaden practitioner training (see, for example, Riskin, 2004).

Aside from helping parties access and employ stress-relieving and stress-management practices to improve their engagement in the resolution process, mediators can be more intentional with their interventions based on understanding the body's involvement in cognitive experience. For example, in listening to a party talk about particularly difficult aspects of their conflict situation, perhaps some painful consequences of the conflict or injuries that have resulted, the mediator's empathic response might include, at the conclusion of the party's telling of the story, a deep inhale and then exhale of recognition, with sympathetic nodding of the head, a breathing technique that can evoke in the speaker an experience of being understood and can elicit or produce a degree of physical relief or release. Sometimes, such empathic intervention by the mediator will trigger the release of emotion and tears that can be an important part of the resolution process.

Beyond any particular body-based intervention that a mediator might use to help parties deal with their stress, awareness of his or her own somatic state will improve practice. The mediator may feel stress in response to the challenge of finding and applying effective interventions and is also exposed to the stressful interactions between the parties, perhaps experiencing reactive responses to some of the subject matter or the behaviors of the parties. Somatic awareness and intentional, conscious breathing will allow the mediator to be more cognitively creative, agile, and resilient.

Process Design Considerations

Caucusing

One of the key mediation process design questions is whether and when to caucus (to meet separately with the each of the parties rather than in joint session). Some mediators practice almost exclusively in the caucus model while others eschew caucusing entirely or almost entirely. Party expectations in some sectors of practice influence whether caucusing is used or not. In some sectors of practice, caucusing seems to be on the rise and joint sessions on the wane.[22] Drawbacks and benefits of caucusing for both the mediator and the parties have been widely discussed and analyzed, the costs and benefits sometimes appearing at cross-purposes for mediator and parties. Whichever approach one favors, and for whatever reasons, the neural perspective helps to illuminate the stark contrasts between the two.

Both caucusing and face-to-face meetings present a two-edged sword. On the one hand, direct perception of one's conflict adversary can activate neural circuits established during the history of conflict between the parties, interfering with settlement efforts. On the other hand, separation of the parties can mean that old perceptions will persist in the absence of new information directly perceived in interaction with the other party or parties. In the caucus scenario, the mediator will carry information from party A to party B that party B may have difficulty taking in without filtering its meaning through the neural networks of past unhappy experience. Even favorable information delivered by the mediator will have to be incorporated into or reconciled with previously established neural structures without the benefit of more direct new information in the present that might amend or restructure established beliefs or understandings. Caucusing will attenuate the ability of parties to shift their perception of the other; the past may remain more frozen in neural structures in the absence of the other's presence. There is no opportunity for the "warming up" to each other that can happen through direct contact, and not much opportunity to change the stories embedded in their neural networks or to create new stories based on new experience with the other. Faces are emotionally expressive and are a primary transmitter of relational information across the social divide. The presence or absence of direct facial cues will be significant, one way or the other.

Mediators often talk about the challenges involved in being the go-between in a caucus process. Parties are having to deal with neural activations in response to the mediator who carries messages from the other side as well as with the activations elicited by the content of the delivered message or offer. The dynamics of perception can become more perturbed and confusing in the shuttle diplomacy circumstance. The parties have no direct information from the other party and will fill in the blanks based on past experience as they attempt to make sense of present offers. This can be a less than ideal situation and particularly unsatisfactory in cases in which there will be an ongoing relationship. Awareness of the neural basis of party experience may help the mediator decide whether or not to use caucusing in a given situation and understand the nature of the challenges he or she and the parties face in either scenario.

Online Asynchronous Mediation

In today's world, conflict resolution processes frequently take place via digital media in asynchronous or synchronous Internet-based negotiations. Often these are text-based only, though video links are becoming more widely used. There are efficiency benefits in using online communication tools. The need to travel is removed. Parties have more time to consider asynchronous messages before responding and more time to carefully craft proposals. In text only communication, the danger of in-the-heat-of-the-moment reactivity is reduced. But as with caucusing, perceptual cues are reduced so drastically that misunderstandings, misinterpretations, and negative or inaccurate projections are even more difficult to avoid than in more standard relational settings. In the absence of richer perceptual information, written words are more likely to activate an internal tone within the reader that might be quite different from the tone intended by the writer, and in a conflict situation of low trust, antipathy, or poor past experience with the other party, it's likely that there will be little match between the two. Some of the same benefits and shortcomings involved in caucusing apply to text-based, asynchronous online communication settings, with maybe more opportunity to cool down or to take time to absorb messages in the online setting. As with caucusing, in separated online interactions, parties will not be triggered by the direct perceptual experience of in-person contact, but they lose opportunities to build new, more positive relational experience.

One of the questions a mediator and parties might ask themselves, in considering whether to use either model, caucusing or online interaction, is how likely it is that the parties will be able to improve communication and relationship dynamics in face-to-face meetings, and also how necessary it will be to continue in an ongoing relationship that will require in-person contact in the post-resolution period.

Site Visits

One of the tried and true interventions in multi-party environmental/public policy collaborative negotiations is a site visit, a group trip made by members of the negotiating table to a location at stake in the negotiations. A forest collaborative will visit a site being considered for selective harvest. Water management negotiators will visit irrigated farmland, a dammed river system for which in-stream flow is being negotiated, or a development site and neighborhood community. In neural terms, site visits provide a common perceptual experience for the parties. That's not to say that the perceptual experience won't activate different meaning associations in each of the parties. But they will at least have a common point of reference, one grounded in a shared external reality to which they can tie their various meaning responses. It is not uncommon that ostensible adversaries at the negotiation table report relational bonding in the common experience of a site visit.

Case Example: In negotiations to build consensus for a hydroelectric facility FERC (Federal Energy Regulatory Commission) relicensing application, I remember the impact of taking a tour of the site with the negotiators (state and federal resource agency staff, local elected officials, the corporate utility operator of the dam, and other interested parties). At one point, walking

(continued)

(continued)

beside a fish ladder leading up and around the dam, we looked down into the concrete channel to see a large salmon some six or more feet below us caught in a pool with not enough water in the system to allow it to continue its journey. The impression was stronger than any words could have conveyed. The image persisted in the minds of the negotiators when they returned to the negotiation table and contributed to galvanizing the parties' motivation to find a sound agreement that traded recreational water behind the dam for sufficient and timely water release for the downstream fishery and healthy riparian habitat, while taking into account power generation needs. The common experience linked the parties together across their different backgrounds and negotiation objectives. They shared the picture of that fish and knew each other more intimately as a result.

Including an Educational Phase

In multi-party, public collaborative negotiation processes, a common process design approach includes five major phases: an assessment phase to determine whether the conditions are suitable for proceeding and how best to proceed; an organizational phase bringing the parties together and preparing the ground work for the negotiations; an educational phase prior to the subsequent negotiation/agreement building, and implementation phases. The educational phase is innovative and often critical for the success of a negotiation. One would expect the educational content to have to do with the substantive subject matter involved in the negotiations, technical and scientific issues, historical background, contextual limitations and opportunities, etc., and those are certainly common and key agenda components. But education about problem-solving, agreement-building, and negotiation skills necessary to participate effectively in a collaborative resolution process can be just as important to the success of the negotiations.

Education about substantive subject matter in multi-party public dispute-resolving or decision-making processes includes what is often termed joint fact-finding (JFF) by which we attempt to avoid adversarial science and the right vs. wrong battle of experts. Instead, we involve the parties in a process to build common understandings of the technical and scientific data that bear on the disputed issues with neutral or independent sources sufficiently trusted by all the parties. A JFF process attempts to address, though typically not explicitly, the various characteristics of neural function I've been discussing: attachment to established neural structures of meaning; the link between what we know and who we are; resistance, in conflict circumstances, to replacing or amending established neural structures with new perceptual information; perceptual tendencies such as confirmation bias and naïve realism, and so on. Educating the parties about the neural dynamics would likely help them grapple with and better understand their internal experience as new information (new perceptual stimuli) meets established beliefs, understandings, and commitments.

Case Example: In the face of a changing energy market, a public electric utility was faced with the prospect of changing its rate structure. Its current volumetric pricing structure (pricing based on electricity consumption) was becoming an unviable business model as consumer shifts to natural gas and solar, changing conservation habits and more energy efficient appliances, heating systems, and building codes, and other factors reduced per capita electricity consumption. Capital and grid costs would have to be covered increasingly through some combination of basic and delivery charges. Any new billing configuration would affect the various consumer constituencies in different ways. Issues of social equity and fairness between low- and high-income groups and low- and high-energy users were in play. The utility had been previously met with harsh community response when it had last proposed an increased basic charge. Rather than once again pursuing a decide, announce, and defend strategy, the utility convened a panel of citizens to deeply delve into the technical details and tradeoffs of various pricing models and to come up with a recommendation for the utility leadership and board to consider. Selection of panel members intentionally included a mix of perspectives and interests. Over the course of several months and many meetings, the panel members educated themselves and were educated by staff, reading documents and receiving presentations from several sources. At the last meeting, the members talked about the process and what their experience had been. One of the members spoke for many when he talked about how he had arrived with some strong beliefs about the issues of basic and delivery charges and tiered pricing but found his beliefs changed by the end of their work, much to his surprise. Two things are notable: 1) this member talked about how resistant he'd been to changing his views over the course of the meetings and how uncomfortable it had felt to him to find the information changing his mind, and 2) the shift in his perspectives was made possible by a JFF process that provided information in an extended experience, and in consultation with others, sufficient to change his mind (change his neural structures). Without such a process, he would likely have remained committed to his views. Members of the general public could not be provided with a similar experience and the challenge then remained how to convey some of the panel's experience to the public when the new rate structure was to be announced.

Linking Progress at the Negotiating Table to Represented Constituencies

In a multi-party process in which the people at the table represent constituencies away from the table, shifting or restructuring the neural understandings of the negotiators can be difficult enough. But with success at the table achieving some consensus agreements, we must address the fact that members of the represented constituencies have not experienced the negotiating table process that produced change in the neural structures of the negotiators. In some cases, those represented, an agency or a corporate player for example, will accept the conclusions and decisions of their negotiator, ratifying whatever agreements were reached at the table. But in other cases, work must be done to duplicate, to one degree or another, the shifts experienced by the negotiators in the neural understandings of those represented. This becomes a process design question as negotiators ask what mechanisms might be used to accomplish the task of bringing their constituencies up to speed with the movement achieved at the negotiating table. There are many options (fish-bowl open meetings, various public involvement techniques, presentations to the home office, mediated consensus-building discussions within a constituency, etc.) but whatever approach is used, recognition of the neural basis of everyone's experience will help to provide rationale for strategic decisions.

> Case Example: A California county was experiencing a contentious dispute over erosion control and riparian setbacks as the local burgeoning wine industry increased its pace of planting vines on ever-steeper hillsides. In response to the fact that the County Board of Supervisors was facing pressures to create a new erosion control ordinance, wine industry representatives and environmental constituency leaders agreed to meet to see if they could reach consensus on the parameters of and draft language for an ordinance, each group fearful that, if left to the Board of Supervisors, the result would not serve their interests. Negotiations were initiated with representatives from each constituency, selected farmers, wine makers, and environmental leaders. As draft agreements were crafted and considered at the negotiating table, conflicts and disagreements arose within the represented constituencies. The environmental constituency was especially not unified or monolithic. Some members were distrustful of the negotiation process itself. Others didn't trust that the individuals at the table would adequately represent and protect their interests. Others were concerned about what they perceived to be unacceptable and coercive power imbalances. Some believed they could better achieve their goals with a public information campaign to influence an upcoming election or, if necessary, with litigation. But a significant element of the environmental community

believed that the growth momentum of the wine industry made continuing development inevitable and that collaborative partnership to seek mutual gains was the most efficient and effective way to achieve their goals. At the table, initial suspicion and distrust between the environmental and industry representatives began to shift. Trust and mutual respect grew as each side recognized and acknowledged the legitimate goals of the other. Concessions were accepted by the industry representatives and ways to expand the pie were identified. The details and language for a mutually agreed-upon ordinance were drafted for submission to the Board of Supervisors, which had agreed to adopt any specifics on which the parties could achieve consensus, as long as those satisfied other criteria to which the Board was responsible. In order to avoid anticipated opposition that threatened to block the agreements reached at the negotiating table, an effort was initiated, with the help of the process facilitator, to bridge the divides within the environmental community, creating a parallel process within the diverse environmental community to address concerns and reservations and produce consensus support for proposals at the negotiating table, an effort that was ultimately successful. Without work done away from the table, progress at the table would likely have been lost.

Notes

1 See, for example, a number of discussions of the issue at www.mediate.com and the first page or two of the 357,000 results, as accessed June 6, 2017, that come up in a Google search for "mediator neutrality."
2 See, for example, discussion in Liebman (2000).
3 See, for example, Lang and Taylor (2000); LeBaron and Patera (2009); Fisher (2003); Bowling and Hoffman (2000); Schön (1983); Argyris and Schön (1996) [1978]; Johns and Burnie (2013) [2000].
4 On this point, see Gary Friedman's (2015) book *Inside Out: How conflict professionals can use self-reflection to help their clients.*
5 A sense of control, of being in control, is felt to be favorable. We strongly prefer the experience of being in control. For some discussion of this and some research illustrating the trait, see, for example, Hood (2012, pp. 167–168).
6 See, as an example, David Rand, professor of psychology, economics, and management at Yale, talk at http://edge.org/conversation/david_rand. In his work looking at the question of what can be done to increase cooperative rather than selfish behavior, Rand asks, "How do you change people's minds about what's right?" Note his terminology, "*change* people's *minds*." To remind, this is a literal not just a figurative event.
7 BATNA is an acronym for "best alternative to a negotiated agreement," meaning the parties' beliefs about the best options available to them for resolving their dispute outside the negotiation process. See Fisher et al (2011).
8 As quoted at https://www.brainpickings.org/2014/05/13/backfire-effect-mcraney
9 As found at www.dictionary.com/browse/agreement?s=t
10 I thank Peter Adler for sharing, pre-publication, his thorough and wise discussion of the controversy, from which I drew my understanding of its history and current status. For his complete account, see Adler (forthcoming).

11 See research papers at https://www.ncbi.nlm.nih.gov/pmc/articles/PMC2737341/ and https://www.ncbi.nlm.nih.gov/pmc/articles/PMC3406601/

12 See, for example, the use of the term "looping" for this type of mediator intervention in Carrie Menkel-Meadow et al (2006, pp. 225–226): "The essence of looping is a genuine commitment of the mediator to understanding each party and demonstrating that understanding."

13 Blaise Pascal spoke on this point in his Pensées when he said, "When we wish to correct with advantage, and to show another that he errs, we must notice from what side he views the matter, for on that side it is usually true, and admit that truth to him, but reveal to him the side on which it is false. He is satisfied with that, for he sees that he was not mistaken, and that he only failed to see all sides. Now, no one is offended at not seeing everything; but one does not like to be mistaken, and that perhaps arises from the fact that man naturally cannot see everything, and that naturally he cannot err in the side he looks at, since the perceptions of our senses are always true" (as quoted in https://www.brainpickings.org/2015/05/20/blaise-pascal-pensees-persuasion/?mc_cid=3cb3d8ae73&mc_eid=13eb06771e).

14 Note the comment in an article on climate change messaging: "The results demonstrate that communication approaches that take account of individuals' personal points of reference (e.g., based on an understanding and appreciation of their values, attitudes, beliefs, local environment, and experiences) are more likely to meaningfully engage individuals with climate change" (available at http://grist.org/climate-energy/the-brutally-dishonest-attacks-on-showtimes-landmark-climate-series/?utm_source=outbrain&utm_medium=web&utm_campaign=outbrain-trending).

15 "Amygdala hijack" is a term coined by Daniel Goleman in his 1996 book *Emotional Intelligence: Why It Can Matter More Than IQ*. Drawing on the work of Joseph LeDoux, Goleman uses the term to describe emotional responses from people which are immediate and overwhelming, and out of measure with the actual stimulus because it has triggered a much more significant emotional threat (from https://en.wikipedia.org/wiki/Amygdala_hijack).

16 "conscious consideration of an internal state, via the orbital medial prefrontal and anterior cingulate cortices, allows us to modulate our emotions and alter our state of mind . . . self-awareness [is] able to change the brain" (Cozolino, 2014, p. 57).

17 "we can continue to learn rapidly and stably about new experiences throughout life by matching bottom-up signal patterns from more peripheral to more central brain processing stages against top-down signal patterns from more central to more peripheral processing stages. These top-down signals represent the brain's learned expectations of what the bottom-up signal patterns should be, based upon past experience. The matching process is designed to reinforce and amplify those combinations of features in the bottom-up pattern that are consistent with the top-down expectations and to suppress those features that are inconsistent. This top-down matching step initiates the process whereby the brain selectively pays attention to experiences that it expects, binds them into coherent internal representations through resonant states, and incorporates them through learning into its knowledge about the world" (Grossberg, 1999, p. 13).

18 Through, for example, the Harvard implicit bias testing program available at https://implicit.harvard.edu/implicit/takeatest.html. But also see the critique of Harvard's Implicit Association Test at http://nymag.com/scienceofus/2017/01/psychologys-racism-measuring-tool-isnt-up-to-the-job.html

19 See, for example Bullock (2016); and Gottman and Silver (1999).

20 "By slowing down our rate of respiration and elongating our exhalation, we can activate the vagal brake, and volitionally elicit the relaxation response. Once this response is initiated and the PNS (parasympathetic nervous system) is dominant, we cease to be governed by the brain's fear circuitry that limits our capacity to effectively think, plan,

reason and respond to others (Brown & Gerbarg 2012). This means we are no longer subject to a narrow range of thoughts, feelings, and perceptions or limited to defensive or escape behaviors (Brown & Gerbarg 2012). In other words, intentional breathing decreases the stress response and increases cognitive and behavioral flexibility, which enhances our ability to be mindfully present in relationships" (Bullock, 2016, p. 19).

21 See, for example, LeBaron and Patera (2009), in which the authors emphasize the importance of understanding and including the psychological foundations of negotiation in training and practice; Fisher (2003); Bowlingand Hoffman (2000); and Friedman (2015).

22 Note research reported by Jay Folberg in his March, 2016 article "The Shrinking Joint Session: Survey Results," available at: www.mediate.com/articles/FolbergJointSession.cfm

6

IMPLICATIONS FOR TRAINING

Preparing practitioners to work with people in conflict is an evolving discipline. For many years, education was available in 25- or 32- or 40-hour trainings and supplemental 8- or 16-hour intermediate or advanced trainings. Quarter- or semester-long undergraduate courses in communication, negotiation, and related subjects began to appear at the undergraduate level. The first Master's degree program was created in 1984 at George Mason University. During my tenure as the first director of the conflict resolution Master's degree program at the University of Oregon between 2006 and 2014, I perpetually felt the constraints that even a two-year program presented on covering the rich wealth of material relevant to conflict understanding and conflict resolution practice. The training of mediators in Austria ranges from 220 to 360 hours of formal instruction and practice, much of which focuses on the psychological dimensions of conflict and communication. This length of time is better than the average 30 to 40 hours of basic training for mediators in the United States, but remains much less than a graduate program. The graduate program at the University of Oregon, substantial as it was in comparison, had only one required course devoted to the psychology of conflict. So the first thing to be said about training conflict workers is that it would be good if we could expand the curriculum and the time devoted to preparing people to work with individuals and systems in conflict.

However extensive the education and training of conflict resolution professionals may become, learning will always be ongoing beyond the limits of a particular academic program or applied training. Conflict understanding is a life-long venture as we continue to mature and reflect upon the challenges of human social relationship. That said, within the practical limitations that we face in any educational program, how might conflict training be adjusted to take into account the neural perspective? A few thoughts:

- Place some emphasis on the emergence of conflict resolution theory and practice within the arc of human history in order to provide a developmental framing for the work we are doing. Conflict resolution seeks to change society and how we manage our social relations in circumstances of conflict. This is no small project. Recognition of the scope and reach of the enterprise will help students understand the importance of the endeavor they are joining.
- Include a foundational component devoted to the basic realities of the human as organism seeking to survive in the three realms, physical, psychological, and social. Grounding their work with people in an understanding of the primal pressures, needs, and fears that parties experience in their lives and that are heightened in conditions of conflict will help practitioners cultivate greater empathy and, consequently, more sensitive practice.
- Devote a substantial training segment to the human organism's neural encoding function that is the basis of learning, memory, cognition, and identity. Not being explicitly aware of the physical basis of our consciousness experience keeps us somewhat in the dark in trying to understand the behaviors we work with. The neural framing can help to normalize conflict, can help to identify and explain some sources or causes of conflict, can make sense of why some conflicts are difficult to resolve or prevent, and can help provide a firm theoretical basis for many of the interventions we teach. Most fundamentally, we work with a particular type of living organism, the human being. The more we understand the nature of the organism and how it functions, the better able we will be to work effectively with it.
- Place more emphasis on the determinative role the stories that people embody about themselves and the world play in human relational behavior. Recognizing that encoded perceptual experience forms our knowledge of the world can help students reflect on their own stories and how past formative experience conditions expectancies, projections, perceptions, and biases.
- Devote more time to a consideration of the nature of meaning, philosophically and biologically, since differences in meaning are at the core of conflict.
- Look for opportunities to further develop the repertoire of approaches and interventions that take into account the neural roots of consciousness experience. There is more work to be done here.
- Engage students in discussions about the responsibility, opportunities, and limits to disseminate conflict understanding to the broader community, to increase social capacity to deal more constructively with conflict, to improve social wisdom. Encourage them to consider how they might develop content and delivery models for public distribution.

- Devote more time to an understanding of culture as a neural construct.
- Explore the ways in which collaborative conflict resolution processes and what we ask of parties in such processes run counter to some fundamental functional aspects of our neuropsychology in order that students better understand the barriers we and parties face in resolving and preventing conflicts.

The specifics of design and content for each of these training components are beyond the scope of this book but offer an exciting and creative curriculum development challenge.

7
CONCLUSION

What we call "interest-based negotiations" and "collaborative problem solving" or, more simply, mediation, can be perceived by parties as risky or threatening for a number of reasons. Resorting to positional litigation can feel safer and easier than entering into a collaborative process of uncertain outcome in which one must take responsibility for the conflict and its resolution. It's not that the outcomes of litigation are not also uncertain and unknown, but we enter into that arena ready to fight with the security of our strongly held positions, positions that we are determined to believe are right, illusory or as wrong-headed as that may be. In conditions of conflict, this kind of certainty is comforting as our neural reality constructs are asserted. Entering into interest-based negotiations requires that we be willing to soften our certainties and be open to perspectives or understandings or ideas different from those we hold and that comprise part of our identity. In the litigation setting, we aim at a known outcome, a win, with our swords drawn and our shields held high, even though we can't be sure we'll receive the outcome we desire, whereas in an interest-based process, we are asked to lay down our weapons of offense and defense, to not know together, and to jointly find an outcome that is undefined to begin with.

As a third party, it can be helpful to understand the neural basis for the resistance parties may experience entering into a collaborative, interest-based conflict resolution process. We believe that, in providing third-party assistance, we offer a good product, a beneficial service, and assume therefore that parties should welcome or, at least, be receptive to the opportunity to resolve their dispute in the framework that mediation, for example, offers. Understanding the neural basis for resistance that parties may experience can help third parties pay more attention to what may be needed to bring parties to the table and to help them participate effectively once they are at the table.

Much of what we expect of the parties in mediation runs counter to the neural experience of people in conflict. Mediation proposes that each party sees only part of the picture, when the parties want to believe that they know the truth. Mediation asks parties to see the issues from the other's point of view, when each wants to believe that they see the situation accurately. Mediation promotes the concurrent legitimacy of different points of view, when each wants to believe that they are right and the other is wrong. Mediation asks parties to move from an either/or to a both/and approach and to relinquish their perception of the other as the enemy. A basic premise of mediation is that the parties will pursue solutions on the basis of mutual needs rather than on independent strategies designed solely to satisfy individual self-interest. Mediation asks parties to actively listen to points of view with which they are in strong disagreement and suggests that it is possible to really listen and understand without necessarily agreeing (and therefore losing one's own point of view). Mediation asks parties to move from the security of strongly held positions to the discomfort and uncertainty of focusing on interests. Mediation encourages parties to creatively engage in building solutions that might be quite different from the solution they had in mind, and to engage in that collaborative problem-solving and agreement-building process with those with whom they have been in sharp disagreement, perhaps even with those whom they have injured or by whom they have been injured. Each of these process expectations runs counter to the default neural dynamics of people in conflict. In some ways, adversarial approaches are a better match with and more comfortably suit our neural experience in conflict circumstances, while consensus-building with our adversaries is at odds with some of our immediate, neurally based responses to conflict. Collaborative conflict resolution demands that we overcome or moderate some of our core neural tendencies in our efforts to construct a joint reality in the face of conflicting beliefs, beliefs that are incarnate in our neural structures.

The work of the conflict resolution field is a bit of a lifting-ourselves-up-by-our-bootstraps project in that we conflict workers are human beings trying to help other human beings be better human beings with each other while we are subject ourselves to the same perceptual and cognitive foibles as are the parties we work with. And we're asking the parties we work with to overcome tendencies and responses that arise from the realities of their physical makeup. The solution to any bootstrap problem is to get help from others. The good news is that we can learn to reduce, prevent, and better manage conflict. Conflict workers can't accomplish resolution for the parties on our own. We are not solely responsible for relational and communicational improvements in a conflict relationship. We work with the parties, not on the parties.

Let's remember that we came out of the caves not so very long ago. We marveled and were afraid. We were vulnerable. We did not understand. We gathered in our in-groups for safety and security, for meaning and belonging. We distrusted and competed with out-groups. Within our in-groups, we contended with power dynamics and sought control. We were compelled to know our environment. We invented. We developed civilizations. We have come a long way, even as we are, in some ways, very much kin to our ancestors. We have progressed on so many knowledge fronts, yet we continue to exhibit much violence among ourselves and with our environment. Our social experience continues to be a mix of cooperation and competition. We have become very powerful with our technologies. We remain weak and afraid and vulnerable.

The state of public discourse today, along with the wars and violence that express the worst of our dominance traits, exhibits in stark relief our propensities in the face of disagreement. Divisions and adversarial polarization in our public discourse can seem to have become worse[1] and perhaps have, though it is difficult to measure and compare with past years, decades, or centuries. But the fundamental roots of vehement and exclusionary disagreement go deep and have been with us from our early beginnings. It's difficult to tell whether present conditions exacerbate underlying internal causes. Whatever the case, certainly our neural function hasn't changed much over the past several millennia. Improving how we respond to differences is not a simple matter.

So much of our conflict behavior is and has been to our detriment, though driven by survival motives and arising from the mix of environmental pressures and our nature. We have been asking ourselves for a few thousand years why we behave as we do with each other and how we can make more just and peaceful societies. It does seem that we are struggling to find more collaborative, less adversarial, and less violent ways to manage our social decision-making. Despite the often-grim daily news from around the planet, there's an argument to be made that the human species is evolving in a generally positive direction, at both the biological and the socio-cultural levels, learning to live together less violently and more cooperatively.[2] Self-knowledge is not simple or easy. But, as I suggested at the beginning of this discussion, there is perhaps something promising in the activities of the species over the recent past, our aspirations and efforts to establish more inclusive democratic political structures, to base social relations on concepts and practices of human and civil rights, to design and implement more equitable justice systems, the advances and revelations in social science research, the appearance and development of the conflict resolution field itself, and the incipient adventure into the workings of the human brain that is the source of our consciousness experience and behavior.

Data from the Human Genome Project suggest that:

> Genetic evolution *greatly accelerated* during the last 50,000 years. The rate at which genes changed in response to selection pressures began rising around 40,000 years ago, and the curve got steeper and steeper after 20,000 years ago. Genetic change reached a crescendo during the Holocene era, in Africa as well as in Eurasia.
>
> *(Haidt, 2013, p. 250)*

The Holocene is the last 12,000 years or so, not such a long time when seen as only 120 of your lifetimes if you were to live to 100. As Haidt asks (2013, p. 251):

> If genetic evolution was able to fine-tune our bones, teeth, skin, and metabolism in just a few thousand years as our diets and climates changed, how could genetic evolution not have tinkered with our brains and behaviors as our social environments underwent the most radical transformation in primate history?

Pair this with the rapidity of cultural evolution and it may not be unreasonable to believe that the new self-understandings arising from the social and neurosciences might lead us to adapt in the positive direction of reduced violence in our social and ecological relations. Might we be too sanguine to hope that cultural evolution, under the selective pressures of climate change and the trends of globalization and communication technologies, will continue the movement toward greater cooperation that has been a defining characteristic of human species development from the beginning?[3]

In their 2007 article, *The Anthropocene: Are Humans Now Overwhelming the Great Forces of Nature*, Paul Crutzen, together with climate scientist Will Steffen and environmental historian John McNeill, describes three "stages" of the Anthropocene: stage 1, the Industrial Era from 1800 to 1945; stage 2, defined as the "Great Acceleration" from 1945 to ca. 2015; and stage 3, a hypothetical new era starting in 2015 in which humans act as "stewards of the Earth System." Steffen et al (2007, p. 618, italics added) describe a number of factors that could support a change for the better:

> The growing awareness of human influence on the Earth System has been aided by i) rapid advances in research and understanding, the most innovative of which is interdisciplinary work on human-environment systems; ii) the enormous power of the internet as a global, self-organizing information system; iii) the spread of more free and open societies, supporting independent media; and iv) the growth of democratic political systems, narrowing the scope for the exercise of arbitrary state power and strengthening the role of civil society. *Humanity is, in one way or another, becoming a self-conscious, active agent in the operation of its own life support system.*

There is a parallel or consonance between confronting climate change and confronting destructive conflict in our human social relations. Both climate change and conflict are symptoms of our psychologies. Both are the products of millennia of species evolution. Both confront us with ourselves. Both pose the question whether we can be in relationship differently than we have been, with each other and with our environment. Both require that we be more self-reflective, responsible, and accountable in our behaviors if we are to change our trajectory.

We desire to promote and achieve greater peace and collaboration even as we often get caught up in conflict and competition. This makes sense given the pain and suffering that often accompanies or results from conflict. The conflict resolution field is a reflection of that urge. To emphasize again, given one interpretation of the evidence, and in spite of examples to the contrary, it can be argued that the arc of human history is moving in the direction of increased respect for diversity, tolerance of different points of view that are acknowledged to be concurrently legitimate, and universal agreements about human and civil rights. The struggles to implement democratic processes for public decision-making, to foster gender equality, to create a fair justice system and a just economic system characterized by an absence or minimization of the abuses of unfettered free-market capitalism or centralized, despotic oligarchy reflect aspirations to live less violently or abusively together.

We tell two primary narratives to explain violence and conflict in the world. One says that we live fallen from a previous state of peace and grace. The Garden of Eden story is one example of this narrative. The other narrative proposes that we are a developing species, evolving from the caves, that living is a challenging experience, that social life, given the characteristics of our psychophysiology, is difficult, and that we are trying to learn how to be responsible in relationship. The Hero's Journey story is one example of this narrative. The one narrative is a fall from grace. The other is a search for grace.

Whether in service to one or the other of these narratives, I think it is fair to state that the conflict resolution field recognizes its limitations and the shortcomings of its practice thus far. We frequently are able to help people achieve settlement of their disputes. We often witness "aha" moments of profound change in perception and understanding. We participate occasionally in instances of transformational change in a relationship dynamic and a shift in or expansion of identity. But also, we are often frustrated by our inability to help people resolve deep-seated conflicts with long history and to prevent or reduce destructive social conflict at all levels, interpersonal, communal, organizational, and inter-group. The promise is there, but our grasp continues often to fall far short of our reach. We can see that there is more to do. We wish we had a magic wand. We may wonder sometimes, with a mix of amusement and half-seriousness, whether drugs in the water supply is the answer. How can we do a better job of helping to reduce, prevent, and resolve destructive conflict? Surely, we ask longingly, people can learn and be helped to behave better than they often do.

The behaviors we work to help people overcome are as much a part of the organism's repertoire as are the behaviors we seek to encourage. As Jonathan Haidt (2013, p. xix) puts it, "human nature is not just intrinsically moral, it's also intrinsically moralistic, critical, and judgmental." These terms, "moralistic, critical, and judgmental," are euphemisms for the neural processes that produce the experiences and behaviors they name. Understanding the physiological workings of the organism may help us better address the consequences of "human nature," a nature that is embodied in the physical structure and processes of the organism. Haidt expressed a hope for his book *The Righteous Mind* (2013, p. xix) that, "it will help us get along" by helping us to "understand why we are so easily divided into hostile groups, each one certain of its righteousness" (p. xviii). Recognizing the neural basis of our cognitive and identity experiences can help us understand why. Otherwise, our conflict behaviors seem to float in some intangible realm with no explanatory foundation.

The practices of athletes and their trainers to improve physical performance are more successful the more they are based upon knowledge of how the body functions. If an engineer is asked to build a bridge, she must know the distance to be covered, the topography, geology, and soil type on each side of the divide, the seismic and wind conditions, etc. Conditions inform design solution. Always, choice of tools is determined by the circumstances of the problem. So it is likely to be for those who work with behavior among people. Relational conflicts are embodied. The psychological is neurological. Therefore, understanding the neurological should help us address the social and psychological.

Philosopher Patricia Smith Churchland speaks about how advances in neuroscience can help address and resolve an assortment of philosophical questions. If we replace her references to the philosophical discipline in the following statement with references to conflict resolution practice, we can hear another perspective on how conflict resolution theory and practice might be advanced if based on understandings of the brain functions that underlie behavior. As she puts it (Churchland, 2002, p. 32):

> If we allow discoveries in neuroscience and cognitive science to butt up against old philosophical problems, something very remarkable happens. We will see genuine progress where progress was deemed impossible; we will see intuitions surprised and dogmas routed. We will find ourselves making sense of mental phenomena in neurobiological terms, while unmasking some classical puzzles as preneuroscientific misconceptions. Neuroscience has only just begun to have an impact on philosophical problems. In the next decades, as neurobiological techniques are invented and theories of brain function elaborated, the paradigmatic forms of understanding mind-brain phenomena will shift, and shift again. These are still early days for neuroscience. Unlike physics or molecular biology, neuroscience does not yet have a firm grasp of the basic principles explaining its target phenomenon. The real conceptual revolution will be upon us once those principles come into focus.

So it is or will be, I'm suggesting, with the impact of neurobiological insights on the conflict resolution field.

This premise is the same that underlies Robert Wright's observations in his 2013 *Atlantic Magazine* article "Why Can't We All Just Get Along? The uncertain biological basis of morality." As he puts it (Wright, 2013):

So maybe the first step toward salvation is to become more self-aware . . . the cultivation of a kind of meta-cognitive skill. This would depend on understanding how our minds work and could help us decide more wisely – presumably not just by showing us the transcendent virtue of utilitarianism, but by making us aware of the biases that routinely afflict judgment . . . Which leads to a question: Um, how exactly do you do metacognition? Well, you could start by pondering all the evidence that your brain is an embarrassingly misleading device. Self-doubt can be the first step to moral improvement.

Put another way, self-knowledge can be the first step in self-management. The dicta "Know thyself" and "The truth shall set you free" come to mind. As Robert Ornstein and Paul Ehrlich (1989, pp. 197–198) ask, "If we learn how we think, how our mind is structured, and how to overcome the innate limitations and biases of mind, can we then learn to act on that knowledge?" Joseph LeDoux refers to the idea expressed by neuroscientist and philosopher Nick Humphrey that, "clever thinking about the way the brain works, not just about how the mind works, may be a key to progress" (LeDoux, 2003 p. 328). And as Don Tucker (2007, p. 269) puts it, "It should not be too much to hope that further advances in science may bring a similar objective perspective to understanding our own minds, thereby offering us ways of participating more deliberately in the process of experience" and:

> Even if the inferences we develop must be applied to domains of experience that are unconscious, the result of this application could perhaps still produce a richer and more powerful quality of experience. A useful scientific theory of mental process could give us a knowledge of what to expect from the workings of the unconscious . . . it is an intriguing possibility that greater knowledge of the unconscious mechanisms of the mind could allow us to participate in those mechanisms more deliberately
>
> *(Tucker, 2007, p. 270)*

and, "It may be that understanding the motivational basis of these processes (of embodied mind) will lead to more effective subjective control of them" (p. 276).

Each new discovery of brain function will shed light on one aspect or another of human behavior and, therefore, on conflict and conflict resolution since these are aspects of human behavior. I expect that conflict resolution practice and theory will evolve as we discover more about how the brain functions and as that information is more widely disseminated to become a part of general understanding. How to leverage that knowledge is yet to be fully explored. How do we best take advantage of the understanding of the neural roots of conflict? At the least, we will have a more solid foundation upon which to explain conflict behaviors and reflect upon conflict resolution practices. Perhaps there is a next phase to be embarked upon in conflict resolution practice, one that is based more explicitly on the realities of our embodied condition. Antonio Damasio's (2010, p. 29) optimistic view is a good note upon which to end this discussion: "The time will come when the issue of human responsibility, in general moral terms as well as on matters of justice and its application, will take into account the evolving science of consciousness. Perhaps the time is now."

Notes

1 See, for example, Hoggan (2016).
2 See, for example, Pinker (2012).
3 "It is inconceivable that you would ever see two chimpanzees carrying a log together" (Michael Tomasello, expert on chimpanzee cognition, as quoted in Haidt, 2013, p. 237).

APPENDIX

Digest of specific practice approaches discussed or suggested in the text

Many of the suggestions below are common to current practice. Some suggest a shift of practice, more of less. In either case, they are founded on an awareness of the neural basis of party experience as a lens through which to understand and craft intervention choices.

- Consider devoting portions of mediation sessions to educating parties about relevant theory. For example:
  - Normalize resistance to changing ideas, beliefs, understandings (brain stability/plasticity balance); there is an attachment to or preference for what we already know, particularly under conditions of conflict and threat.
  - Ideas, beliefs, understandings exist as physical neural structures; changing one's mind is a physical event and is not always easy.
  - There is a close connection between what we know or believe we know and our identity; some conflicts involve our identity more than others (for example, conflicts that involve values).
  - There is a power to language as it enters into us as a physical event that threatens or attempts to change us; there is the potential for violence and the attendant responsibility.
  - In language exchange, there is an easy potential for misunderstanding; words can easily have different meaning associations for the parties without them recognizing it.
  - We can better manage our responses to the other party when we understand the neural activation phenomenon.
  - Biases exist in all of us (implicit, confirmation, fundamental attribution, naïve realism, transference, etc.)

- o There is a dorsal (self-to-world) and ventral (world-to-self) balance to our experience.
- o Ingroup/outgroup identification is accompanied by a number of consistent patterns.
- o Memory can be an inexact representation.

- Beware moving too quickly from identification of issues, being sure to explore and determine what the issues actually signify or mean for each of the parties.
- Be sensitive to the pace and degree of narrative revision the parties are being asked to consider and make adjustments accordingly.
- Be aware of the reality of the neural stability/plasticity balance and adjust interventions and process management accordingly, being sensitive to variations in willingness and ability to change.
- Help parties consider how a proposed settlement can or does fit into their larger life context. If the fit is not quite seamless or complete, what additional agreements might improve the fit?

  - o Work to insure that any progress at the negotiating table is maintained upon return to home context; ask direct questions about what might impede or hamper the durability of agreements reached.
  - o Help parties find and articulate a positive self-role within the new narrative reflected in the settlement agreements.

- Help parties talk about their emotions without getting flooded by the emotions; normalize strong feelings and help them use their emotional experience as part of their decision-making process.

  - o Take some time after the expression of strong emotions for the parties to recover before continuing with the negotiation dialogue.

- Consider ways in which it might be possible to help parties understand and articulate their conscious or unconscious expectancies, both those conducive to and those at odds with negotiation progress.
- We aware of behaviors that might reflect a tipping of the dorsal (self-to-world) and ventral (world-to-self) balance one way or the other and find ways to support parties in recovering or establishing a better balance.

  - o Dorsal extreme (too much speaking) --> more attention to the other's experience.
  - o Ventral extreme (too much attention to the other) --> more attention to expression of the self's experience.

- Pay particular attention to the key words involved in party dialogue and actively inquire to learn, and help the parties learn and make explicit, what these words signify and mean to each of them.
- Recognize, and help the parties understand, that stress and threat impact negotiations (for example, by reducing creative problem-solving, inhibiting

language production, inhibiting the ability and willingness to hear and understand the other's experience); look for ways, with the parties' involvement, to reduce stress and threat.

- Look for opportunities to couple somatic awareness with negotiation dialogue and to supplement reason-based verbal engagement with somatic interventions. (For example, helping parties breathe to relax, move or stretch to relieve body tension, take a walk in a peaceful or bucolic setting, laugh when appropriate to the circumstances.)
- Recognize that party beliefs, understandings, and knowings form important parts of their identity; work hard to help the parties shift differences and disagreements from right/wrong, good/bad framings.
- Pay attention to underlying dynamics of trust/distrust and address directly when relevant.
- Consider whether experiences of betrayal or trauma have been part of the historical conflict narrative and whether it might be helpful or necessary to address these experiences in order for the parties to resolve the presenting issues and create a new narrative. Are apologies a possible part of recovery? Ask the parties.
- Be aware of and acknowledge, most commonly only to oneself, your internal responses to the parties in order that you not let those unavoidable responses interfere with your multi-partiality.
- Understand impasses as opportunities rather than roadblocks. Look for the element(s) in the negotiation and the relationship between the parties that are preventing the gears from turning. Use the neural theoretical framework as one lens for considering what's getting in the way.
- Do not be cavalier in asking parties to shift from positions to interests. Recognize what is involved in neural terms. Consider what the parties might need to willingly make the shift.
- Pay attention to the usefulness or wisdom of having parties extensively recount to you the history of the conflict from their point of view prior to joint session. How much is enough? How much is too much? What is the benefit measure for you, for the party, and for the negotiation?
- Help the parties shift from competing stories (right/wrong) to concurrent stories (equally legitimate) in order to provide the foundation of safety, acknowledgement, and respect necessary for subsequent joint problem-solving.
- Be sure that the parties have achieved sufficient trust and safety (in the process, in feeling heard and understood) before moving to the consideration of solution options.
- Look for opportunities to increase interactional responsiveness and attunement between or among the parties (shared stories, humor, shared meals, site visits) in order to build trust.

REFERENCES

Adler, P.S. (forthcoming). "Rocks on the Road: Inside the Pandora's box of culture," in *Essays on Mediation*, edited by Ian Macduff, Alphen aan den Rijn: Kluwer.

Argyris, C., & Schön, D.A. (1996) [1978]. *Organizational Learning: A theory of action perspective*. Addison-Wesley OD series 1. Reading: Addison-Wesley.

Arrow, K., Mnookin, R. H, Ross, L., Tversky, A., & Wilson, R.B. (eds) (1995). *Barriers to Conflict Resolution*. New York: W.W. Norton and Company.

Bara, B., & Bara, B. (2010). *Cognitive Pragmatics: The mental processes of communication*. Cambridge: MIT Press.

Barsalou, L. (1999). "Perceptual Symbol Systems", *Behavioral and Brain Sciences*, 22: 577–660.

Barsalou, L., Wenchi Yeh, Luka, B.J., Olseth, K.L., Mix, K.S. & Ling-Ling Wu (n.d.a). *Concepts and Meaning*. Working Paper. Dept. of Psychology, Chicago: University of Chicago.

Barsalou, L., Niedenthal, P.M., Barbey, A.K., & Ruppert, J.A. (n.d.b). "Social Embodiment," *The Psychology of Learning and Motivation: Advances in Research and Theory*, 43: 43–92.

Bergen, B. (2012). *Louder than Words: The new science of how the mind makes meaning*. New York: Basic Books.

Birke, R. (2010). "Neuroscience and Settlement: An examination of scientific innovations and practical applications", *Ohio St. J. on Disp.*, 25: 477.

Bor, D. (2012). *The Ravenous Brain: How the new science of consciousness explains our insatiable search for meaning*. New York: Basic Books.

Bowling, D., & Hoffman, D. (2000). "Bringing Peace into the Room: The personal qualities of mediators and their impact on the mediation," *Negotiation Journal*, 16(1): 5.

Bruner, J. (1973). *Beyond the Information Given: Studies in the psychology of knowing*. New York: Norton.

Bullock, B.G. (2016). *Mindful Relationships: Seven skills for change. Integrating the science of mind, body and brain*. Scotland; Handspring Publishing.

Burke, P., & Stets, J. (2009). *Identity Theory*. Oxford: Oxford University Press.

Burton, R. (2008). *On Being Certain: Believing you are right even when you're not.* New York: St. Martin's Press.

Bush, R., & Folger, J. (1994). *The Promise of Mediation.* San Francisco: Jossey-Bass.

Churchland, P. (1996). "The Hornswaggle Problem," *Journal of Consciousness Studies,* 3(5–6): 402–408.

Churchland, P. (2002). *Brain-wise: Studies in neurophilosophy.* Cambridge: MIT Press.

Churchland, P. (2011). *Braintrust: What neuroscience tells us about morality.* Princeton: Princeton University Press.

Churchland, P. (2013). *Touching a Nerve: The self as brain.* New York: W.W. Norton & Company.

Cozolino, L. (2014). *The Neuroscience of Human Relationships.* New York: W.W. Norton & Company.

Crosswhite, J. (2013). *Deep Rhetoric: Philosophy, reason, violence, justice, wisdom.* Chicago: University of Chicago Press.

Damasio, A. (1994). *Descartes' Error: Emotion, reason, and the human brain.* New York: G.P. Putnam's Sons.

Damasio, A. (1999). *The Feeling of What Happens: Body and emotion in the making of consciousness.* New York: Harcourt Brace.

Damasio, A. (2010). *Self Comes to Mind: Constructing the conscious brain.* New York: Pantheon Books.

Dehaene, S. (ed.) (2001). *The Cognitive Neuroscience of Consciousness.* Cambridge: MIT Press.

Dehaene, S. (2014). *Consciousness and the Brain: Deciphering how the brain codes our thoughts.* New York: Penguin Books.

Duggan, M. (1996). "A Nested Theory of Conflict," *A Leadership Journal: Women in Leadership,* 1 (July): 9–20.

Edelman, G. (1989). *The Remembered Present: A biological theory of consciousness.* New York: Basic Books.

Edelman, G. (1992). *Bright Air, Brilliant Fire: On the matter of the mind.* New York: BasicBooks.

Edelman, G. (2005). *Wider Than the Sky: The phenomenal gift of consciousness.* New Haven: Yale University Press.

Edelman, G. (2006). *Second Nature: Brain science and human knowledge.* New Haven: Yale University Press.

Edelman, G., & Tononi, G. (2000). *A Universe of Consciousness: How matter becomes imagination.* New York: Basic Books.

Fauconnier, G., & Turner, M. (2002). *The Way We Think: Conceptual blending and the mind's hidden complexities.* New York: Basic Books.

Feinberg, Todd, E. (2009). *From Axons to Identity: Neurological explorations of the nature of the self.* New York: W.W. Norton & Company.

Feldman, J. (2006). *From Molecule to Metaphor: A neural theory of language.* Cambridge: MIT Press.

Fisher, R., Ury, W., & Patton, B. (2011). *Getting to Yes.* New York: Penguin Books.

Fisher, T. (2003). "Who's Minding the Mediator? Mindfulness in Mediation," *ADR Bulletin,* 5(10), available at: http://epublications.bond.edu.au/adr/vol5/iss10/1

Folberg, J. (2016) "The Shrinking Joint Session: Survey Results," available at: www.mediate.com/articles/FolbergJointSession.cfm

Franks, D.D., & Turner, J. H. (eds) (2013). *Handbook of Neurosociology.* New York: Springer.

Freud, S. (1990). *The Psychopathology of Everyday Life*. New York: W.W. Norton & Company.

Friedman, Gary (2015). *Inside Out: How conflict professionals can use self-reflection to help their clients*. New York: American Bar Association.

Fuller, T. (2015). "Those Who Would Remake Myanmar Find That Words Fail Them," *New York Times*, July 19.

Fuster, J.M. (2003). *Cortex and Mind*. Oxford/New York: Oxford University Press.

Fuster, J.M. (2013). *The Neuroscience of Freedom and Creativity*. New York: Cambridge University Press.

Fusting, E. (2012). "Making the Brain a Friend Not Foe: What interventionists should know about neuroscience," *AM. J. Mediation*, 6: 41.

Gallese, V. (2011). "Embodied Simulation Theory: Imagination and narrative," *Neuropsychoanalysis*, 13(2): 196–200.

Geary, D. (2005). *The Origin of Mind: Evolution of brain, cognition, and general intelligence*. Washington: American Psychological Association.

Gendlin, E. (1997). *Experiencing and the Creation of Meaning: A philosophical and psychological approach to the subjective*. New York: Northwestern University Press.

Gilligan, M. D. (1996). *Violence: Our deadly epidemic and its causes*. New York: G.P. Putnam's Sons.

Gleick, J. (2011). *The Information: A history, a theory, a flood*. New York: Pantheon Books.

Goldman, W. (2011). "Mediation, Multiple Minds, and Managing the Negotiation Within," *Harv. Negot. L. Rev.*, 16: 297.

Goleman, D. (1996) *Emotional Intelligence: Why it can matter more than IQ*. New York: Bantom Books.

Gottman, J.M., & Silver, N. (1999). *The Seven Principles for Making Marriage Work: A practical guide from the country's foremost relationship expert*. New York: Three Rivers Press.

Grossberg, S. (1999). "The Link Between Brain Learning, Attention, and Consciousness," *Conscious Cogn.*, 8: 1–44.

Haidt, J. (2013). *The Righteous Mind: Why good people are divided by politics and religion*. New York: Vintage Books.

Hamilton, C. (2010). *Requiem for a Species*. Washington: Earthscan.

Harinck F., & Van Kleef G.A. (2012). "Be Hard on the Interests and Soft on the Values: Conflict issue moderates the interpersonal effects of anger in negotiations", *British Journal of Social Psychology*, 51: 499–790. doi:10.1111/j.2044-8309.2011.02089.x

Hasson, U., Ghazanfar, A.A., Galantucci, B., Garrod, S., & Keysers, C. (2012). "Brain-to-Brain Coupling: A mechanism for creating and sharing a social world," *Trends Cogn Sci.*, 16(2): 114–121, doi:10.1016/j.tics.2011.12.007.

Heyes, C., & Huber, L. (eds) (2000). *The Evolution of Cognition*. Cambridge: The MIT Press.

Hoffman, D., & Wolman, R. (n.d.). "The Psychology of Mediation," *Cardozo Journal of Conflict Resolution*, 14(3): 759–806.

Hoggan, J. (2016). *I'm Right and You're an Idiot: The toxic state of public discourse and how to clean it up*. Gabriola Island: New Society Publishers.

Hood, B. (2012). *The Self Illusion: How the social brain creates identity*. New York: Oxford University Press.

Johns, C., & Burnie, S. (2013) [2000]. *Becoming a Reflective Practitioner*. 4th ed. Chichester and Ames: Wiley-Blackwell.

Johnson, M. (1987). *The Body in the Mind: The bodily basis of meaning, imagination, and reason*. Chicago: University of Chicago Press.

Johnson, M. (2007). *The Meaning of the Body: Aesthetics of human understanding*. Chicago: University of Chicago Press.

Kahneman, D. (2011). *Thinking, Fast and Slow*. New York: Farrar, Straus, and Giroux.

Kandel, E.R. (2006). *In Search of Memory: The emergence of a new science of mind*. New York. W.W. Norton & Company.

Keltner, D. (2009). *Born to be Good: The science of a meaningful life*. New York: W.W. Norton & Company.

Klein, S.B., & Nichols, S. (2012). "Memory and the Sense of Personal Identity," *Mind*, 121(483): 677–702.

Kouzakova, M., Harinck, F., Ellemers, N., & Scheepers, D. (2014). "*At the Heart of a Conflict: Cardiovascular and self- regulation responses to value versus resource conflicts*," *Social, Psychological, and Personality Science*, 5(1): 35–42 January.

Lack, J., & Bogacz, F. (2012). "The Neurophysiology of ADR and Process Design: A new approach to conflict prevention and resolution," *Cardozo J. Conflict Resol.*, 14: 33.

Lakoff, G. (1987). *Women, Fire, and Dangerous Things: What categories reveal about the mind*. Chicago: University of Chicago Press.

Lakoff, G., & Gallese, V. (2005). "The Brain's Concepts: The role of the sensory- motor system in conceptual knowledge", *Cognitive Neuropsychology*, 21(0): 1–25.

Lakoff, G., & Johnson, M. (1999). *Philosophy in the Flesh: The embodied mind and its challenge to Western thought*. New York: Basic Books.

Lang, M., & Taylor, A. (2000). *The Making of a Mediator: Developing artistry in practice*. San Francisco: Jossey-Bass.

Leary, M., & Tangney, J. eds. (2012). *Handbook of Self and Identity*. New York: Guilford Press.

LeBaron, M., & Patera, M. (2009). "Reflective Practice in the New Millennium," *Hamline J. Pub. L. & Pol'y*, HeinOnline, available at: http://law.hamline.edu/files/4-LeBaron-Patera-Reflective_Practice_FINAL_May_09.pdf

LeDoux, J. (2003). *Synaptic Self: How our brains become who we are*. New York: Penguin.

Lehrer, J. (2009). *How We Decide*. New York: Mariner Books.

Liebman, C.B. (2000). "Mediation as Parallel Seminars: Lessons from the student takeover of Columbia University's Hamilton Hall," *Negot. J.*, 16: 157.

Malle, B., & Hodges, S. (2005). *Other Minds: How humans bridge the divide between self and others*. New York: Guilford Press.

Marcus, G., & Freeman, J. (eds) (2015). *The Future of the Brain*. Princeton: Princeton University Press.

Matthiessen, S. (2008). *Mindfulness-based Approaches to Conflict, Without and Within*. Available at: www.mediate.com/mediator/attachments/15911/MindfulnessBased ApproachesToConflict1008.pdf.

Maturana, H., & Varela, F. (1987). *The Tree of Knowledge: The biological roots of human understanding*. Rev. ed. Boston: Shambhala.

McRaney, D. (2012) *You Are Not So Smart*. London: One World Publications.

Menkel-Meadow, C., Porter Love, L., & Kupfer Schneider, A. (2006). *Mediation: Practice, policy, and ethics*. New York: Aspen Publishers.

Mercier, H., & Sperber, D. (2011). "Why Do Humans Reason? Arguments for an argumentative theory," *Behavioral and Brain Sciences*, 34 (2): 57–74; discussion 74–111.

Mercier, H., & Sperber, D. (2017). *The Enigma of Reason*. Boston: Harvard University Press.

Moore, C. (2014). *The Mediation Process: Practical strategies for resolving conflict*. San Francisco: Jossey-Bass.

Nagel, T. (2012). *Mind and Cosmos: Why the materialist neo-Darwinian conception of nature is almost certainly false.* New York: Oxford University Press.

Nichols, S. (2000). "The Mind's 'I' and the Theory of Mind's 'I': Introspection and two concepts of self," *Philosophical Topics*, 28: 171–199.

Ornstein, R., & Ehrlich, P. (1989). *New World New Mind: Moving toward conscious evolution.* New York: Doubleday.

Pinker, S. (2012). *The Better Angels of our Nature: Why violence has declined.* New York: Penguin.

Popper, K. (1995). *In Search of a Better World: Lectures and Essays from Thirty Years.* New York: Routledge.

Porges, S. (2011). *The Polyvagal Theory: Neurophysiological foundations of emotion, attachment, communication and self regulation.* New York: W.W. Norton and Company.

Riskin, L. (2004). "Mindfulness: Foundational training for dispute resolution," *J. Legal Educ.*, 54: 79.

Sapolsky, R. (2017). *Behave: The biology of humans at our best and worst.* New York: Penguin Press.

Schön, D.A. (1983). *The Reflective Practitioner: How professionals think in action.* New York: Basic Books.

Schulz, K. (2010). *Being Wrong: Adventures in the margin of error.* New York: Ecco.

Schwartz, C. (2015). *In the Mind Fields: Exploring the new science of neuropsychoanalysis.* New York: Pantheon Books.

Seung, S. (2012). *Connectome: How the brain's wiring makes us who we are.* Boston: Houghton Mifflin Harcourt.

Steffen, W., Crutzen, P., & McNeill, J. (2007). "The Anthropocene: Are humans now overwhelming the great forces of nature," *AMBIO: A Journal of the Human Environment*, 36(8): 614–621.

Strauss, A. (1997). *Mirrors & Masks: The search for identity.* New Brunswick: Transaction.

Tamietto, M. & de Gelder, B. (2010). "Neural Bases of the Non-conscious Perception of Emotional Signals," *Nature Reviews Neuroscience*, 11(10): 697–709.

Tucker, D. (2001). *Embodied Meaning: An evolutionary-developmental analysis of adaptive semantics.* Institute of Cognitive and Decision Sciences Technical Report, No. 01-04.

Tucker, D. (2007). *Mind from Body: Experience from neural structure.* Oxford: Oxford University Press.

Tucker, D., & Luu, P. (2012). *Cognition and Neural Development.* Oxford: Oxford University Press.

Tucker, D., Luu, P., & Poulsen, C. (2016). "The Neurodevelopmental Process of Self-Organization", in: *Developmental Psychopathology*, edited by Dante Cicchetti, 3rd ed. Hoboken: Wiley & Sons.

Weitz, D. (2011a). "This is Your Brain on Mediation: What neuroscience can add to the practice of mediation," *NYSBA New York Dispute Resolution Lawyer*, 4: 36.

Weitz, D. (2011b). "The Brains Behind Mediation: Reflections on neuroscience, conflict resolution and decision-making," *Cardozo J. Conflict Resol.*, 12: 471.

Woit, P. (2006). *Not Even Wrong: The failure of string theory and the search for unity in physical law.* New York: Basic Books.

World Health Organization (2010). *Injuries and Violence: The facts.* Geneva: WHO.

Wright, R. (2013). "Why Can't We All Just Get Along? The uncertain biological basis of morality," *Atlantic Monthly*, November 1.

Zalewski, D. (2015). "Life Lines", *The New Yorker*, March 30, 2015.

INDEX

human development viii
human rights viii
Humphrey, N. 159

I-language 111, 134
identity xix, 1–3, 8n2, 14; beginnings
  15, 18; construction 66, 68–70;
  relationships 71, 105; stability 32;
  stories 108–13
impasse 90–1, 116
information 16, 18, 19–20, 25n43, 76
instantiation 26n55
intention 59–61
intentional control 41
interdisciplinary nature of conflict
  resolution ix, 156
interests 94–6
internalizing disorders 41–2
intuition 9n10
isolation 57
issues 92–4

James, W. 8n1, 13
Johnson, M. 19, 25n46, 71, 78n3,
  81n42
joint fact-finding (JFF) 144–5
joint sessions with parties 106–8,
  114–16, 142

Kahneman, D. 11n33, 48n18
Kant, I. 53n71
Klein, S.B. 52n63
knowing 18, 19, 75–8
Kouzakova, M. *et al.* 138–9
Kuhn, T. 32

Lack, J. 45, 133
Lakoff, G. 48n15
language acquisition 16–17, 18–19, 36;
  see also communication
language activation 36
law viii, x
learning 14, 15, 16–20; and change xi,
  2, 7–8, 75–8; pre-natal beginnings
  15, 16
LeBaron, M. 149n21
LeDoux, J. xxiii n15, 9n12, 22n5, 22n11,
  26n59, 27n70, 27n74, 48n16, 49n31,
  54n88, 81n36–7, 148n15, 159
limbic system 29
listening 125–9
litigation 153
location and setting 121–3

long-term memory 44
Luu, P. xxi, xxii n3, xxiii n21, 6, 8n3,
  8n6, 13, 16, 18, 22n10, 23n14, 23n18,
  23n27, 24n28, 24n31–2, 24n37,
  25n40, 27n62, 27n72, 29, 32, 36, 37,
  38, 39, 40, 41, 42–3, 48n8, 49n24,
  50n37, 50n39, 50–1n43, 51n53,
  52n58, 52n60, 52n69, 53n73–6,
  53–4n79–83, 56, 78, 82n45, 83n57

McNeill, J. 156
McRaney, D. 80n20, 114–15
Maneli, M. 83n56
Maturana, H. 82n52
Mayer, B. ix, x
meaning-making 6, 16–21, 90
mediation 85, 96, 153–4; caucusing
  141–2; online asynchronous mediation
  142–3; process 106–7; settlement 97–9;
  site visits 143–4; *see also* practice issues;
  practice: process design considerations;
  practice: stages of process; practice:
  theoretical issues
mediator influence 89–90
meditation 27n71, 51–2n55
memory 2, 14, 19, 43; consolidation
  22n10, 37, 41, 43–4, 45; explicit
  memory 46; implicit memory 46–7,
  86; long-term memory 44; pre-natal
  beginnings 15, 16; working
  (short-term) memory 43, 45–6
Menkel-Meadow, C. *et al.* 148n12
Mercier, H. 64, 65, 66, 78–9n6
mindfulness 140–1
mirroring 74–5
moral values x
motivational significance 43, 128

Nagel, T. xxii n2
naïve realism 64
Necker Cube xii, 30
negotiation 146–7
nervous system x–xi, xii, xvi, xix, 2, 3, 5;
  see also neural encoding function; neural
  encoding: key characteristics
neural activation 33–7
neural encoding function xi–xiii, xix, xxi,
  2, 12–14; prenatal beginnings 15–16;
  birth and meaning making 16–21
neural encoding: key characteristics 28;
  connectivity, coherence, consistency
  28–31; dorsal and ventral systems
  40–3, 128; expectancy 38–40; memory